D1594125

ROWAN UNIVERSITY
LIBRARY
201 MULLICA HILL RD.
GLASSBORO, NJ 08028-1701

GINNING COTTON

GINNING COTTON

An Entrepreneur's Story

A. L. Vandergriff

Texas Tech University Press

© Copyright 1997 Texas Tech University Press

All rights reserved. No portion of this book may be reproduced in any form or by any means, including electronic storage and retrieval systems, except by explicit, prior written permission of the publisher except for brief passages excerpted for review or critical purposes.

This book was set in Cheltenhm and Futura printed on acid-free paper that meets the guidelines for permanence and durability of the Committee on Produc-tion Guidelines for Book longevity of the Council on Library Resources. (∞)

Design by Lisa Camp

Printed in the United States of America

Library of Congress Cataloging-in-Publication Data
Vandergriff, A. L. (Arvel Loyd), 1910-
    Ginning cotton : an entrepreneur's story / A. L. Vandergriff.
       p.   cm.
    Includes index.
    ISBN 0-89672-371-2 (cloth : alk. paper)
      1. Cotton gins and ginning—United States—History. I. title.
    TS1585.V36 1997
    677'.2121—dc21   96-52347
                                                 CIP

97 98 99 00 01 02 03 04 05 / 9 8 7 6 5 4 3 2 1

Texas Tech University Press
Box 41037
Lubbock, Texas 79409-1037 USA
800-832-4042

TS
1585
V36
1997

3 3001 00811 1931

Foreword

The customary and the commonplace are frequently overlooked in our estimation of our values and historical nexus points. Such may be said of that invaluable and ancient special gift of flora, cotton. The desert provided this unique plant long before the people of the Stone, Bronze, and Iron Ages utilized it. Since then, this plant of wonder has given its special and generous values to humankind throughout the globe: both simple and elaborate cloth, clothing, and tapestries, and the sails that carried news of a larger world—the sails of Magellan and Vasco da Gama as they explored and demonstrated new worlds. In this latter role, Columbus required the canvas sail to reach the Americas, and it was in the Americas that Eli Whitney's cotton gin was to change the economies of lands and revolutionize a global industry. Whitney's simple device foreshadowed constant improvement in the ginning process; i.e., separating the seed from the cotton fiber.

Many engineers and inventors have provided innovation and improvement in the gin industry since Whitney, but no one has achieved such a host of accomplishments as A. L. Vandergriff. Many of his breakthroughs have been awarded important patents, but his overall contributions are so unique that they demand more public recognition. Vandy's impact on the global cotton industry cannot be adequately appreciated without visiting the entire saga of cotton, and the story of cotton's growth as an ever improving servant of humankind, as both food and fiber, would require extensive exposition in the telling. In this book, we invite you to follow a brief history of the cotton-ginning industry. The modern gin makes machine picking and harvesting economically possible, and Vandy's role in this seminal aspect of the world's economy deserves much praise. Without such important adaptations at the processing level of the cotton industry, rayon, polyester, or wool might well be the order of the day. Only by advancements in gin technology was it possible to develop important by-products; for example, cottonseed oil, meal, and cake. In these chapters, Vandy modestly documents the machinery and ideas that have provided, and continue to provide, important aspects of this progress.

Henry Quick

Contents

Dedicated to my wonderful wife Marie Miller Vandergriff. She kept the home fires burning, looked after our finances, raised our wonderful son Loyd and traveled with me whenever possible—a wonderful loving relationship for almost 59 years until her death in 1992.

Preface

I wish to thank numerous people who have helped me in the work recorded in this book. A brief, chronological synopsis of my endeavors, naming some of my innovations in the field of cotton-ginning machinery, appears in the Introduction.

I would like to thank my friends at Elbow Gin in Visalia, California, Robert Faris, manager and Mike Price, superintendent, for allowing me to use their plant as a laboratory for some of my ideas. They and their crew played a major role in this success story. My thanks also go to R. C. Swartz for his outstanding engineering work on the 164; and I am grateful to Consolidated Cotton Gin Company, Inc., of Lubbock, Texas, particularly Russell Sutton, for allowing me to continue to work in an area to which I have devoted most of my life. I would like to express my appreciation to the fine young men who make up their engineering department; in 1994, we introduced the Consolidated 198 Saw Gin Stand, the world's first twenty-bale-per-hour stand, a proud product of Vandergriff Research.

Readers of this book will no doubt recognize developments by the author that are now credited to others. My documentation will be questioned by some, and that is to be expected. I have seen many so-called industry leaders come and go, but I have preferred to continue my efforts and work with those who choose to pursue solid developments.

Today, it is a thrill for me to watch a modern gin plant operate, knowing it is heavily influenced by my research over the years. It provides me with a great deal of quiet satisfaction to watch automatic unloading systems, presses, seed-cotton drying, extracting, and cleaning systems, all performing efficiently at tremendous capacities.

I hope my many friends who read this book enjoy it, and that they will realize how much I owe to them. I would especially like to thank Henry Quick for some truly expert editing early on; and my son Loyd, who spent endless hours wrestling with the manuscript, editing and typing and retyping until we reached the final product.

Introduction

My work with the manufacturers of cotton-ginning machinery started in the 1930s, my first experience in the engineering phase of the business being with the Hardwicke Etter Company, of Sherman, Texas. I was privileged to travel and work with the chief engineer, John A. Streun. His formal education was practically nil, but he was a mechanical genius. He developed a line of gin machinery that was competitive with that of other manufacturers of the day (for an explanation of the word *gin*, see Chapter 6). Of special note was his Burrs Out machine, developed in the early 1920s to handle the bollie cotton of West Texas. During my time with Hardwicke Etter, I listened, learned, and accumulated many ideas for future use.

During World War II, I served in the navy. Soon after returning to Hardwicke Etter, I moved to the Lummus Cotton Ginning Company to set up a research and development department. The management and long-time employees there were not receptive to improvements in their line of equipment, but I did have the support of the ownership, which allowed me to hire my own people—people who would help me make great changes in virtually the entire line of equipment.

My first key acquisition, in 1947, was Don Van Doorn, who had not even seen a cotton gin up to this time. He, along with the likes of Joe Dugger, William C. Pease, Karl Smith, and others—who like him had never seen a cotton gin before—helped me accomplish many goals. Don is still with Lummus, where he continues to be a valuable asset to both Lummus and the industry.

In those early days, we were able to develop a line of equipment second to none for its time. We put together systems that would successfully handle and process what is now known in history as the "second revolution"—machine-picked cotton. Many of our designs from this time are still in Lummus plants today.

In 1959, I left Lummus to become president of Continental Gin Company. I inherited a company that was in the midst of severe downsizing and restructuring. The firm was under new ownership that had little experience in operating a company. The people remaining in top-level management from the earlier regime were bitter at a so-called outsider being brought in, and partly as a consequence of this little of my time could be devoted to the development of new products. Even so, we did develop some valuable innovations.

Frustration at Continental Gin Company led me to accept a position in 1964 with the J. G. Boswell Company, based in Los Angeles, California. The J. G. Boswell Company is a large integrated farming company with operations in California, Arizona, and Australia. There, as vice-president and general manager of the processing division, I was able to play a major role in developing solutions to problems that faced large farms, such as Boswell, and the gin industry as a whole. We improved the capacity of the gin stand, developing the first drying system to handle more than forty-bale-per-hour capacities, but still faced the age-old obstacle to increasing capacity of the plant, the press. The trading rules of the time required twenty-one pounds of tare on the bale, which would limit capacity to fifteen to eighteen bales per hour no matter what you did to the rest of the plant. My position with Boswell afforded me the opportunity to force the industry to change from *gross weight* to *net weight* trading. This permitted the strapping of a naked bale, which allowed the press to become fully automated with a cycle-time of about one minute. This work was completed in the early 1970s, and strapping a bale naked rapidly become the standard, including pushing the bale through a stuffer—all started at Boswell.

These developments led to plants with capacities in the sixty-bale-per-hour range. An important factor in achieving these levels was the Vandergriff Moisture System, which humidified and precompressed the lint to allow the press to function effectively at high capacity.

After leaving Boswell in 1976, I became an independent consultant for various companies and individual gin plants including Boswell, Westlake Farms, Elbow Gin, and Sayler American. The arrangement I had was that they would make their plants available for experimental work and pay for material and manufactured parts. In turn, they were able to use any improvements resulting from the research. I was able to sell enough patented developments to continue to pursue improvements in drying systems, gin-stand performance, and the development of a new gin rib.

By 1986, I had limited my work with individual ginning companies to Elbow Gin. They have an excellent organization, capable personnel, and we have been able to keep their 1959 Model Gin Plant "retro fitted" so that it continues to be competitive in terms of capacity and fiber quality. My work continues there with pleasure, and innovations are continuing.

Also in 1986 I designed the first completely new gin stand since the introduction of the sixteen-inch saw gin at Continental in 1962. This 1986 design ultimately became the highly successful Consolidated 164 Saw Gin. A 198 model (conceptually the same as the 164) was introduced in 1994 and became the first twenty-bale-per-hour gin stand.

I formed Vandergriff Inc. in April of 1989. In September 1994 after a twenty-year teaching career, my son Loyd joined the company. He has been a tremendous asset in helping me manage the company and expand our operations.

1   My Early Life

Exposure to cotton gins came early in my life. I was born Arvel Loyd Vandergriff to Blanche and Schelley Vandergriff in 1910. At the time I was born, my dad was operating a cotton gin. He continued to do this until 1916, when he purchased his own gin plant on a leveraged buyout. The plant was a 3-80 saw, a Continental of the Munger variety shown in figure 1, one of the earliest 80-saw gin plants. (The industry often uses "gin" to refer to both a gin stand and plant. The gin stand is a single unit within a plant.)

The plant was in two stories, with a line shaft under the floor driven by a steam engine. I found it fascinating to see the steam engine get started and set all the wheels turning. The plant had a conventional two-story press with swinging doors that opened from the top, not the side. The doors were counterweighted so that the operator could let them down and get the bale out. The counterweights also helped to lift the doors back into place. The press had a hydraulic pump that

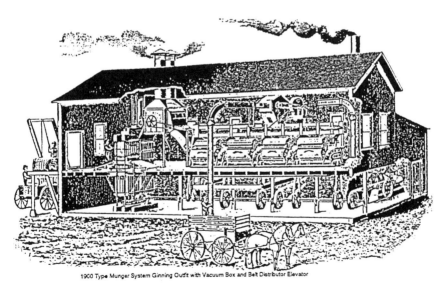

1900 Type Munger System Ginning Outfit with Vacuum Box and Belt Distributor Elevator

Figure 1. Munger plant, early 1900s

Figure 2. Munger Press

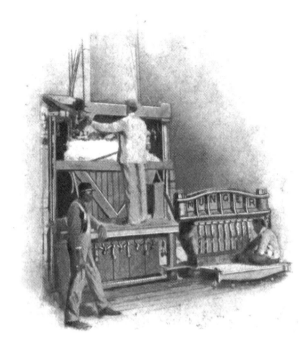

used water, not oil, because oil was expensive. The pump was powered by steam from the boiler. It had a steam tramper with no feeder for the press (figure 2).

My job at nine years of age was to sit on a stool, or to stand, like the young man in figure 2, and rake the cotton from the lint slide into the press box. When the press-box hopper was full, I pulled a lever that operated the steam tramper, thus pushing the cotton down into the press below the dogs that held the cotton down. Then I repeated the process.

A big problem I had was with the condenser. It always made a big-ended bale unless I raked the right amount of cotton to the right side of the tramper to make the bale come out level. If I messed up on this it would be dangerous; the wooden press did not perform well pressing a big-ended bale. Somewhere along the line I learned that placing a bag of sand in the bottom of the lint flue helped rectify this problem. The big-ended bale was caused by a swirl in the flue. The flue ducts from the gin stands entered on a spiral that continued all the way back to the condenser, and this allowed too much cotton to spiral to the inside of the condenser. This caused the cotton to accumulate on my left side, so I had to rake cotton to the right side. By breaking up this spiral with a bag of sand, it evened up the feed to the condenser and lessened the problem considerably. I worked in this gin for five seasons, until it burned in 1924. We collected enough insurance to pay off our debt, but came out of this venture with nothing.

In 1925, when I was fifteen, my dad took a position in Sulpher Bluff, Texas, running a gin for an oil mill. My job at this plant was to fire the boiler. This involved hauling many cords of firewood on a two-wheel cart to the boiler. The working season was very short and the rest of the year we had to find other things to do, such as working on the farm—sharecropping—doing a variety of tasks. This went on until I left home at nineteen, in an effort to finish high school.

I had had difficulty in finishing high school because of the seasonal work I did to help my family survive. All during my growing years, I had not gone to school for more than six months at a time. Most of the time, the schools were held for six-month sessions, which I never got to finish because of working at the gin in the fall. In the spring, I had to drop out and go to work on the farm. So, until I was eighteen, I had gone to school sparingly. I was not going completely without an education, however: I would borrow my more fortunate friends' books and read them. I learned a lot on my own and did my best to educate myself.

When I was eighteen, I did get to go to school for sixty days at the local high school in Sulphur Bluff. I was doing well, but again had to drop out to work. One day I was riding by the school in a wagon and the principal noticed me. He came out, stopped the wagon, and said, "Arvel, why don't you come back and take your final exams?" I told him I felt I had not attended enough and was concerned, but he told me he wanted me to give it a try, so I took him up on his offer. I passed the exams, and got high school credit for sixty days of attendance, or one quarter. These credits, however limited, would be vital when I tried to enroll in the high school at Sulphur Springs, thirty miles away the next year.

I had played a lot of baseball, and one of the guys on my Sulphur Bluff team attended Sulphur Springs High and played football. He asked me if I would like to try out for the Sulphur Springs High football team. I jumped at the chance, even though I had never played football or even seen a game. I went to Sulphur Springs and met the coach. He liked me—and the fact that I was a big guy didn't hurt matters. They were having a two-week training session prior to the start of school and he asked me to attend. It was held at a farmhouse out in the country; we slept and ate there as well. Readers can only imagine how confused I was at the first practice, having never played the game before.

When school was about to open, the coach introduced me to the principal. All I had was my sixty-day report card from Sulphur Bluff. Although the principal was concerned about my poor attendance and lack of credits, he allowed me to enroll as a senior, provided I promised to attend summer school. In the meantime, because Sulphur Springs was thirty miles from my home, the coach had made arrangements for me to stay at the local fire station and sleep on a cot. I ate at a local restaurant, with my meals being paid for by one of the team's fans. I didn't ask questions; I was just glad to eat.

Staying at the fire station, I made it through the football season and went into the basketball program, at midterm I went home to visit for the first time and found my family in dire straights. My dad was in bed with rheumatism and could not work, and I felt compelled to stay home and try to provide for my family. I went to the bank and borrowed $100 to plant a crop on a sharecrop basis. The bank advanced $90 and kept $10 for interest. They allowed me to have the $90 at $10 a month for nine months. We struggled for this nine-month period, and by midterm the next year I was determined to go back and try to finish high school.

By then I was twenty years old and had no further football eligibility, but I did have a tremendous desire to get my diploma. I went back to school, told the principal my problem, and he told me that if I could find a place to sleep and get my meals, he was sure I would have no trouble graduating; but, he said, my class load would be heavy. I stayed at the house of a cousin, Dillard Vandergriff. The principal required that I take six subjects, which would not leave me a lunch hour. I studied until one or two in the morning, every day, and made good grades. I received a small cash scholarship for having the highest grades in the senior class for that term, graduated with the class, and got my high school diploma. It seemed nothing short of a miracle.

By the time I graduated in 1931, the school's football coach had taken a job as an assistant coach at Austin College, in Sherman, Texas. He arranged for me to have a scholarship, provided I could make the team. I hitchhiked seventy-five miles to Sherman, hiking much more than hitching. I spent the first night in Sherman at the coach's home and he arranged for me to stay in the college gym in a small room with a cot in it. I stayed there the entire first year of college. For breakfast, at times I had to depend on the college's head coach—a famous pro football player by the name of Cecil Griggs. For my other meals, evenings I worked at a drive-in, an arrangement that lasted only a short time because the drive-in went out of business. I then got a job waiting tables at a downtown boardinghouse, which meant that I walked two miles each way, three times a day, to serve the three meals per day required of me. This lasted through the 1931-32 school year.

All this time I had little or no money: I shaved time and again with the same razor blade, sharpening it on a water glass. But I was able to play football against some football greats, such as Sammy Baugh and Johnny Vaught of Texas Christian University. When the football season was over, the county high school basketball teams arranged to play a number of their games in the gym where I was living—the only enclosed gym in the county. I lucked into refereeing their games and received a small amount of money for this, a situation that enabled me to live comparatively well.

In 1933, a neck injury cost me my football scholarship. On Christmas Day 1933, I married a lovely lady by the name of Marie Miller, who lived near the college campus. Our marriage lasted almost 59 years until her death from cancer in 1992. This marriage was certainly the crowning achievement of my life.

I had to stay out of school for part of the 1934 year because of my neck injury. While I was recuperating, I taught school in the small community of Posey, Texas. I went back to college in the summer of 1936 and graduated with a major in math and a minor in chemistry and physics.

The Years with the Companies

2

Hardwicke Etter Company, 1937-43, 1945-47

After graduating from Austin College, I taught elementary school in Sherman, Texas for two and a half years; it was the heart of the Depression and jobs were tough to come by. During the Christmas holidays of 1937, I paid a call to Joe Etter, president of the Hardwicke Etter Company to see if I could get some money for our church. I was active in the Baptist church at Sherman, and Etter was a prominent member, well known for his financial contributions. I was chairman of the building committee, which was trying to raise enough money to build an educational building. I walked into the company office and asked the receptionist if I could see him. Etter's desk happened to be close by and he said, "Oh yes, Vandy, I want to see you." I had never met him, but he invited me to sit down and immediately started talking about employing me. The day before at a board meeting there had been a discussion about approaching me to see if I would be interested in working for the company. Much as I enjoyed my teaching job, it did not take long to reach an agreement. Because of my early experience in my father's cotton gin, I saw the chance to pursue a career with a cotton-gin manufacturer as an exciting challenge, not to mention being potentially more lucrative.

Hardwicke Etter started as a mill-supply store in the early 1900s. I believe around 1920 they got the agency for Skimmer Steam Engines and it proved to be very profitable for them. These engines were just beginning to be used to power cotton-gin plants. In the 1920s, a large percentage of the gins in Texas and Oklahoma were powered by Skimmer Steam Engines sold by the Hardwicke Etter Company.

During this period, they developed a seed scale for weighing the cotton seed as it was ginned. The scale consisted of hoppers mounted above each other on a rack. The top hopper received the seed from a screw elevator as it was ginned. This top hopper was supported by scale beams, and when the bale was finished the weight was recorded and the seed was dumped into the lower hopper. Seed was then conveyed out of this hopper to storage, while the seed from the next bale filled the top hopper. This process enabled the gin to pay the farmer, if he chose to sell his seed to the gin, based on actual weight. Prior to that time, the seed weight was arrived at by a formula based on a percentage of the seed-cotton weight, or by deducting bale weight from seed-cotton weight and then deducting an estimated amount for trash. It was the generally accepted opinion at Hardwicke Etter that this was the first successful seed scale used in cotton gins.

In the early or mid-1920s, the company hired John A. Streun, a man short on formal education but long on mechanical ability and ideas, who would have a tremendous impact, not only at Hardwicke Etter but throughout the entire industry. Streun developed an extraction method to deal with the bollie problem— a situation that was becoming common in the industry. Streun's Big Burr machine would set the standard for years to come. This subject is discussed in detail in the section on extractors (Chapter 8).

In view of Streun's reputation in the industry, I was excited about the prospect of working with him. I stayed around the office for about a month, learning whatever I could from any source I could find. The company had purchased a car for me, and I was anxious to get out into the territory and begin my training, which would consist of traveling with a veteran salesman in West Texas. After some delay, a kind soul told me they would not send me out bareheaded; I would have to buy a hat. Up to this time, no one had informed me of this; apparently, it was assumed I would be smart enough to know that bareheaded men did not sell cotton-gin machinery. I bought a white hat and I was off to Lubbock to begin my training.

After an initial training period, I was sent to territories where the salesman was ill, or where there was no salesman at all. I worked in several different territories and began to develop a good rapport with Streun, and traveled a lot with him. During this time, it became clear that I was being groomed to be his successor as chief engineer. When I went into the U.S. Navy in 1943, it was understood that when I returned this arrangement would be continued. However, during the war, the plant, like most industrial operations, had been converted to making war materials, and Streun had brought in his son to help. The son decided he would like to continue with the company after the war, and thus he would occupy the position I had been training for. When I returned, I was placed back in the sales department. I did well there, but it was not what I wanted to do: I wanted to be more on the engineering side of the operation.

3

Lummus Cotton Gin Company, 1947-59

Prior to leaving for the navy, I had been approached by the Lummus Cotton Ginning Company, of Columbus, Georgia and offered a position there. Because I was unhappy with my reassignment at Hardwicke Etter, I decided to join the Lummus firm in June 1947. I was employed to set up a research and development department. My qualifications in this area were limited, but so were the numbers of experienced personnel available for such positions.

As a one-man department, I experienced a rocky start. The established employees did not believe that their machinery needed improvement and they did not expect me to be around for long. I did, however, receive encouragement from the chairman of the board, John P. Illges, Sr. He visited Lummus once a week, on Monday mornings, and he always came by my desk, which was isolated in one corner of a storage room. He never failed to ask how I was doing, was I getting full cooperation, and did I need anything. I could not tell him the truth, I knew it was a battle I had to win or lose on my own.

My first project was to design a new feeder. The John E. Mitchell Company of Dallas was dominating the feeder business, and if we could keep some of this business it would be a big help. However, before I got far into this project, I was sidetracked to work on a press. Thaddeus Grimes, a ninety-year-old engineer, had been working on a standard-density press that was to be delivered in the near future to a customer in West Texas. Most of the press was finished, but some drawings still had to be made when Grimes suffered a heart problem. I finished the engineering work and Grimes and I followed the press to the field. We took the train to Amarillo and continued to Plainview by car. As soon as we arrived Grimes experienced health problems and returned home immediately.

The Anderson Clayton plant was located at Aiken, Texas, a few miles out of Plainview. The plant had a turn-out valve in the lint flue so that either a standard flat-bed bale or a round bale could be produced. A standard bale at that time was rectangular in shape, roughly twenty-seven inches thick by fifty-four inches long and almost forty-two inches high, although the height could vary depending on the compression. These bales weighed about five hundred pounds, including twenty-one pounds of tare (strapping and jute bagging). The weight would vary depending on the compressed height. A round bale was formed by passing the bat from the gin condenser between a series of compression rollers that wound the bat into a high-density cylindrically shaped bale with an approximate weight of only 250 pounds. It was a beautiful and practical bale. Anderson Clayton Company of Houston, Texas owned the patent to this press.

The new press had been installed late in the season to replace an old round-bale press and was designed to make a higher density bale, with dimensions of twenty inches by fifty inches by thirty-two inches. The new press was put into operation, but before the first bale was finished, the cast-iron parts of the tramper gave up and the pieces scattered widely in the press room.

I returned to Columbus, had replacements for the cast-iron parts fabricated from steel plate, and took them back to Aiken to test the press further before the season was over. No other problems serious enough to shut the press down completely arose during this short testing period, but there was still plenty to be done. The dogs and the dog-locking mechanism proved to be too weak and would have to be redesigned for the next season. The doors had hydraulic locks (Grimes was an excellent hydraulics engineer) and the door pressure was too great; the locks held, but the pressure ruptured the oil lines. The lower boxes and the top baling boxes had the same dimensions. I concluded that if the bottom boxes were slightly smaller so that the bale could expand slightly as it was pressed into the top boxes, the pressure on the doors would be reduced. I put a quarter-inch plywood shim in each side of the lower box, which relieved the pressure on the doors enough to solve our immediate problems.

This press was designed, at Anderson Clayton's request, to make twenty-inch by fifty-inch bales instead of the standard fifty-four-inch length. They reasoned that the shorter bales would stack on top of each other, thus fitting more cotton into a railroad boxcar than did the traditional longer bale. We believed that we would not have any problem with the industry accepting this shorter-bale approach, especially because a big operation like Anderson Clayton wanted it. Anderson Clayton bought several of these presses, most of which are still in operation, but this bale dimension was never accepted by the trade.

I continued to be active in press work for some time, but then turned the details over to Donald Van Doorn, who had come to work for me soon after my arrival. I completed the designing of a new feeder during the winter and ran into problems trying to get it tested in our demonstration plant. The Lummus service department refused to help with the installation but I was able to get the service manager overruled. The tests were run, production drawings were made, and the first set of feeders was sent to Santa Rosa, Texas, in the Rio Grande Valley. Five of these feeders were installed over Lummus 80 saw gin stands in July 1948. The machines operated well and became a production item in 1949. The details of the design of this feeder are covered in Chapter 8.

During this time, I was also working on a number of other projects, including the Multi-Jet Air-Blast Gin Saw Doffing Nozzle. This was first designed as an attachment to replace the existing air-blast nozzle on the Lummus 80 saw gin. Because it used individual jets for each saw, this multijet air-blast approach used a small amount of air and intensified both the top and bottom moting arrangements on our gin stand. (The subject of moting is discussed in detail in Chapter 6.) I experimented with the first set of these in a Lummus plant at Dothan, Alabama, during the 1947 season. For the 1948 season, a later model of these multijet nozzles were installed in the 3-80 saw Shannon Plantation Gin at Lake Cormorant, Mississippi. During this time, spindle-picked, mechanically harvested cotton was in its early stages, and water was used on the spindles. There was practically no defoliation, so the cotton was loaded with green leaves. The plant was equipped with one short dryer and two cylinder cleaners, with Mitchell Feeders over the gins. The cleaning done by the moting systems after the installation of the Multi-Jet Air-Blast nozzle was amazing (see figure 37 in Chapter 6). The process created more interest across the cotton belt than anything new since system ginning.

With the new feeders beginning to sell well, the press under control for the moment, and the multijet cleaning system in demand, I could devote more attention to other projects. Having seen the potential for the multijet method of separation, Don Van Doorn came up with the idea of separating trash particles from the lint by directing the lint at an open slot at a high velocity, with the commingled mass meeting an incoming current of air. The trash particles, having a greater mass, would continue their initial direction; the lint would be turned in another direction. We experimented with this device in our plant and were pleased with its simplicity and effectiveness. We had to provide a vacuum in the flue system sufficient to turn the lint as it approached the slot. This made it necessary for the condenser receiving the lint to operate and discharge the lint between the doffing rollers under considerable negative pressure. A high-volume fan was needed in the air discharge of the condenser to provide this vacuum. The doffing rollers had to be redesigned in order to strip the lint from the condenser screen and be able to discharge it.

These jets, which Van Doorn called superjets, complemented the multijet installed in the Shannon Plantation Gin. Because they operated in the same manner as the multijets, the results did not create as much excitement as we had with the multijets themselves. Also, the multijet doffing was not designed to operate

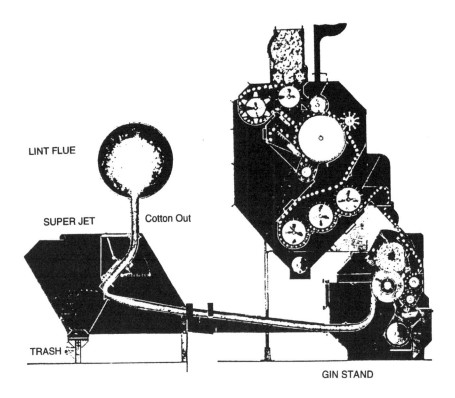

LINT FLUE

SUPER JET   Cotton Out

TRASH

GIN STAND

Figure 3. The Lummus Super-Jet

against enough pressure to allow the superjets to operate at optimum efficiency. The velocity of the air and lint as it approached the jet slot had to be created by the induced air from the "jet effect" of the air-blast nozzle. When these jets were installed behind the regular air-blast nozzles, they had more zip, making them more effective. The superjets (figure 3) became a popular item with our sales department. This little unit probably did more to enhance the prestige of Lummus than anything we did for some time. Some textile mills specified that they would receive only cotton from gins equipped with superjets.

Many gin owners who bought Lummus Super-Jets did not have condensers that would handle the four- to five-inch WC vacuum necessary to make them work properly. However, the fact that they had superjets made their cotton more desirable, at least for a few years.

During this time, there was so much interest by the mills in getting cotton that was not "over-ginned" that some contracted with the growers for cotton to be ginned according to their own instructions. This always included superjets, and usually included minimum drying and cleaning—in some cases, no drying at all. Because the grower was paid a fixed price for his cotton regardless of the grade, sometimes this led to careless harvesting; eventually this method of purchasing cotton was for the most part abandoned. But the Lummus Super-Jet maintained its place in the gin plant, and has done so up to the present. Other manufacturers were licensed to manufacture the Lummus Super-Jet; the Murray Company of Texas sold a large number of these units. From the time this unit was introduced until I left Lummus in 1959, 2624 were sold. Thirty-five years later, virtually all Lummus gin plants sold are still equipped with superjets.

The patent on this unit was issued in Van Doorn's name and assigned to Lummus. The engineering and the working out of the practical application was left to me and the people on my staff, including Don; hence, the management decided that I also should share in the royalties.

Karl Smith, a valuable member of our team who made some of the original drawings, has an interesting story about the origin of the idea for the superjet. We had placed the battery condenser under vacuum to aid the multijet air-blast gin-doffing system. We had this system in our experimental gin plant. In the rectangular elbow in the duct going to the condenser, a slot had been cut accidentally in the outside of the curvature of the elbow. While ginning, trash would pop out through the slot, and because the flue was under vacuum there was no lint loss. According to Karl, I told Van Doorn to dress this up; apparently, I said: "Let's sell it," or something like that. Whether or not the story is true, Van Doorn did an excellent job in designing a valuable unit. This was the beginning of a long and successful career for him with Lummus. Several years later when I was promoted to executive vice president, Van Doorn succeeded me as VP in charge of engineering, a position he held for many years.

It is explained in the section on gin saw doffing that a brush-gin saw doffer will not push against as much pressure as an air-blast doffing system. With the Lummus Super-Jet, it is desirable to have the highest velocity possible, and this favors the air-blast doffing system's higher velocity. The throat of the Super-Jet is adjustable to control the pressure in the flue against which the doffing system must operate. Many customers wanted to use this unit, but more and more were switching to brush-doffing arrangements, which limited the superjet's efficiency. In view of this, we designed a booster jet to go in the duct between the gin stand and the superjet. This was similar to the air-blast nozzle, and required an additional blower. This modification did not increase the efficiency of the unit significantly, and we soon abandoned this approach and settled for the velocity that could be produced by the brush-doffing system.

In the 1980s, more than thirty years after the introduction of the Super-Jet, I designed another version of the superjet cleaner for a California gin. This unit had a modified version of the concept abandoned at Lummus, incorporating a booster jet in the duct from the gin stand to the jet cleaner. The booster jet is built into it, near the jet slot. It is placed in the top of the duct so that it increases the velocity of the air conveying the cotton without interrupting the smoothness of the flow. This was a distinct improvement and made the unit very efficient.

Another significant improvement in the new unit is that the foreign matter discharges into a sealed chamber. These units operate under vacuum; the negative pressure pulls air into the slot against the air flow from the gins and turns the lint back into the duct, where it continues out of the unit into the discharge flues. With the Super-Jet, this air enters through the foreign-matter discharge chamber, and the foreign matter has to discharge through the incoming air (i.e., against the current). This allows some of the lighter foreign matter to be carried back into the slot. To overcome this problem, the top of the chamber was closed and a narrow inlet for air was placed just under the jet slot (see figure 4). Because the chamber is under vacuum, enough air is pulled through the air inlet to turn the lint back into the slot, which allows the foreign matter to discharge into a dead-air space. The conveyor in the bottom of the hopper receiving the foreign matter is sealed at the discharge to prevent air from flowing back into the chamber, bringing trash back with it. This unit operated in the California gin for several years. When I joined Consolidated Cotton Gin Company as a consultant, I made this type of unit available to them. It is now known as the Super-Mote and has proven to be a valuable asset in their line of equipment.

The Super-Mote unit can be used with no positive pressure on the inlet duct conveying the cotton to it. The incoming air generated by the vacuum can be limited, and the negative pressure can pull on the incoming cotton-conveying duct, creating a conveying velocity up to the booster jet that allows the cotton to reach the discharge slot at good velocity. This makes it practical to use this unit in connection with roller-gin lint cleaning, where a positive conveying air often is not available. Presently, several manufacturers make some type of air-jet lint cleaner, the Lummus patent having expired several years ago.

Entering 1950, our main project was redesigning the gin stand with ninety saws and giving it a cosmetic treatment—at which Van Doorn excelled. By this time, William C. Pease III, an electrical engineer, had also joined our team. As

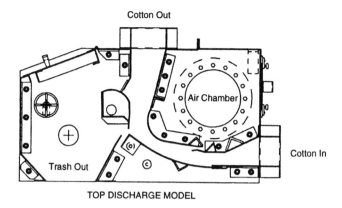

TOP DISCHARGE MODEL

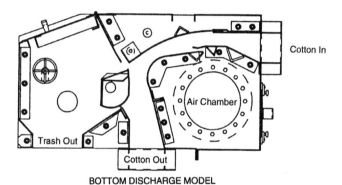

BOTTOM DISCHARGE MODEL

Figure 4. The Vandergriff Super-Mote

previously mentioned, Van Doorn had no experience in cotton ginning when he arrived, and neither had Pease. In a way, this was an advantage because experienced industry personnel were often negative about design changes. Van Doorn and Pease did not know enough about ginning to say whether or not a project could be done, and they were willing to take the risks necessary to improve our products. This allowed us to set the standard for the industry.

Another important member of our team was Joe Dugger, one of the earliest members of my staff. Dugger, who was excellent in the area of mechanics, contributed greatly. In late 1949, a young, local engineering student joined our staff—Karl Smith. He had a head full of ideas and participated in most of the major projects. Karl carried more than his share of the load in field testing and modifications, learning fast and well. In 1958, he left to follow another line of work. He became well known and respected in the industry and I have enjoyed working with him on various projects. Our friendship and mutual respect has endured for more than forty-five years.

The Model 90 saw gin stand was ready for production in time for the big push for new plants that occurred during the Korean War. By 1 April 1951, we had sold all the machinery we could manufacture for that year. We sold and delivered, on time, between forty to fifty 5-90 saw plants in 1951-52. Most of these orders were shipped to California and Arizona, where, during the Korean War, restrictions had been lifted on the amount of acreage that could be planted.

When I had arrived at Lummus, some of the engineering bottlenecks were unbelievable. To cite one of many examples: when a cylinder cleaner was sold, the installation information was given to a draftsman for him to engineer, but he also had to engineer the cleaner frame. The delay, however, was not only in engineering: the factory could not make up cleaner frames and supports to be placed in stock; they had to be made up after the job was engineered. This type of antiquity (they called it *custom design*) existed throughout the engineering department. Fortunately, we took the time in 1950 to design standard frames, supports, platforms, and so forth (see figure 5) and were ready for the big rush in 1951. Looking back, I am amazed at how we got so much done—and so quickly, too. Many of the standards that we established are still in use.

The plants sold that year were all fairly standard and the new Model 90 saw gin stands performed well. We did make one change during this season: the Multi-Jet Doffing System did not provide adequate doffing when used with the superjets, because of back-pressure needed to make the superjets operate. We therefore modified the multijets to use a larger volume of air. This reduced their cleaning efficiency, but the effectiveness of the superjets was improved; hence, the net result was about the same. This modification in the doffing system is covered in the section on gin doffing.

During this period, incoming feed-control units were not being used in gin plants. I was not satisfied with this situation, so I designed a system to alleviate the problem. This was to be the beginning of feeding the cotton into the gin plant at a controlled rate—an important milestone.

The unit consisted of a surge bin that was placed under the separator receiving the incoming cotton. A set of feed rollers were placed in the bottom of the bin to feed the cotton out at a controlled rate. This was done by varying the speed of the rollers—a rate controlled by the operator. Toward the top of the bin

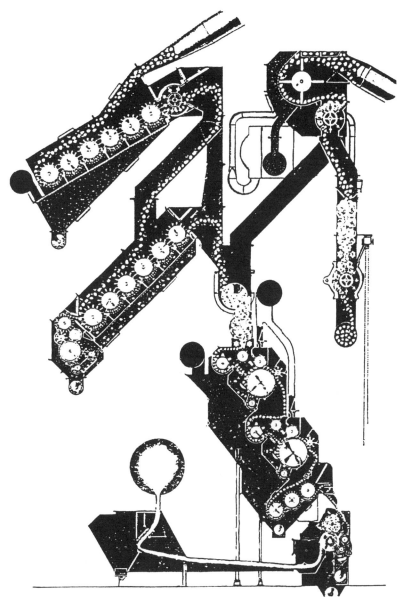

Figure 5. Standardized cylinder cleaning arrangement. More than forty years later, this arrangement is still in use in Lummus plants.

is a *sensor*, which is triggered when the bin is about to fill. When this sensor is actuated, the vacuum to the separator is blocked and no more cotton can be fed into the hopper. As the cotton feeds out, another sensor sends a signal to unblock the vacuum line when the bin is about to be empty, starting the flow again from the farm vehicle delivering the cotton. This is one of the many projects we worked on in 1950-51. Today, these units are standard and make use of micro-switches with a feeler in the hopper to sense the position of the cotton in the bin. The switch actuates a solenoid-operated air cylinder attached to a butterfly valve in the vacuum line between the unloading fan and the separator receiving the incoming cotton.

Many plants in the 1950s did not have compressed air to operate air cylinders, so I designed a cutoff valve that would be actuated by the vacuum in the line. Figure 6 shows such a valve as it was installed in the Model 90 saw plants. It was also sold for use in the older plants.

The device consisted of a surge bin (as described above) located under the receiving separator. A vane or sensor is projected into the bin near the top. When the hopper is filled, the vane is pushed back against the wall of the bin. A linkage is connected to the shaft supporting this vane, and this linkage connects to a small butterfly valve on the end of the bin. The vane in the top of the hopper closes the butterfly valve and the vane in the bottom opens the valve. This valve has a four-inch vacuum line connected to it. In the main vacuum line from the unloading fan to the separator is an ingenious valve for blocking the flow of air when actuated by the vacuum from the butterfly valve. A cutoff valve (consisting of a flat quarter-inch plate disk the diameter of the pipe) is mounted in the vacuum line in a rectangular box and attached to a shaft inside the box, right-angled to the pipe. On the opposite side of the shaft a flat plate is mounted at a right angle to the cutoff disk, and enclosed in a separate chamber. This plate acts as a diaphragm. The small vacuum line from the butterfly valve connects to the bottom of the chamber containing the diaphragm. To the other side of the butterfly valve, a small line connects to the top of the chamber containing the cutoff valve, so that it is always under vacuum during operation. The butterfly valve is normally open so that the vacuum on the diaphragm holds the cutoff valve in the up (open) position. When the hopper fills, the butterfly valve closes, cutting off the vacuum on the diaphragm that holds the cutoff valve open, and allows it to fall across the pipe, cutting off the vacuum to the separator and thus cutting off the flow of incoming cotton. The *rate of feed* is controlled by the speed of the feed rollers in the bottom of the surge bin. Their speed is controlled by Love-Joy variable-pitch sheaves on a small gear box mounted on one of the feed roller shafts. This is driven by a small 110-volt motor mounted on the side of the bin. The pitch of the driven sheave is

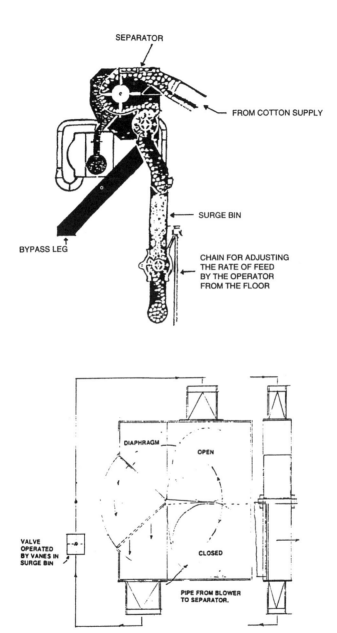

SEPARATOR

FROM COTTON SUPPLY

SURGE BIN

BYPASS LEG

CHAIN FOR ADJUSTING
THE RATE OF FEED
BY THE OPERATOR
FROM THE FLOOR

DIAPHRAGM

OPEN

VALVE
OPERATED
BY VANES IN
SURGE BIN

CLOSED

PIPE FROM BLOWER
TO SEPARATOR.

CROSS SECTION OF CUT-OFF VALVE FOR SNUFFY'S STILL

Figure 6. Snuffy's Still: the beginning of feeding cotton at a controlled rate.

controlled by a chain suspended from the unit, so the operator, by pulling the chain in either direction, can increase or decrease the speed of the feed rollers.

From this description and figure 6, readers will understand why the people who put it together at the experimental gin named it Snuffy's Still. It was later replaced by units with much larger surge bins and more sophisticated sensors and control methods. However, a number of these units were sold, and the only legitimate complaint about them was the limited size of the surge bin. This limitation was the result of placing the receiving separator above the distributor, so that there could be a leg to the distributor to bypass the precleaning equipment. There were times when the operator chose to bypass the overflow rather than run this cotton back through the precleaning equipment.

The 1951 season brought us another interesting challenge. Practically all of the plants we sold that year were 5-90 saw plants. Some of these plants went to West Texas in the area that was stripper harvested. There was so much foreign matter—stems, limbs, and burrs—that it was difficult to unload the cotton from the farm trailers. I was told by veterans in the area that nothing larger than a four-stand plant was practicable because of this problem of unloading. I ignored this advice and sold four 5-90 saw plants. Sure enough, the standard unloading fan was not adequate. I immediately installed another fan adjacent to the original unloading fan and piped the discharge of the unloading fan into the inlet of the new fan. The vacuum in the line between the fans and the separator increased according to the laws of fans in series, and the unloading problem was solved.

The word began to get around in the trade about the Lummus fan arrangement and these double fans were shipped to West Texas in large quantities. Most of those who ordered the double fans did not pay much attention to their speed, which resulted in a lot of collapsed pipe, but no one seemed to mind. They could unload cotton, and installing reinforced pipe seemed to be only a small problem. Years later, I was still encountering situations where plant capacity was limited by unloading capacity. It is ridiculous to spend money for new ginning equipment and then not be able to put enough cotton into the plant to utilize this equipment. When we were testing a trailer-dumping system in the late 1960s, we built a plant that had large unloading telescopes as an auxiliary unloading system, and one man could unload fifty bales per hour. Of course, it took additional power, but that is cheap compared with having the equipment and not being able to unload enough cotton to allow it to operate at maximum capacity. The industry had a lot to learn about unloading telescope and pipe sizes to get the most efficiency out of these high-capacity unloading systems. Customers seemed to have little interest in this problem; they just wanted to keep the gins running. With proper duct work, a separator, and telescopes, one fan can be adequate—but the industry rapidly adopted fans in series, called supercharged fans, and thirty-five years later they are still referred to in the same manner.

By the early 1950s, most of the company employees were slowly accepting me and the new program at Lummus. One veteran engineer however, demanded that I go or he would. I was informed about this by John Illges, the president, and I realized this was a tough decision for him. I told him I would gladly accept his decision. Illges told me the next day that he had accepted the other man's resignation. I soon became vice president in charge of engineering.

Sales continued to escalate.

Presses and Automation at Lummus

Also in the early 1950s, we started an extensive program of redesigning our cotton-gin presses. One incentive was to make them more adaptable to automation—the system we were applying to the rest of our line of equipment. One of the early needs was a simple method of determining when there was a bale in the press. In many areas, the cotton was still transported to the gin in one-bale lots; hence, there was no need for this because all the cotton in the lot was pressed into the box, and the press was turned for the tying operation. But in some areas, particularly in the west, cotton arrived in trailers containing more than one bale and some means was needed to divide the load into bales. In many cases, one of the press operators would pull against one of the press dogs to determine the pressure, and with experience he would guess pretty close to when there was a bale in the press. As more and more plants started driving the press feeding tramper from a separate motor (instead of with a belt from a common source of power for all of the plant) it became common to have ammeters to read the tramper load. At first these ammeters sounded a signal when a preset load level had been reached; the press was then turned manually.

Soon the press turning was motorized, and when the ammeter signaled that a bale was in the box, the signal actuated the press-turning motor and the press turned automatically. This was the beginning of automating the press, a process that has developed to the extent that now the bale is strapped and delivered to a conveyor belt (to the outside of the building) automatically.

A principal reason for redesigning the presses was to make them rigid enough for the limit switches to be actuated and not be affected by instability. Van Doorn and Pease were integral parts of this effort. By the early 1950s, we had the most automated and best-looking equipment on the market (figures 7, 8).

Burr Extraction

A problem we recognized early on was that our master extractors were not competitive in the stripper-cotton areas. This was particularly true when compared with the Hardwicke Etter Big Burr machines that had dominated this market for many years. Recognizing this, we designed a new machine similar to Hardwicke Etter's. I had plans for a different approach when we had time to develop it, but cleaning systems and lint cleaners were to occupy us for quite some time. We did develop these burr machines for the stripper areas, and this work is covered in detail in the section on stick machines (see Chapter 8).

Immediately following the introduction of the Big Burr machines, I started working on the design of a burr-extraction machine that would employ a unique method of separation we called the *sling-off principle*. I discovered this while I was developing the Thermex Feeder in the late 1940s. When a commingled mass of cotton and trash was applied to the extraction cylinder, rotating with a peripheral speed of twelve hundred to sixteen hundred feet per minute, the trash, particularly burrs and sticks, would sling off the cylinder in a tangential direction. The cotton fibers would be engaged by the teeth of the cylinder and remain with it until doffed. In this first machine, the doffing brush was relocated to expose about ninety degrees of the circumference of extracting cylinder, permitting the burrs, sticks, and other foreign matter that had followed the cylinder under the stripper roller to sling off the cylinder. This material, along with some cotton, would be passed to another extractor cylinder, where the cotton would be reclaimed. This machine was introduced into the West Texas area in the early 1950s and was well received. I later was granted a patent on it.

The sling-off principle was applied as an attachment for the Big Burr machine. It was later used in a completely new machine and became almost standard equipment in gin plants worldwide. It was also one of the most copied machines to be introduced in many years. This is discussed in depth in Chapter 8 covering extractors.

Fiber Quality

Another problem we recognized and addressed early in our work was fiber quality. We believed it was our responsibility to supply the industry with equipment that would process machine-harvested cotton, which would provide an acceptable grade for the grower and a product the mill could live with. As a first

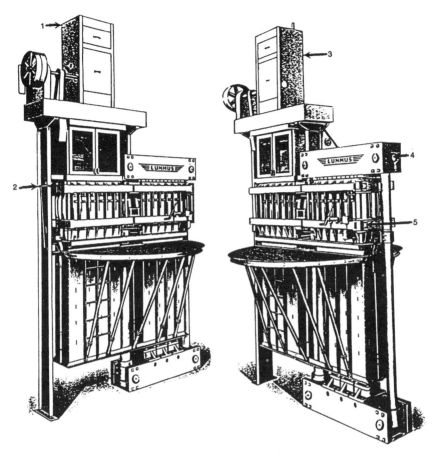

1 Tramper enclosed in sturdy steel casing for safety of the operators—dust proof for protection of moving parts. All ball bearings mechanically sealed and prelubricated.

2 Tramper control lever starts, either manually or automatically, but only after all locks are in safety position. Also serves as turning lock, which permits either manual or automatic turning. Latches automatically in new position when press is power turned.

3 Tramper may be equipped with automatic bale weight control if uniform electric power is available for a 10 HP motor.

4 Gauge which tells at a glance hydraulic pressure actuating compression.

5 Hydraulic door locks: 2 or 3 easy strokes close door latches without noise or wear, shock-free opening.

Figure 7. Lummus standard-density press

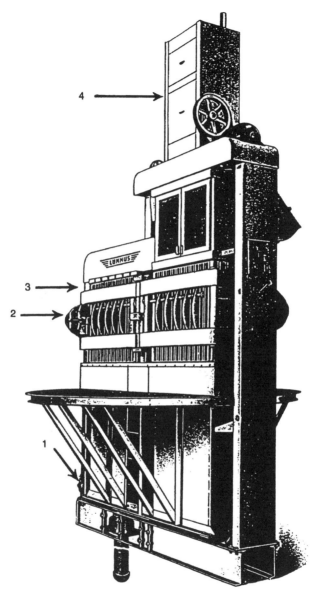

1 Automatic hydraulic control, after press is turned, starts the ram and stops at the limit of its stroke.

2 Hydraulic door latches release without noise and without wear. Closed by one stroke of handle.

3 Simplified ram control.

4 Heavy-duty, enclosed tramper automatically starts after press is turned—either by power or by hand—but only after everything is safely locked into operating position. Stops automatically when desired bale weight is reached.

Figure 8. Lummus Auto-Pak press

step we decided to hire a cotton-fiber technician. (At that time there were a few cotton-fiber technicians—I believe these technicians had been trained by USDA fiber scientists in Washington, DC—and were working with the U.S. Department of Agriculture and other public agencies.) We set up a laboratory with the standard equipment available at the time. One piece of equipment was a Shirley Analyzer (for checking the non-lint content of the lint), another a USDA Fractionater (for measuring trash content of seed cotton; we made this according to USDA specifications). We also used a Pressley Strength Tester and a Suter Webb sorter (for making fiber arrays to determine the length distribution of the fibers in a sample).

We learned very early the obvious; that any mechanical processing, precleaning, ginning, or lint cleaning would break some fibers. But what did fiber breakage mean? One result of fiber breakage was a change in the length distribution of the fibers. We chose to study this change through the use of fiber arrays. A given variety of cotton grown under normal conditions produced a fiber of fairly stable length distribution; that is to say, a certain percentage of fiber would be shorter than one-half inch, or any other length one might choose to observe. In an effort to determine what each processing machine did to the length distribution, we chose to use the change in fiber shorter than one-half inch as a measure. One particular variety we studied had about 11 percent of the fiber shorter than one-half inch when hand-pulled from the seed. We then ginned this cotton with increasing levels of cleaning. The results of this study (Table 1) told us that if we used only a feeder and a gin, we increased the percentage of short fibers by 33.6 percent; add one six-cylinder cleaner and we find an additional 2.75 percent increase; add a second cleaner and get a further 4.75 percent increase; add a stick machine, get a further 5.44 percent increase. Saw-type lint cleaners under four different conditions showed a short-fiber increase range from 8.5 percent to 13 percent. The use of twenty-one cylinders of precleaning and a stick machine, along with the feeder, gin, and a lint cleaner, resulted in an overall short-fiber increase of more than 50 percent over the hand-pulled fibers.

We made raw-stock nep counts at the various processing levels (see Table 1). Generally, the nep counts followed the short-fiber increases—each 1 percent increase in short fibers resulting in a 2 to 3 percent increase in neps.

Our efforts to determine how these short-fiber increases due to processing affected spinning quality yielded predictable results. These results were not as clear-cut as the short-fiber measurements, however. Mill processing is essentially a continuation of the cleaning processes in ginning (except for carding, which tends to level out some of the difference in both gin and mill processing). There is indication that cotton cleaned to a high grade in the ginning process will produce more acceptable finished products when minimum processing is used in the mill.

In the early years of mechanical harvesting, having found that spinning quality was related to fiber breakage, we attempted to limit the gin processing to a reasonable level and live with the resulting grades. However, with poor to no defoliation, and the heavy use of water on the spindles of the pickers, there was a rush to install multiple stages of seed-cotton cleaning and drying. This resulted in excessive fiber breakage, and the mills complained bitterly. Better methods of defoliation and harvesting and gin processing were needed.

Lummus Feeders

When I designed the new feeder briefly described earlier in this chapter, I designed it so that hot air could be introduced into it. This air entered over the stripper roller above the saw; a scroll then directed it around the roller and back over the saw to strip back trash. I named the feeder the Thermex Feeder because of this drying feature. I remembered how much drying we were able to get with the hot air in the Mitchell Feeders when they were the only drying available for seed-cotton conditioning.

The heat in the feeder proved so effective that I added another section of extraction to the heated feeder. This proved to be popular in gins with limited drying systems and, with this success, I added a third stage, which produced even better results. I have never seen a better cleaning system for the low capacity of the 80 and 90 saw gins.

A serious problem of this arrangement was the height: the Triplex had little room above the distributor for the conventional precleaning arrangement that was needed for machine-picked cotton. We had made so many alterations to a gin plant that I did not want to risk moving the precleaning equipment to some location other than standard. Although its height was a problem, the concept of introducing hot air into the feeders proved to be popular. During my time at Lummus, 1378 Thermex Feeders (figure 9) were sold.

Lummus Lint Cleaning

Continental Gin Co. and others were beginning to have good success with saw-type lint cleaners. They referred to these cleaners as re-gins. Re-ginned cotton had a bad name with the cotton mills, and understandably so. It was common practice for the loose cotton from various sources—sample rooms, warehouses,

Table 1*

CLEANING VERSUS FIBER PROPERTIES

	Fibers Shorter than 1/2"	% Increase	Nep Count
Hand Pulled Lint	11.3%	—	3
Feeder & Roller Gin	11.4	1%	7
Feeder & Saw Gin	14.7	30%	18
Feeder, Gin & L. C.	16.6	47%	24
Feeder, 6-Cyl. Cleaner & Gin	15.1	34%	20
Feeder, Cleaner, Gin & L. C.	16.7	48%	26
Feeder, Cleaner, Gin & S. J.	14.8	31%	20
Feeder, 2 Cleaners & Gin	15.4	36%	23
Feeder, 2 Cleaners & L. C.	16.7	48%	29
Feeder, 2 Cleaners, Gin & S. J.	15.1	34%	23
All pre-cleaning & Gin	15.5	37%	25
All pre-cleaning, Gin & S. J.	15.5	37%	24
All pre-cleaning, Gin & L. C.	17.1	51%	32

Add one cleaner - 14.7 - 15.1% = 2.72% Increase
Add two cleaners - 14.7 - 15.4% = 4.75% Increae
**   Add three cleaners - 14.7 - 15.5% = 5.44% Increase
Add lint cleaner - 14.7 - 16.6% = 13% Increae
Add lint cleaner - 15.1 -16.7% = 10.6% Increae
Add lint cleaner - 15.5 - 17.1% = 10.32 Increase

*   Table 1 is a composite of a lot of tests and the results most likely could not be repeated on a single test basis. Also today's machines under today's conditions may produce different results. These results are reported to illustrate the trend in the change in length distribution as the level of processing increases.

**   Twenty-one cyclinders of cleaning and stick machine. Test done at Lummus Cotton Gin Co. Fiber Lab, 1954-55.

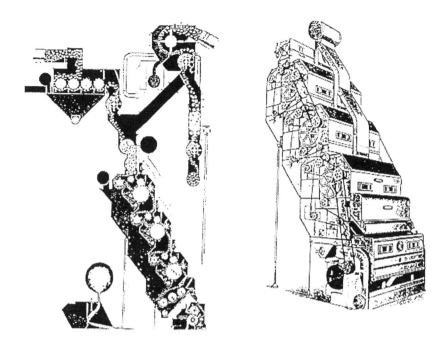

Figure 9. Lummus Triple Thermex Feeder

and so on—to be concentrated, run through a machine called a re-gin, and baled. This cotton might not be of good quality, because it had been treated rather badly and was a mixture of various qualities. To the mills, a saw-type lint cleaner sounded like about the same kind of treatment.

These saw-type lint cleaners were soon improved to the point that the cotton from them was combed to an attractive smoothness, in addition to the cleaning done by them. To a classer's trained eye, this smoothness was readily apparent— and this combed cotton looked good. There was no way, of course, to know what had actually been done to the fiber in the process of cleaning and combing.

We knew from our fiber tests that we could furnish a better spinning product with superjets, and a number of mills refused to accept the re-ginned cotton for quite some time. However, we recognized that the classers, except in isolated cases, were going to continue to favor the combed cotton. Therefore, we started working toward developing a method of combing the cotton—preferably by a method that would not be classed as a re-gin.

By chance, I knew about a Shirley Opener that operated on the same principle as the Shirley Analyzer mentioned earlier in this chapter. This machine did a combination of combing and cleaning without grid bars and it seemed to have some features that would result in less fiber stress than the so-called re-gins. We obtained one of these machines and set it up for testing. Modifications were necessary to feed it from a gin condenser, and some components had to be enlarged. After a year of redesigning and testing, we were ready to give the machine a field test. We went back to A. V. Shannon of Shannon Plantation Gin at Lake Cormorant, Mississippi, but Shannon had built a completely new Lummus plant. The machine was designed to receive a batt from a horizontal direction and we were attempting to feed it with a batt approaching from the vertical. We used a curved metal sheet to turn the batt the necessary ninety degrees. To get this curved scroll sheet in the right place to perform this function was tricky. In trying to work out this problem, I let my right hand get caught between a pair of five-inch feed rollers that were feeding the lint to the curved scroll and almost lost my hand.

My injury delayed the development of this machine significantly, but we did get production models in the field the next season. They were popular in our own plants, which had condensers that made a good batt, and we sold more than six hundred of them in one year. However, when used with some of our competitors' condensers, on threading up at the beginning of a bale, or during start up, the first cotton to come out would be a roll of lint (called a hard roll) that had accumulated between the screen drum of the condenser and the doffing rollers. It was difficult for the Little Comber, as we called it, to digest this hard roll—a problem that was too much of a handicap to overcome, although some customers insisted on putting them in anyway. Our salesmen were not inclined to turn down an order if the customer insisted, and in spite of difficulties, we had a successful run of sales with Little Combers.

A unique feature of these machines (figures 10 and 11) was that the feed bar was made in short segments, each about two inches in width and individually spring loaded to move down with the thickness of the batt. By contrast, the feed plate, or feed bar as it is more commonly called, used in the lint cleaners made by others, followed the pattern of that used for years with the toothed cylinder (called a licker-in cylinder), used to feed cards in the textile mills. They were in one piece and in a fixed position with the other lint cleaner. The feed roller over the feed bar floated under heavy spring tension, holding it about one thirty-second of an inch off the feed bar. If the batt was thick enough in one place to push the feed roller up, the remaining length of the batt would be released. These short sections of feed bars used on our combers were an advantage with this type of a lint cleaner, but were not suitable for lint cleaners with grid bars.

As the lint was fed over the comber feed bars and into the combing cylinder, the teeth of the cylinder would not stress the batt until the fibers were about one staple length away from the pinch point. The idea was that as the teeth combed through the fibers, they would be released from the pinch point before being broken by the stress. This feature certainly had some merit. The teeth on the cylinder were radial—so the fibers were not seated into them, they merely followed the rotation of the cylinder along with the air current generated by the surface of the cylinder. As the fibers left the feed bar, the particles of trash, having a greater density, left the cylinder in a direction at a tangent to its surface. By placing the lint-duct opening so that this tangent was outside the outer edge of the duct, the trash was separated from the lint. A short section of the lint duct was hinged, to be adjusted to make the cleanest separation, lose the minimum amount of lint, and separate the maximum amount of trash.

This cylinder with radial teeth was self-doffing, and the lint was carried to the condenser over the lint slide by vacuum. These units were used on 5-90 saw plants producing at about ten bales per hour, which was above their most efficient range but they filled a need for a time. There was considerable skepticism about the use of the little twenty-four-inch secondary condenser to receive the lint at this rate, but this one performed well. This was an excellent method of separation, but for good separation, the rate of flow—as with any of the machines of this type—is limited. The separation efficiency was not much better than that of the superjet cleaners, but the combing action resulted in a smoother sample, which pleased the cotton classer.

The success of these little units was short-lived: we were experiencing the advent of a formidable competitor. A West Texas ginner, Ennis Moss, had been working on the development of a saw-type lint cleaner for some time, and the use of his machine was becoming widespread. Our combers were being replaced by this unit, and in an effort to salvage something from the situation, for a short time we acted as an agent for these units in our plants.

During this period, Ennis Moss and I became good friends. He was still using closely spaced twelve-inch gin saws on a mandrel, with spacers similar to a gin saw. I told him about the textile wire being used in several applications in the mills (we were using it ourselves on our comber cylinders). The wire was a thin strip of drawn metal, one edge expanded and the other edge with teeth cut on it—teeth that could be just about any shape or size. The other edge was of such a shape that a circular spiral groove could be cut in a solid metal cylinder, the wire

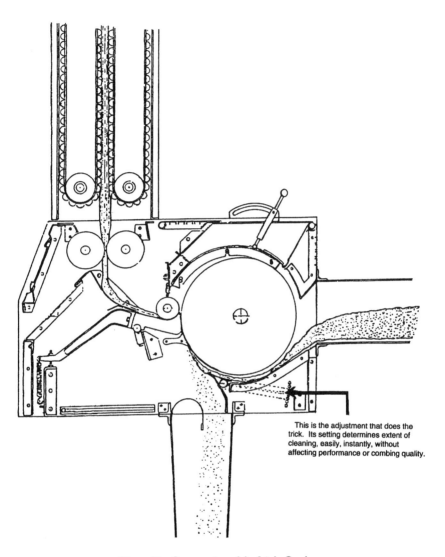

This is the adjustment that does the trick. Its setting determines extent of cleaning, easily, instantly, without affecting performance or combing quality.

Figure 10. Cross section of the Little Comber

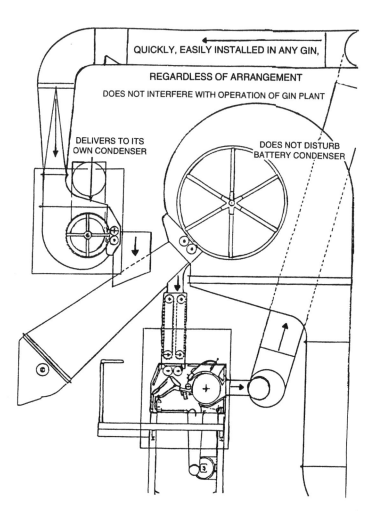

QUICKLY, EASILY INSTALLED IN ANY GIN,

REGARDLESS OF ARRANGEMENT

DOES NOT INTERFERE WITH OPERATION OF GIN PLANT

DELIVERS TO ITS
OWN CONDENSER

DOES NOT DISTURB
BATTERY CONDENSER

Figure 11. Complete layout of the Little Comber arrangement

pulled into this groove under tension, and then the edge of the groove be pressed
in against the wire with a special tool to lock it into position.

I helped Moss get some samples of this wire and he made good use of it.
He started manufacturing cylinders using a tooth that was ideally suited to seating
the fibers in them and holding them as they passed over the grid bars. This was

the secret of minimum fiber damage and good lint cleaning and combing. John T. Gordin, an experienced sales executive, had joined Moss early in his sales effort, and the Moss-Gordin lint cleaner blitz left the competition groping in their trail of dust.

We had earlier started adding grid bars to our Little Combers, and this helped. A factor that we could not cope with was the blending done by the Moss-Gordin units. In areas where there was frost before the cotton harvest, the fibers had stained spots from the deteriorating boll. When these spots showed in the sample, the price was discounted severely. This was particularly bad on the Texas high plains, where this blending of spots alone was cause for a ginner to buy Moss-Gordin lint cleaners. We redesigned our lint cleaner to include a stationary feed plate and a full set of grid bars, but did not give up the self-doffing combing cylinder. With this arrangement, we gradually regained a reasonable share of the business. All of our other equipment was well accepted, and we were gaining in prestige with the passage of time.

Another phase of ginning that we had not addressed seriously was seed-cotton conditioning, more commonly referred to as drying. I spent a lot of time studying this situation and developing a new approach. I patented the Super Volume Cotton Conditioner, which added significantly to the company's volume of business (see Chapter 10).

Last Days at Lummus

I left Lummus in 1959 to become president of the Continental Gin Company. One of my last major projects with Lummus was the development of the Super 88 high-capacity gin stand (discussed in detail in Chapter 6). This stand had a profound affect on Lummus and the industry in general.

At the time of my leaving, I had three important patents pending: the Stick Machine; the Super Volume Cotton Conditioner, and a joint patent with William Pease on the Super 88 Saw Gin. I am very proud of our accomplishments at Lummus during my tenure there. It was in a sense a golden age for the industry—so many advances took place, and in almost all phases of ginning, our equipment set the standard. This could not have been done without the help of the fine, capable staff I worked with over the years. Looking back on this experience, I consider it to have been one of the most enjoyable and productive times of my career.

4　Continental Gin Company, 1959-64

Sometime in 1958, the Continental Gin Company was sold by the Wood-ruffs, the family of Coca-Cola fame, to a group of New York investors. The business had been deteriorating for some time and the price the investors paid was next to nothing. This new group wanted to turn the company around as soon as possible, and after extensive investigation as to who was who in the industry, they approached me.

That was in early 1959. I turned down their first offer. Lummus was not anxious to lose me, and in an effort to keep my services they made me executive vice president. The new owners of Continental were persistent, however, and six months later made me another offer. I accepted their offer on 1 December 1959, and was made president and CEO, which included holding the positions of senior vice president and a director of the parent company, Fulton Industries—prestigious positions that involved working with capable, well-intentioned people.

A big factor in my decision to take this position was the opportunity to become president of a company so rich in ginning heritage. Robert Munger had had a big impact on my life, and I consider him to be one of the giants of the industry.

As a young man, Munger operated cotton gins in Mexia, Texas in the 1880s. Among other things, he was responsible for the idea of conveying cotton from the farm vehicles to the gins by "air power," but the most outstanding example of his resourcefulness was his invention of *system ginning*. It revolutionized the industry. The most important components of system ginning were (1) the unloading of the cotton from the wagon and conveying it into the plant by air; (2) distributing the cotton to a battery of two or more gins by belt conveyor; (3) using a common lint flue to receive the lint from the battery of gins and carry it to a single condenser; and (4) from the condenser having it fed into a double-box press to permit continuous operation.

Munger obtained a number of patents on these developments and by the mid-1890s he built a large factory in Dallas, Texas to manufacture this equipment. Before the end of the century, he joined with the Pratt Gin Company, Prattville, Alabama, in building an additional manufacturing facility there. Munger's system

Figure 12. A. L. Vandergriff,
president, Continental Gin
Company 1959-64

ginning was dominating the field. The merger of Munger and Pratt and four other companies formed Continental Gin Company in 1900. I believe that the history of the cotton ginning industry could rightfully be divided into two periods: from Whitney's invention in 1794 to the late 1800s and from Munger's system ginning to the present.

Munger also patented the first high-density press in 1902, but it was not adopted by the industry because at that time the compresses were not willing to rebate compression charges back to the gin. Without this savings the gin could not afford a gin compression press. It took at least fifty years before the industry could take advantage of this cost-saving idea. The problem was solved when the J. G. Boswell Company began shipping non-standard packaged bales direct to the mill, which forced the industry to switch to net weight trading.

It is no wonder I was so excited—extremely excited—on assuming the presidency of Continental Gin: my father, as mentioned in Chapter 1, had purchased a Munger plant in 1916, manufactured by the Continental Gin Company. One of the first things I did when I traveled to the Continental headquarters in Dallas was to go to the old files and find the original record of this transaction.

When I joined Continental, the company was in the process of a major restructuring. They had a large industrial division, including an oil-mill machinery division and a materials-handling division, but it had been decided, prior to my arrival, that all manufacturing facilities except ginning would be liquidated. Financial analysis indicated that the cotton-gin division had the best potential for profit. I inherited the task of disposing of some fine people under stressful circumstances. Naturally, this liquidation process was unpopular throughout the company, which added to my problems in dealing with remaining personnel.

I soon learned that some of the upper-level management were bitter about ownership bringing in an outsider to run the company. Along with these problems, I learned that the warranties on some of our product line, most of which was not performing satisfactorily, were not being serviced. The cost of maintaining the warranties was excessive. Under these circumstances, the company could budget only limited amounts for research and development.

Despite these drawbacks, we were still able to develop and market some important products. Prior to my arrival, the decision had been made to build a sixteen-inch saw gin, and a short model had already been produced. The model had a flaw: the size of the roll box increased in proportion to the increase in the diameter of the saw. Although a logical assumption, from experience I knew this would fail, so I moved my design experience into the project. My efforts in this area are discussed in Chapter 6.

Other products developed during my time at Continental were a stick machine based on my Lummus success, unit lint cleaners, and the first rotabar roller gin, which I patented. There is much controversy and misinformation about the development of the rotabar roller gin (see Chapter 12).

We also developed a fixed-box press. In my continuing efforts to improve the bale package to make it more economical, in the 1960s my Continental staff designed a press to produce a bale with a twenty-inch by fifty-four-inch dimension, instead of twenty-seven-inch by fifty-four-inch. Our reasoning was that a twenty-seven-inch bale had to be compressed to a twenty-inch dimension to make higher densities. In compressing the twenty-seven-inch dimension to twenty, the layers of lint in the bale would be wrinkled and formed into hard strips. These hard strips would not break up in the standard mill-opening equipment, and considerable hand labor was necessary to process them. By making a twenty-inch bale at the gin site, it could be compressed in only one direction, thus avoiding this serious problem at the mill.

The height of a press that would make a twenty-by-fifty-four-inch bale would have to be determined empirically, because we used an unusual arrangement on the tramper side, calculated to make a higher density bale, with less load on the press structure and hydraulic system. This feature consisted of placing a small double-acting cylinder under the follow block on the tramper side. A follow block is a heavy member forming the bottom of the press box. When the press is turned to place the box in position to be pressed by the hydraulic ram, this block is pushed up against the cotton by the ram. The block follows the cotton up to a position to be strapped, thus the name "follow block." This block has slots to allow the straps to be pushed through and around the bale. The cylinder pushed the follow block up in this box so that the lint was pressed against it as it was fed into the charging hopper and pressed by the tramper. As the press box filled, the follow block was pushed down, thus precompressing the lint.

This press was designed as a so-called down-packing unit. A standard 8 3/8-inch double-acting ram and cylinder was used on the compression side. We found that we could make eighteen to twenty pounds per cubic foot with the normal two thousand pounds-per-square-inch hydraulic system. This made a beautiful little bale. Unfortunately the rest of the industry was not ready to accept a smaller high-density bale. Again, some adjustments would have to be made at the compress to handle this bale. This design was abandoned.

A few years later, after the industry was forced to accept net-weight trading during my tenure at J. G. Boswell Company, the idea of the twenty-inch bale became popular. The ginning industry had the know-how to produce a high-density bale as far back as Munger's ginner's compress in 1900. The mills finally accepted a bale made at the gin, but these bales could not be called high-density because of the bad name derived from the twenty-seven-inch bale compressed to twenty inches. None of these bales were compressed from the sides. For quite some time, gins were making twenty-four-pound density bales twenty inches wide, but because there was no monetary advantage, except to the few who were shipping direct to the mills, use of these presses was slow to catch on.

To get the mills to accept the higher-density bales made at the gins and avoid the stigma of "high density," the industry compromised by calling this gin-compressed bale a Universal Density (UD) bale. Munger would have appreciated this. In the 1980s, the compresses—which were rapidly becoming primarily warehouses—finally started rebating the gins for production of UD bales. Almost all gins now have UD presses, with almost identical dimensions to the Munger Gin compressed bale.

I did not enjoy my executive duties at Continental and wanted to devote more time to research and development. So I began to do some prospecting. James Boswell, of the J. G. Boswell Company of Los Angeles, California, was my customer at both Lummus and Continental and I had visited with him frequently. On one of my visits late in 1963 I discussed my interests with him. I made it clear that I wanted to work as a consultant, and not on an exclusive basis. We agreed on a plan and he promptly confirmed it in writing.

I left Continental on good terms with the ownership. They made great efforts to keep me, but I had decided that there was great opportunity for consulting in the cotton-gin field, not only at Boswell but in other parts of California and in Arizona. Initially, my position at Boswell was as a consultant, with the freedom to work with other organizations as time permitted. The real attraction at Boswell was that they were a large operation, with integrated facilities, and were well financed.

5   J. G. Boswell Company,
        1964-76

The J. G. Boswell Company is one of California's, and the nation's, biggest farming operations. Its corporate headquarters is in Los Angeles, and its processing headquarters in Corcoran, California. It is a diversified operation, with interests in safflower, cattle, cotton, and cottonseed oil. In early 1964 I moved my family to LA, bought a home in the mountains overlooking the Santa Anita racetrack, and began to work with some of the finest people I have ever been associated with.

My first project was to design a new gin plant for the processing division—a three-stand 119 saw Continental plant, well equipped with a fixed-box, standard-density press. Once this project was under way, Boswell informed me that their cottonseed oil mill needed a way to process safflower. I accepted this challenge, and worked with the Stanford Research Institute on a method to crack the seed and separate the meat and hulls.

During this time, James Boswell was pressuring me to take charge of the processing division in Corcoran and become vice president and general manager. After six months of negotiation, I accepted the challenge. The autonomy I would have in research and development and the opportunity for stock and stock options were too much to resist. I moved my family to the processing headquarters in Corcoran.

In this position, I had limited time available to devote to gin improvements. In addition to the duties associated with running such a big operation, the company also had, as mentioned earlier, an oil mill and a feed yard. The yard had up to twenty thousand head of cattle. These responsibilities could be expected to consume much of my time, but I continued with the plans to design a three-stand 119 saw plant, with several others to come later.

When the construction of the first plant was well under way, in 1964, I began restructuring the entire processing operation. On my arrival at Boswell twelve gin plants were operating and ginning slightly less than one hundred thousand bales. These plants were operated primarily by itinerant labor, with a production level of about three hundred bales per employee. My plan was to increase the production rate per employee. I also worked to stabilize the work force with better qualified, better paid, permanent employees. One phase of the effort was to increase the production rate of the gins. The gin plants were all 5-90 saw Continentals, well maintained and producing about 200-220 bales per day.

The first significant improvement in the overall production rate came as a result of my Vandergriff Capacity Booster Roll Box, designed in 1964. I had the first of these units installed in Boswell's Buena Vista Gin that year, and this alone increased its capacity to about three hundred bales per day. The rest of the plant was strained to handle this increase in capacity, especially with the old Continental perfection feeders. Drying was limited by the use of a single fifty-inch twenty-three-shelf tower and a seventy-two-inch counterflow dryer. Most of the plants had fourteen-foot antique burr machines that made no contribution to the efficiency of the cleaning. No plants had stick machines, although for their machine-picked cotton this was not a significant factor. However, the overall results of my capacity boosters were so good that we installed them in the remaining Boswell plants after the first season. (These capacity boosters are discussed in detail in Chapter 6.)

We continued to juggle machinery into different combinations, experimenting with various ideas for seed-cotton cleaning and drying. This effort was driven by a plan to build a plant that eventually would replace at least half of the twelve gin plants, one that could be operated with about the same labor as one of the old plants. I envisioned a plant with a forty-bale-per-hour capacity, compared with the standard seventeen- to eighteen-bale-per-hour capacities of top caliber plants of this time. Such a plant could not be built without encountering bottlenecks in every direction. They would start with the unloading of cotton from the field conveyances and continue through pressing and packaging. Almost everything I did in the way of planning for the first three years of my stay was done with this goal in mind.

In the meantime, we were making slow progress on improving the labor situation. I inherited a situation in which gin superintendents chose their own crew, and could hire and fire at their discretion. This resulted in gins being operated by family units, with little regard to qualifications. In an effort to improve the situation, we set up a personnel department and required all personnel to be cleared through it. Gin superintendents still had some latitude in choosing people and maintained the right to fire at their discretion. It took time and effort to change the old system, but the end result was that the personnel office had a list of employees and applicants who were known to be capable and reliable.

An important advantage of the new system was that it also prevented problems with unions. The union was active during this time, especially in the San Joaquin Valley, and if we were to employ large numbers of itinerant workers, the union would have had just cause to be a problem. By being selective with our hiring techniques, we got qualified people, paid them accordingly, and the unions never found fertile soil. We also reached a level of above two thousand bales per employee during my stay, compared with the three hundred mentioned earlier.

In 1965, I started to experiment with drying systems that would allow cotton to be processed at the higher production rates needed for the high-capacity plant I desired (see Chapter 10 on seed-cotton conditioning). This effort, which involved using larger volumes of air and shorter exposure times, proved to be successful and removed one huge bottleneck for the proposed forty-bale-per-hour, high-capacity plant.

In 1964, 1965, and 1966, we built one new 3-119 Continental plant each year, and each was capable of capacities higher than the old 5-90 saw plants. But they still had capacities below my expectations. One of the primary reasons was the saw spacing that Continental was using at the time (0.787 of an inch). Not only did this not work for getting maximum capacity; but it also wasn't desirable in terms of lint residual. I had recognized the problem while I was at Continental and knew it would have to be addressed by considerable narrowing of the saw spacing.

In the meantime, I was working on a new design for a gin rib that I felt would alleviate this problem. Tests were encouraging and in 1967, having completed all 3-119 saw gin plants, I had this rib installed. It helped with the residual-lint problem, but I realized that the saw spacings would still have to be narrowed. The rib became known in the trade as the Western Rib (see the section on high-capacity stands in Chapter 6). The new plants each had a capacity of slightly more than four hundred bales per day, which strained the packaging system at the press. I began to formulate plans for the automation needed to achieve my goal of forty bales per hour.

It was also in 1967 that I made the first combination seed-cotton cleaning and drying system capable of processing forty bales per hour—a necessary component of the superplant. It was not easy to test this development because Continental and other manufacturers were skeptical of the feasibility of a forty-bale-per-hour plant. I turned to local shops for the trial run. The pilot system, installed in our Melga gin, contained several firsts for the industry and laid the groundwork for the drying system we would use in the superplant (see Chapter 10).

In this 1967 season and the one following, we explored methods of unloading forty bales per hour from paired ten-foot by thirty-foot field trailers. We worked with people from Continental Gin Company and Signode Strapping, of Chicago, seeking to automate the press. Our staff was working on an idea for turning the trailers upside down to dump the cotton into a pit, thence onto a conveyor belt to be picked up by air and fed into the gin. By the early spring of 1968, we had completed enough of the design phase to begin work. The strapping tests at Continental, although not completely satisfactory, satisfied me that we were close enough, conceptually, to be able to iron out remaining problems in the plant itself.

One of the stickiest problems we faced in packaging was how to strap with steel a bale with twenty-one pounds of jute. Even stickier was how to work with the long-established USDA trading rules: the purchaser of a bale of cotton could deduct twenty-one pounds from its gross weight. Furthermore, if it proved that there were not twenty-one pounds of tare, then the original seller lost the difference between actual tare weight and twenty-one pounds. The heavy wrapping material used to make up this tare weight had to be applied by hand—an approach that limited the ginning rate to less than twenty bales per hour. If we fully automated the packaging at a rate of forty bales per hour or more, there would not be time to dress the press with the traditional wrapping material; it would be necessary to apply the straps to the bale automatically before applying the wrapping. In effect, the bale would have to be strapped "naked" and packaged after it left the press—a process not acceptable under the current rules, and our cotton would not be eligible to be sold and shipped through normal trade channels. We would have to get these rules changed, which would be no easy task, or ship straight to the mills.

This situation was the subject of a number of discussions at Boswell, particularly with the cotton merchandising division. At this time, much of our cotton, anyway, was sold directly to the mills; it did not go into the normal trade channels. It was decided that if we could successfully produce an acceptable automated package, the cotton could be sold directly until such time as we might get the rules changed to permit net-weight trading (in other words, the elimination of the twenty-one pounds of tare).

The superplant was ready for operation for the 1968 season—no small feat. But many portions of the operation were rushed, which led to complications for us later. We did not have time to fine-tune many of the cutting-edge aspects of the technology.

The plant was equipped with six 119 saw gin stands capable of producing our goal of forty bales per hour. However, in spite of my improved gin rib, the amount of residual lint on the seed was not as low as on our twelve-inch 90 saw gins (figure 13).

As we have seen, I had already concluded that the only way to get the necessary improvement was to narrow the saw spacing. I believed 20 percent more saws in the same space offered a good prospect (see Chapter 6) and would lead to development of the 141 saw gin. The plant (figure 14) contained many features not standard for the time.

Figure 13. Continental Gin Company's six 119 saw gin stands, J. G. Boswell Company, 1968.

The trailer-dumping arrangement went into operation, but not without problems. Under this arrangement, two loaded trailers, each ten feet by thirty feet long, were rotated and completely turned over. Our main problem was with the mechanism that locked down the trailers as they rotated. Occasionally, we would dump a set of trailers into the pit and the ranch department's hoist trucks became proficient at fishing them out. We also had installed a telescope to unload the cotton in the event of difficulties with the dumping mechanism. This telescope came in handy during the first season of operation. A single nineteen-inch telescope with fans powered by 250 hp supplied plenty of vacuum to unload up to fifty bales per hour. This bulk-handling method (figure 15) ushered in a new era in unloading cotton for ginning.

We anticipated problems with the automated packaging of the bale—trying to strap the naked bale at the press. Most critical was our inability to prevent lint cotton from getting into the strapping chutes, which would cause the strapping heads to fail in locking the ties. We had explored several alternative wrapping materials to use until this problem could be solved, and settled on a full cardboard carton as a temporary solution to the problem. This would not maximize the plant's

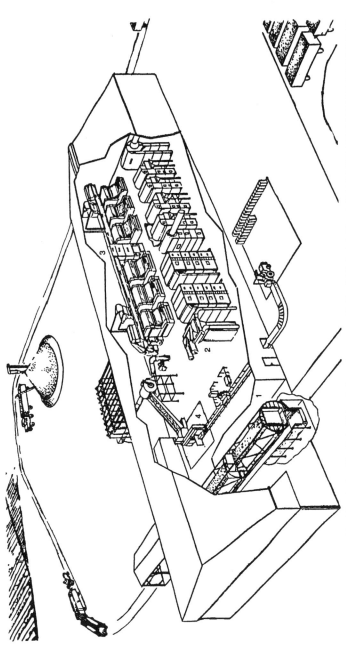

1 Trailer dump capable of dumping two 10' wide by 30' long trailers onto a moving belt in a pit where the cotton is fed automatically into the gin.

2 A single line drying and cleaning system using 50,000 CFM of air and 24 M BTU for drying. The drying air follows the cotton through the cleaning machines and at the inlet of each of the four groups of cleaning equipment the cotton is split, about one-third into a bad stream which is processed through the cleaning machines in that group and the remaining two-thirds bypasses back into the conveying air. The one-third which has been through the cleaning group rejoins the conveying air and the process is repeated at the next group.

3 The distributor is fed from both ends with the overflow in the center and three 141 saw gins on each side of the overflow. These were the first 141 saw gins, and supplied at the request of Vandergriff, but against the manufacturer's wishes.

4 Another first in this plant was an automated press with a cycling and packaging time of one minute. The new package brought about a revolution in bale packaging, and forced gross weight trading to be replaced by net weight trading to accomodate the new packaging materials.

Figure 14. J. G. Boswell Co. El Rico high-capacity plant, 1968

Figure 15. Trailer-dumping, J. G. Boswell Co., 1968

capacity because of the time required to place the two halves of the carton in the press box, but it would buy us time to work on the strapping-chute problem. It did, however, make a beautiful package, as can be seen in figure 16. Another benefit was that the mills liked it. The uniqueness of it created a lot of interest in the industry and in trade channels. This would be extremely helpful to us in achieving our goal of net-weight trading.

At the end of the first season, we found ourselves in a precarious position, because the Signode Strapping Company had decided that the potential business from the industry did not justify the continued expense to them involved in solving our strapping problems. We were using nine straps, eight in the normal position and one around the entire length of the bale. Each strap had a separate strapping head, and all were hydraulically operated. There were a lot of failures with this method of operation and frustration ran high, which is normal when innovative, groundbreaking ideas are being incorporated. Surviving the so-called learning curve can be difficult. The Boswell management were wonderfully patient.

The erratic performance of the heads was primarily because the hydraulic oil for operating them came from the same tank that supplied the rest of the press. The oil temperature would go too high for normal performance of this little

Figure 16. Packaged bale from automated press, J. G. Boswell Company, 1968

hydraulic unit and the strapping heads would malfunction. Solutions to this problem—and there were several—would have to wait for another season.

For Signode to pull out of the project at this time would have been a disaster. I traveled to Signode headquarters in Chicago to talk with top officials. I was well received; they were sympathetic to our problem, but were not willing to commit themselves to continue the project. I used the occasion to visit with the engineering department that had designed the system and found that they were pursuing the problems of both the strapping heads and the lint in the strapping chutes. They were designing new heads that were driven by electric, instead of hydraulic, motors. I left encouraged that this research would continue, even though I did not have a firm commitment.

To further complicate matters for us, Mother Nature entered the picture: between the 1968 and 1969 seasons we experienced a flood of unprecedented proportions. So much water ran off the mountains into Tulare Lake that all our gins in the region were threatened. Boswell lined the huge levee they had there with old cars in an attempt to protect the new plant from the growing body of

Figure 17. Packaged bales on truck for shipment

water. A smaller levee was built outside of Corcoran to protect the town itself. We removed two of our gin plants, but held out as long as we could with the big plant, knowing that to take it out at this critical stage would be a disastrous setback. Reluctantly, in July 1969 we decided to remove the plant—an operation that was done in great haste, with cutting torches, hammers, and chisels as tools of choice. At one point I watched a feeder fall off a truck that was leaving the yard. Readers may imagine the thoughts that went through my mind.

In September, when the waters no longer posed a threat, we reinstalled the gin. We put it back almost as fast as we took it out, which led to more problems at start-up time—difficulties in addition to the fundamental technical problems we had faced all along.

My trip to Chicago paid dividends. We got new strapping heads for the 1969 season and the strapping chutes had been gated. We still were not sure that this would solve the lint problem in the chutes and were forced to stay with the cardboard cartons for yet another season. However, we now used only partial boxes—short top and bottom sections, with the center of the bales open. This was a slight saving in cost and meant less cardboard to dispose of at the mill.

By this time, the National Cotton Council and the USDA were well along with the plans for net-weight trading. The bale-packaging committee had been established and I became an active member. We went through the 1969 season with the half cartons, which were well accepted. We were not, however, running at the desired capacity.

Net-weight trading was approved by the USDA during this season, which opened the door for other suppliers to begin to work with different packaging materials for the upcoming 1970 season. The importance for the industry of obtaining net-weight trading cannot be overstated: it opened the door for high-capacity gin plants and the universal acceptance of the UD pressed bale. It broke the shipping constraints that had impeded the progress of the cotton-ginning industry since 1902 when Robert Munger tried to market his original high-density bale.

During the 1969 season, the gated strapping chutes in the follow blocks were tested and improved. We felt confident that we had solved the problem of lint in the chutes. For the 1970 season, we chose to strap the bales naked as originally planned. After the bale left the press, it was pushed onto a conveyor, down a chute, and then we applied a polyethylene bag. Prior to the season, we had searched for a heat-shrink tunnel—a place to shrink the polyethylene tightly on the bales. We did not find a suitable unit so our Boswell staff designed one. This served our purpose well and we were producing a beautiful bale—one that could be stored outside, on the ground, without damage. The packaging material was generally too delicate for the normal trade channels, however. Our bales were loaded directly into a boxcar and handled as little as possible before reaching their destination at the mill.

The warehousing industry fought hard against our sealed package. A sealed package meant that cotton could be stored anywhere, bypassing cotton ware-houses. One argument used was mildew: cotton would mildew in the sealed package when stored. To refute this, we shipped a hundred bales to a mill in North Carolina and left them for a year. There was no mildew.

Of greater concern for the warehouses was the loss of the weight-gain factor—a significant economic consideration for them. They had been receiving unsealed bales at 4.5 to 5 percent moisture; to "add weight" they humidified the bales and shipped them out at 7 to 8 percent moisture—a gain of at least fifteen pounds per bale that added to their profits considerably.

In 1972, I developed a system to supply moisture to the cotton at the condenser to allow our press to operate more efficiently at higher capacities. A side benefit to this was the increased moisture content of the lint going into our sealed bale—allowing us to get the moisture up to 7 or 8 percent, in the sealed package. Thus, we would get the benefit of the weight gain. In a matter of a few years, we sold several million dollars worth of water, had much better performance from our press, and the mill customers were happy with the moisture content. This method of humidifying lint is discussed in detail in Chapter 11—the chapter on condensers.

I knew that ultimately all our gins would convert to naked-bale automatic strapping. I also knew it would be more efficient to do this at a central location and began working on such an arrangement in 1972. It took several seasons to work out the best arrangement. The unwrapped baled cotton was brought in from the gin on trucks. At the gin, we placed a bar code on the strapping to identify the gin location. At the packaging center, the bales were unloaded onto a conveyor belt, weighed, and assigned a permanent number. This information was fed into a central computer, with the number and weight becoming a permanent part of the bale's history. In addition, the section of the ranch on which the cotton was grown, along with other pertinent information regarding its growth and the method of culturing and harvesting it became part of the record. The bale then traveled by conveyor to the sampler, which cut both sides of the bale at the same time. This sample was pulled and placed in a tray to be sent to the classing office.

Following the sampling, the bale entered a stuffer and was automatically pushed into a polyethylene bag. At first, we used a heat-shrink tunnel to shrink the polyethylene. Later, we found we could use a bag of the proper size and push the bale into it tightly enough that shrinking was not necessary for the package to be neat. The only other operation at this point was the use of a heat sealer to seal the open end of the bag. The bale moved on a conveyor, was dumped outside the packaging center, and arranged with other bales in groups of ten. These groups of ten could be picked up by an automated wagon and delivered to the proper lot in the bale yard. There, bales were unloaded hydraulically. This was an efficient arrangement. The very competent Boswell staff cooperated with me in working out all the critical details.

By 1972, all our gins were equipped to strap naked bales and transport them to the central packaging facility. We were handling 3000-3200 bales per day. With numbers like this, the bales, stored in the bale yard in neat rows, were an awesome sight. Our bale yard was capable of storing up to two hundred thousand bales.

With the advent of net-weight trading, a number of gins across the country had followed our lead and gone to strapping naked bales at the press. Very few were using polyethylene bags, but all had some type of light, inexpensive wrapping material and lightweight strapping, either to be strapped automatically or hand strapped. A popular way of strapping at this time was use of the Titan tie—a lightweight steel strap that could be hand tied rapidly. This method was used extensively across the cotton belt. Now, thirty-five years later, almost all gins, both in the United States and the rest of the world, wherever significant amounts of cotton are processed, use this method of packaging. Bales are strapped naked, conveyed to a stuffer, then pushed into some form of bagging material—generally polypropylene or lightweight jute.

In our early discussions with Signode, they indicated they would need to sell a million pounds of strapping a year to justify their efforts in designing a strapping system for cotton ginning. In about the third or fourth year of using this method, the Boswell company alone bought a million pounds of strap. Signode was certainly pleased, and they continued to remain involved in this area of automation at the press.

In 1972, Boswell went through a major restructuring and I was reassigned. I continued as vice president, advising on design and construction of processing facilities, with emphasis on technology. I continued to work on packaging, as well as other areas. During this time, we did much of the original testing on dust-and-noise control for the Environmental Protection Agency.

By the early 1980s, five gins were handling almost three times the volume of cotton that the twelve had when I arrived fifteen years earlier. I "retired" from Boswell in 1976. My time there was very productive. I am particularly proud of my work involving the construction of the first forty-bale-per-hour high-capacity gin plant and, in light of the initial skepticism, a personal triumph. For the industry itself, it was revolutionary: a turning point. The vision and dreams I had for this plant demonstrated to the industry that high-capacity plants could be a reality.

After leaving the J. G. Boswell Company I again worked as a consultant, working with various companies, and started more extensive research in many phases of cotton processing.

Independent Research

6

The Gin Stand:
At the Heart of Cotton Ginning

Eli Whitney generally gets credit for the invention of the cotton gin, although his unit as patented in 1794 was a crude device (figure 18). In his first efforts, he apparently was not aware of an important and fascinating characteristic of the fuzzy cotton seed. In his unit, a supply of seed-cotton was fed into the ginning chamber, and as it was engaged by the teeth, or points, on a rotating cylinder, it formed a rotating mass. This rotating action continued until the lint was removed from the seed. The bottom of the chamber was then opened, allowing the seed to fall.

The key fact that the roll in the ginning chamber commingled, or clung together, was noted by H. Ogden Holmes, whose patent was issued two years after Whitney's (1796). Holmes left an opening in the bottom of the ginning chamber, thus allowing the ginned (or separated) seed to be discharged continuously (see figure 19). It was logical to conclude, as apparently Whitney did, that such an opening would not be selective, permitting unginned seed to be discharged. This accounts for his keeping the chamber closed until the lint had been removed from the batch in the ginning chamber. With the Holmes version of the gin, only the ginned seed would be released, unless the opening permitted the rotating mass to sag drastically into the opening, which would result in a severe rupture in the surface of the mass as it passed the opening. I realized early in my work with gin stands the importance of controlling this sag in relation to saw spacing, saw speed, etc. to obtain the proper seed discharge rate and residual lint on the seed.

Since 1796, when Holmes received his patent—he had circular saws spaced at regular intervals on a cylinder that passed between ribs restricting the passage of the seed—the saw gin has been used almost exclusively. The controversy that followed these inventions, as to which inventor should be given credit, was bitter, but history has been kind to Whitney: by virtue of his earlier patent date, he has been accepted as Father of the Cotton Gin.

The word *gin* as applied to cotton gins is said to be an abbreviation of the word *engine*. Engine is a suitable name for the little machine that Eli Whitney invented in 1794 to separate cotton fibers from the seed, because an engine may be defined as a machine in which physical power is applied to produce a physical

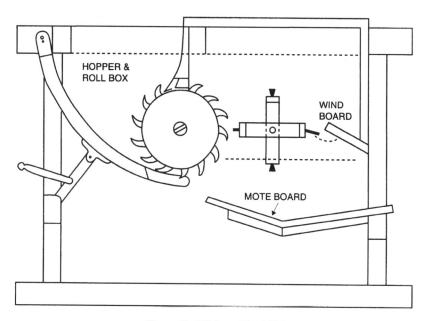

HOPPER &
ROLL BOX

WIND
BOARD

MOTE BOARD

Figure 18. Whitney Gin, 1794

effect—and that is the essence of Whitney's idea. The word *gin* was applied to the single machine, because originally the gin stand was the only basic machine in a plant. Later, mechanical feeders were added, and the two units together came to be referred to as the gin. They were later used in batteries of more than one unit, fed by a distribution system. As the technology evolved, cleaners, dryers, separators, condensers, blowers, and presses were added, and today a gin is a complicated and sophisticated plant.

Typical Gin Stand

Today, the term *gin* refers to a complete plant, regardless of its size. It is still sometimes used, as originally, to refer to the particular machine that separates the lint from the seed; more usually, however, this machine is referred to as the *gin stand,* and when reference is made to the size of a plant, it will be described as having a certain number of stands (usually from one to six). Figure 20 shows a cross section of a basic gin stand.

For those who are not familiar with a gin stand, a brief description of the major components will be helpful. With the modern gin, the seed cotton, which

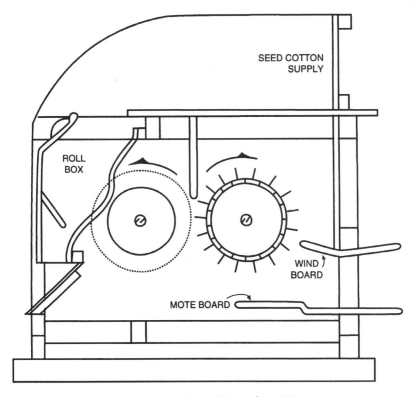

Figure 19. H. Ogden Holmes Gin, 1796

has been dried (conditioned) and cleaned, is delivered to the gin by a feeder (which may also be a cleaner) at a regulated rate. The rate may be controlled automatically, usually with the control being sensitive to several factors, among them: (1) the load required to turn the saw cylinder; (2) the density of the roll acting against a pressure plate; and (3) the manual control of the operator. The cotton from the feeder enters the *huller breast* of the gin. This is a chamber into which the saws project, through the huller ribs, to pick up the cotton. The incoming cotton falls onto a roller that has pins (it is called a *picker roller*). These pins kick the cotton against the saw teeth. The hulls and other particles of trash rejected by the huller ribs fall back on the picker roller, which allows them to pass between it and the gin saw. The hulls may go directly to a trash conveyor or pass through a reclaimer section that picks up stray locks of cotton and reapplies them to the saw, dropping only the hulls into a conveyor. The picker roller on gins that include huller-breast

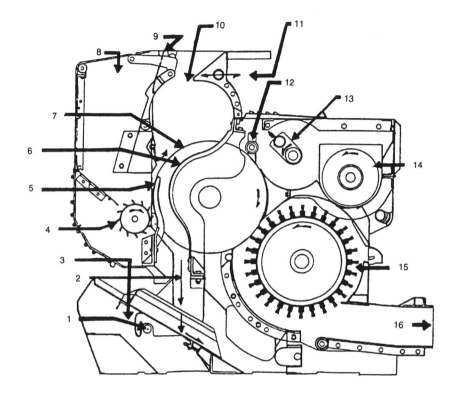

1 PIVOT POINT	9 BREAK LINE BETWEEN HULLER BREAST & GINNING BREAST
2 SEED PASSAGE	
	10 ROLL BOX
3 HULL PASSAGE	
	11 BREAST ASSEMBLY MOVES OUT UNTIL GIN RIB CLEARS SAWS
4 PICKER ROLLER	
5 HULLER RIB	12 FREE TURNING SHAFT
6 GINNING RIB	13 MOTE BOARD WIPER
7 GIN SAW	14 MOTE CONVEYOR
8 SEED COTTON IN	15 BRUSH DOFFER
	16 LINT DUCT

Figure 20. A typical gin stand with basic components identified

reclaimers (such as the Model 30 huller front on the Continental Gin Co. gin stand) are adjustable, to and from the saw, to accommodate cotton with a lot of hulls. The picker roller can be backed away to let the hulls, or burrs, pass, and any cotton passing with the hulls will be reclaimed. On gins without a reclaimer, the picker roller is also adjustable to and from the saw. With clean cotton, it is operated close to the saw; when cotton that has more hulls gets to the huller breast of the gin, it is backed away to let them escape. The cotton that is picked up by the saws is carried into the *roll box* (roll boxes are discussed further in this chapter).

The huller breast received its name when it was found that hulls could be separated from the cotton at this point in the manner described above. The name *breast* apparently originated with Eli Whitney, who referred to the front side of his gin as the breast. For many years this huller breast was the only means used for separating hulls. It was quite satisfactory for hand-picked cotton.

Chapter 8 describes the development of the single-rib huller gin and the double rib huller gin. The gin saw blades project through the huller ribs (figure 20). In such gins, the teeth engage the cotton fibers still attached to the seed and take the mass through the seed roll to the gin ribs. The seed roll is encased in a cavity formed by the upper surface of the ginning ribs, the upper ends of the huller ribs, and a front scroll beginning above the upper end of the huller ribs and curving outward and upward to form a curved front of the roll box. Another scroll begins at the top of the ginning ribs, continuing on, roughly with the curvature of the gin ribs, to form the back of the roll box. The shape of the cavity is basically circular, but as can be seen in sketches of early roll boxes, there were many variations.

The gin ribs have sharp edges in the area where the saws enter the gap, and the spacing is such that the cotton seeds are rejected while the lint attached to the teeth passes through the gap and is removed by the doffer. The rib gap, historically, has been, and still is, close to one-eighth of an inch; it varies slightly with different manufacturers. The radius of the curvature of the gin rib may have varied considerably over the years, but the ribs in all of today's twelve-inch saw gins use a radius of about 4.5 inches. About fifty to sixty degrees of the upper curvature of the gin rib is utilized as the lower back section of the roll box. The curved scroll at the top of the gin ribs usually has a radius of five to six inches.

As we will see in the later discussion of the technical aspects of the seed roll, the shape and direction of the front scroll is the critical part of the roll box cavity. In the early (round) roll boxes, the curvature of the front scroll was essentially the same as the back scroll, but in later, loose-roll gins, this radius is greater than that of the back scroll (figure 21).

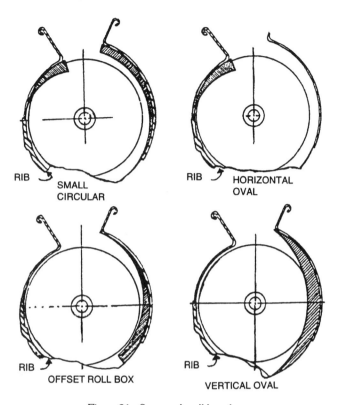

Figure 21. Some early roll box shapes

A critical element is how the lower front of the roll box approaches the seed-discharge passage; in other words, how it affects the sag. In operation, the seed roll rotates as the saw blades pass through it and engage the fibers. Less than ninety degrees of the saw blades project into the seed roll, and as they pass through the commingled mass of lint and seed, the mass is rotated. As the fibers, attached to the saw teeth, enter the rib gap, some of them remain in the gap, but most remain attached to the teeth. As the fibers in the gap accumulate ahead of the saw, they become so dense that the saw has to move them up for it to pass through the rib gap.

Once this mass of fibers starts flowing up the gap, the seed roll turns, and the action creates a singing sound. This slight sound indicated to old-time ginners like my father that the seed roll was turning. In the days of the round roll boxes, seed rolls stopped quite often, and ginners listened for this sound to know whether a roll had stopped or not. Without this rotation, there is no ginning. The seed roll will quickly become so tight that it stops the rotation of the saw (the disk-brake effect). This turning of the seed roll, and the resultant seed discharge, is the most important and least understood aspect of the operation of a saw gin stand. The curvature of the gin rib, the width of the rib gap, the angle at which the leading edge of the gin saw-tooth enters the rib gap, the shape of the relief section, and its location above the ginning point—all these, along with the contour of the scroll sheets forming the roll box cavity are critical parts in the efficient performance of the gin stand. I will discuss the role of the gin rib in the stand in some detail; most of these relationships have been established empirically over a long period of time, some as far back as a century or more.

Gin Rib Design

The gin rib is one of many critical components of the gin stand. Working in conjunction with the saws, the ribs are responsible for removing the seed from the cotton. They also play an important role in the critical area of seed discharge. Their contour and their relationship with the saws in terms of spacing and saw-tooth penetration into the rib gap can be critical to the efficiency of any high-capacity gin stand.

Since the time of the earliest gins, the gin ribs have been made from a sand casting. Literally hundreds of shapes, curvatures, and gimmicks have been used to aid the ginning process in various ways. A number of variations in rib design can be found in the U.S. Patent Office. For the last forty or fifty years, the design has been well standardized for the twelve-inch saw gin (see figure 22).

The first point to establish in rib design is the location of the ginning point—the point where the tooth enters the rib gap. With the Lummus rib in figure 22, this point is theoretically 1.75 inches past the vertical centerline of the saw. This is further back than the placement in designs by any other manufacturer and places the seed roll further back on the saw. (This is illustrated in the discussion of seed discharge passages in the high-capacity gin section.)

The tooth angle at the ginning point is established by using the same center as that of the saw blade, and drawing an arc of a circle as shown, with a radius two inches less than that of the saw. A line tangent to this arc through the ginning point establishes the direction of the leading edge of the teeth as they enter the rib gap. The point of the teeth should enter the rib gap a few degrees ahead of the throat. My experience with the Lummus rib indicates that it is designed to have a tooth lead of about seven degrees. When this is known, the center of the curvature of the ginning section of the rib can be established (see figure 22). Draw a line

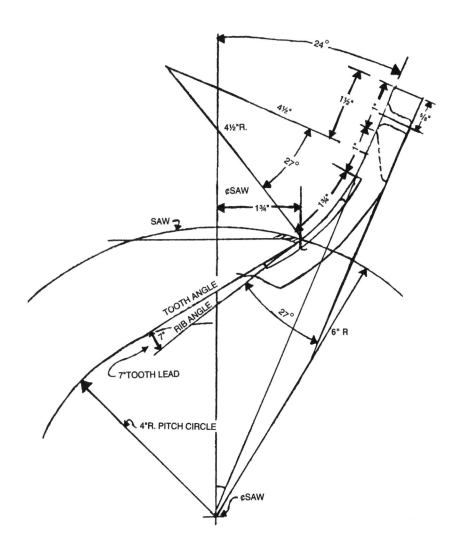

Figure 22. Standard Lummus gin rib

through the ginning point seven degrees inside the line of tangency to the pitch circle: the center of the curvature is along this same line. The radius of the curvature is 4.5 inches from the ginning point along this line. This curvature continues from below the ginning point upward until it becomes tangent to the straight section of the upper end of the rib, a distance of twenty-seven degrees from the ginning point. From this point to the top of the rib, the line is about twenty-four degrees off vertical. (It has been noted that the ginning point is further back past the centerline of the saw: the designer chose to stop the rib curvature as shown.) A more uniform curvature of the roll box, which joins the top of the rib, would have resulted if the rib curvature had continued to vertical. However, the back scroll of the roll box has been designed to compensate for this odd angle.

The saw teeth pass between the ribs at the ginning point. The space between the ribs at this point is referred to as the *rib gap*. This, as mentioned earlier, is generally about one-eighth of an inch. In the case of the Lummus rib, the gap is slightly less than one eighth (0.1171 inch)—arrived at from the gin rib at the ginning point being 0.500 inch and the saw spacing being 0.6171 inch. Subtracting the 0.500 from the 0.6171 gives a 0.1171 rib gap. Other manufacturers use slightly different gap dimensions and the design of other ribs will be detailed.

The other twelve-inch saw gin being manufactured today—a product of Vandergriff Research—is produced by the Consolidated Cotton Gin Company, of Lubbock, Texas. The rib I designed for this gin is shown in figure 23. The ginning point is one inch back of the vertical center line of the saw. This places the seed roll much further forward on the saw than in the Lummus rib. Further discussion of this can be found in the section on roll box design and the section on the Consolidated 164 saw gin.

Note in figure 23 that I brought the curvature of the top section of the rib around to vertical. As stated earlier, this allows for a smoother flow of the seed roll from the rib to the back scroll of the roll box. The center of the rib curvature of the ginning section is 4.5 inches, as on other twelve-inch saw gins. The tooth lead is eight degrees, when the gin breast is in its recommended position.

The Consolidated gin stand breast pivots at the bottom, and the top moves in and out of ginning position. There are stop bolts at each end of the main frame, against which the breast rests in the ginning position. These bolts can be screwed in or out to change the position at which the breast assembly (containing the gin ribs) stops. Backing the stop bolts out to stop the breast sooner will decrease the tooth lead. I know of no research that has established the optimum tooth lead. Performance has always been satisfactory if the point of the tooth led the throat slightly. Commonly, this is determined by placing a piece of thin card—a business

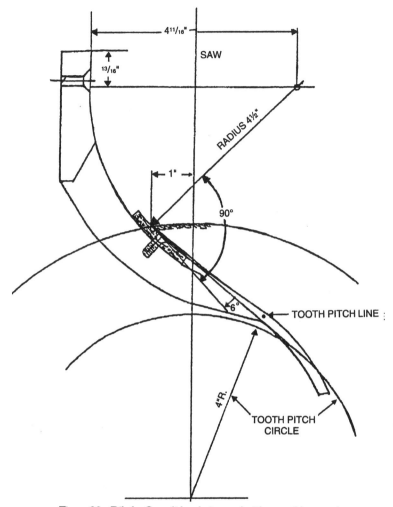

Figure 23. Rib for Consolidated gin stand with reversible wearplate

card is often used—into the teeth ahead of the ginning point. The saw is then turned slightly against the card. If the point of the tooth makes a deeper impression in the card than the throat, the lead is adequate although this does not indicate how much the lead is.

Of the three manufacturers making this equipment, Consolidated is the only one having much flexibility in this in-and-out position. Continental's gin stand has huller ribs, which necessitate maintaining a recommended projection of the saw through the ribs to pick up the incoming cotton. Continental has stop bolts similar to Consolidated's, but maintaining the proper projection through the huller ribs limits the movement that would change the tooth angle, decreasing its effectiveness.

The tooth angle in the Lummus gin stand has a minimum adjustment, because the gin breast is stopped in a fixed position. There are no adjustable stop bolts. I have no hard evidence that a greater or lesser tooth angle is better. However, I have observed that pulling the top of the gin breast back seems to result in increased capacity. But this pulls the seed roll back on the saw and changes the seed discharge passage. Any increase in capacity may be the result of this, and not of a change in the tooth angle. I plan to pursue this further.

The Consolidated gin rib (figure 23) is the first completely new rib design since the one I helped design for the Continental sixteen-inch gin in 1960. A new feature that is a part of this Consolidated rib is the reversible and removable wear plate at the ginning point. This feature, which has been a part of this gin stand since it was designed in 1986, has played a significant part in the success of this gin stand. The wear plate, of hardened steel, is held on by one screw. The ginning point is near the upper end, which makes it possible to change ends to obtain a new surface. The wear plate is 0.460 inches wide and the saw spacing is 0.580 inch, leaving a rib gap at the ginning point of 0.120 inch. This entire gin rib is molded from stainless steel; it is not necessary to plate it to prevent corrosion.

The rib for the other current manufacturer of gin stands is shown in figure 24. It is found on the sixteen-inch saw gin manufactured by Continental Eagle Co., of Prattville, Alabama. The most notable feature of this rib is that it is mounted only at the top; the bottom is left open. When I left Lummus, we had a nagging problem of lint collecting in the bottom of the ribs, blocking the seed passage. This was caused primarily by our air-blast gins. When I arrived at Continental, the engineering department was exploring possibilities for designing a sixteen-inch saw gin. I had experimented with the top-only idea at Lummus and would have adopted this new design had I not left. It has proved to be a valuable asset to Continental.

Note in figure 24 that the ginning point is only three-quarters inch back of the vertical centerline of the saw. Note also that the upper end of the rib is vertical. The pitch circle has a radius of about three inches less than the saw radius; that is, about five inches. The rib drawing locates the center of the rib curvature with a radius of five inches. From this it can be determined that the tooth lead is about eight degrees. This angle is subject to variation, depending on how the gin is adjusted.

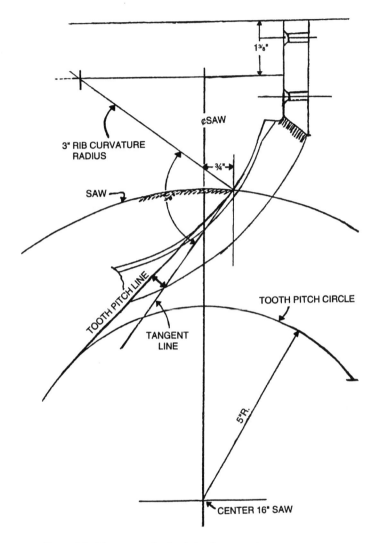

Figure 24. Top-mounted-only rib for Continental sixteen-inch saw gin

The relief at the top of this rib (figure 25) differs from the other two described. As the fibers, which are not attached to the saw, move up the rib gap, they must pass around the end of a raised section of the rib to return to the seed roll. On the surface, this may appear to be a good relief method. However, it has a weakness in that the surface of the seed roll is not pressing against the fibers to

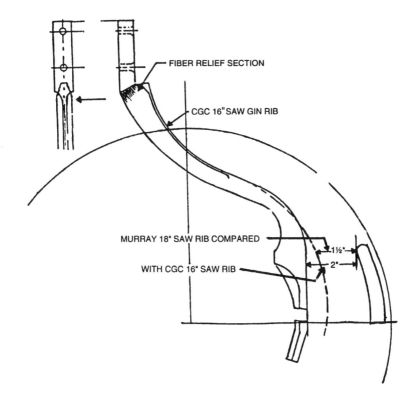

Figure 25. Relief area at the top of the Continental Gin Company rib (figure 24)

pull them back into the seed roll. This encourages wads of fibers, particularly damp or wet ones, to stop occasionally before being pulled back into the seed roll.

This rib is a sand casting. The ginning surface, a distance of about three-quarters inch at the ginning point, is hardened by placing a steel plate in the mold at this point. This chills the metal and hardens it. Other methods may be used, such as induction-heating the rib at this point, then chilling it. We started using this method at Lummus.

In operation, the saw teeth load up with fibers as they pass through the seed roll. The teeth pull these fibers into the rib gap. A lot of the fibers are not well enough seated into the teeth to make it through the gap; they are pulled back into the seed roll at the relief point. These fibers must move freely up the gap and into the relief section of the rib, where they are free to follow the surface of the seed roll. With the type of rib gap shown in figure 26, it is easy for these fibers to flow

Figure 26. Relief section of
rib that allows smooth flow of
fibers back into the seed roll.

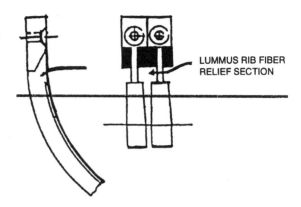

LUMMUS RIB FIBER
RELIEF SECTION

through this section of the rib and follow the surface of the seed roll. Consolidated and Lummus, as well as the Continental twelve-inch saw gin, all use this type of relief at the top of their ribs.

When machine-picked cotton arrived at the gins in the 1950s, some were ill prepared to handle the hard knots of fibers involved (known as spindle twists). The gin ribs did not have sufficient relief above the ginning point to release these knots once they were pulled into the rib gap. Some gin saws—those with a straight tooth—were badly damaged by the knots wedging in the rib gap. There is generally enough upward pressure from the saws to push the knots up the gap between the tapered sections of the ribs, but many ribs did not have enough open section at the top to allow the knots to slip back into the seed roll.

While I was with Continental Gin Company, we had a serious problem with these spindle twists wedging in the top of the ribs. There was no relief section in the 90 saw gins and the 120 twelve-inch saws. We improvised a relief section by running a three-eighths-inch drill bit between the ribs at the top. This provided enough relief to stop most of the saw damage, although the slim, straight saw teeth still were a problem. At Continental, there was considerable resistance to adding a slight roach to the back of the saw teeth for strength, but the spindle twists spelled the end of teeth that did not have added strength. Drilling out the top of the ribs was only a temporary solution to the problem of relief at the top of the rib. On ribs that were still at the manufacturing stage, it was a simple matter to mill a slot on each side of the rib to provide a relief section (see figure 27 for example). We made no changes in the casting or any other part of the rib, and today Continental continues to mill this slot, in this same manner, on twelve-inch saw gin ribs.

On gins in which this area can be exposed, it is fascinating to watch the top back of the gin ribs in operation. A long trail of fibers is pulled into the rib gap at

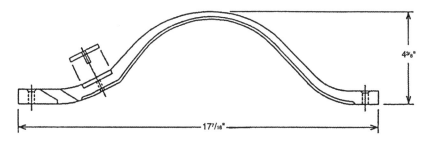

Figure 27. Vandergriff rib with reversible wearplate for Lummus gin stands

the ginning point, but the fibers are still attached to the seed roll—mostly, in fact, to the seed in the seed roll. They move up the rib gap above the ginning point at about the surface speed of the seed roll. When they reach the relief section at the top of the rib, they are pulled back to the surface of the seed roll and follow its rotation until they are reengaged by the saw teeth on the next round. The process is repeated until the fibers, removed from the seed, follow the saw to the doffing section of the gin stand. If for some reason the fibers are prevented from moving up the rib gap, the ginning by the saw in that rib gap ceases. The saw will continue to pull fibers into the gap, but if they are not able to move up, the saw will quickly overheat and could cause a friction fire. This failure to move up may be caused by roughness along the ginning edges of the rib, which may be from a manufacturing defect or from the ribs having been repaired by building up the rib at the ginning point.

Gin operators can have problems obtaining replacements for gin ribs. An example is the case of the Murray gin, which is no longer manufactured. The Murray was made with twelve-inch and eighteen-inch saws and a lot of these gins are still in operation.

The ribs for the twelve-inch saw gin are close in design to that of other twelve-inch saw gins, although none of these are interchangeable. The saw spacing on the twelve-inch saw gin is 23/32 of an inch (0.71875 inch). Until recent years, this was the closest spacing in the industry. In addition to the different spacing, the top of the rib is eight degrees back of vertical as compared with the Lummus, which is about twenty-four degrees back. Consolidated and Continental are zero degrees off vertical. The Murray eighteen-inch saw gin rib is very long and difficult to cast accurately. It is eight degrees off vertical, the same as the twelve-inch. The curvature of the ginning section is 6 3/8 inches. This rib is discussed further in the section on the conversion of the Murray eighteen-inch saw gin, later in this chapter.

For a number of years I have worked on the development of a fabricated gin rib with a replaceable wearplate at the ginning point. It has been difficult producing an accurate fabricated rib at an acceptable cost to the industry.

I am now having a rib produced from a forging that is machined accurately on computer-controlled machines—the most accurate rib ever produced in quantity. This rib allows for easy installation, compared with the conventional rib that must be adjusted and shimmed to allow it to line up with the saws. It is presently being produced for Lummus gin stands (figure 27). The rib has a wearplate at the ginning section 1 1/2 inches long by 3/16 of an inch thick. It is oil-hardened to a uniform Rockwell C 58, and is held on by a three-sixteenths-inch dowel that goes through the wearplate and is pushed into a hole in the rib. To change the ends of the wearplate, the plate can be lifted out or the pin can be pushed back from the back enough to turn the plate. When both ends are worn, the pin can be pushed back through the plate and it can be turned over to present two new surfaces. However, if the saw is allowed to run against the wearplate for any length of time, it may cut a notch, and if the notch is deep enough it may not be practicable to turn the plate over. However, the wearplate is easily replaceable at reasonable cost.

Gin ribs also wear ahead of the wearplate. To compensate for this wear and increase the life of the rib, there is a one-sixteenth-inch ledge ahead of the wearplate. Without this initial ledge, the rib would soon wear down below the plate; the corners of the wearplate will cause a tag to form between the ribs. This happens with carbide inserts and is a serious problem.

I have redesigned the forged ribs for the Continental Gin Company sixteen-inch saw gin (figure 28). This rib provides all the advantages of the one I designed for the Lummus and Consolidated gin stands, but has important differences. It is more efficient than the conventional rib for Continentals. The relief section is like the one on the Lummus and Consolidated rib. This allows for smooth flow of fibers back into the seed roll. As mentioned earlier, lack of a good relief section on the conventional Continental rib can lead to tagging and the formation of wads in the gap. The saw can no longer engage the fibers at this point. Also, as with the Lummus rib, the curvature of the ginning section is a 4.5-inch radius, compared with the five-inch radius on the standard Continental rib, relieving the pressure as the seed roll turns past the top of the gin rib. These two modifications help create optimum seed roll conditions. Other modifications include those for the promotion of seed discharge.

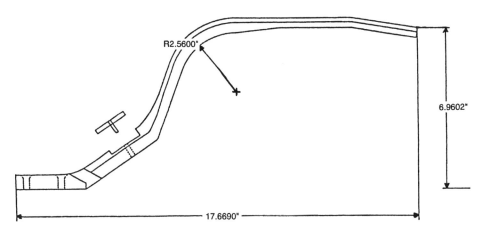

Figure 28. Vandergriff gin rib with removable reversible wearplate (patent #44,310,949)

Gin Saws

A gin stand has a saw cylinder with saw blades with teeth that remove the lint from the seed. The saw blades have followed established standards for many years without much change. The twelve-inch saw has been standard on most gins since the turn of the century; however, there are now sixteen-inch and eighteen-inch saw gins.

Gin saws are made from a good grade of high-carbon steel. The standard thickness for Lummus is 0.036 of an inch; for Continental Gin Company it is 0.037 inch; and Murray used 0.045 inch. Figure 29 is a sketch of an enlarged view of gin saw teeth specified for Continental's twelve-inch saw. Note that the thickness at the point is 0.010 inch to 0.014 inch. In the 1990s, the higher horsepower used on the saw shaft, which also provides for a higher capacity per saw, requires a thickness at the point of the tooth in the range of 0.015 inches so it does not break under the severe stress. The slight roach shape in the back of the tooth is important, giving it the strength to avoid having the tooth turn back under ginning pressure. This tooth design is essentially that used on all twelve-inch saws.

Punching this circular disk from a flat sheet and then punching the center hole for the shaft adds stresses to those already in the sheet. This results in the finished disks not being perfectly flat. For many years this stress was relieved by

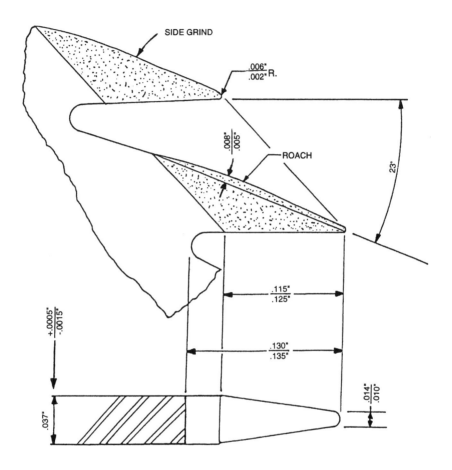

Figure 29. Gin saw tooth detail

hammering the disk on both sides with a chisel-pointed hammer until it would lie perfectly flat on a finished surface. This required no small amount of skill and patience. In the 1950s, the industry started stress-relieving the disks by a heat treatment. The disks were stacked on a mandrel, clamped with considerable pressure, and placed in an oven and brought up to the required temperature, which resulted in a very flat saw.

I have had experience with all three of the standard thicknesses and there is no doubt that the 0.045-inch is better. It is more rigid, stands more heat from friction without buckling, and requires little training to get it to run straight between the ribs. The negative aspect of switching to this thickness is found in the spacers between the saws (space blocks). These have to be reduced in width to accommodate the extra saw thickness. Most space blocks are aluminum castings and can easily be machined. This procedure has not been understood or widely adopted. Some saw cylinders are equipped with space blocks of steel corrugated metal. These are difficult to machine. To make a change in these cases requires new space blocks. This is a one-time cost that can be justified, but because it is not being pushed by the manufacturers, the change is coming slowly.

The pitch angle of the saw teeth on the twelve-inch saw is nearly standardized. The leading edge of the tooth is tangent to a circle two inches less than the radius of the saw, as described in the section on gin-rib design. The teeth on the sixteen-inch saw have a pitch angle tangent to a circle with a five-inch radius; the eighteen-inch saw teeth have a pitch angle tangent to a circle with a six-inch radius—all these radii from the center of the saw.

The twelve-inch saw for most gins is made with 264 teeth per saw. The Lummus standard is 282 teeth per saw. I have a slight preference for the 282 teeth, but no reliable data that I know of exists to support this preference.

Huller Breast

The huller breast serves to separate out some of the hulls as the cotton is fed into the gin stand roll box. Each manufacturer has come up with its own versions of this process.

Continental Gin Company came up with the most prominent method of removing these hulls. Their Model 30 Front—named for the year this arrangement was introduced and patented by Thomas Elliot, then president of Continental—is shown in figure 30. This front included a small reclaimer-saw cylinder located under the picker roller, so that the hulls and any cotton would pass under it. The cotton was picked up by the saw teeth and the hulls were pushed over the end of the hull board and dropped into the trash conveyor. The reclaimed cotton was then doffed from the saw by a small-diameter rotating brush cylinder; thence, it went back onto the picker roller and at this point it was reapplied to the gin saw.

Another arrangement was used by Lummus. It consisted of a double-spiral picker roller arrangement that reclaimed the cotton from the hulls rejected by the huller ribs (figure 31). Following World War I, much of the cotton in West Texas and western Oklahoma was being harvested by pulling the bolls off the plant. Even though hull extraction was being used ahead of the gins, many hulls were broken

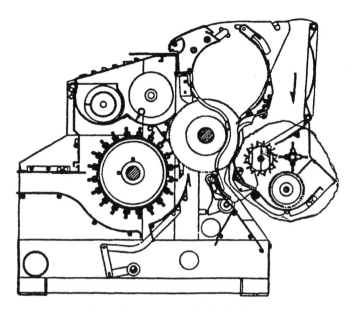

Figure 30. Continental Model 30 Front

and were reaching the huller breast. For these hulls to pass between the picker roller and the saw, the picker roller had to be moved back from the saw. This arrangement allowed some cotton to pass with the hulls. Lummus chose to use two spiral picker rollers, one above the other. The top roller conveyed the rejected hulls to the ends, where they dropped to the lower roller. There, the hulls were conveyed to the center as they were reapplied to the gin saw. The hulls discharged through a chute into the trash conveyor under the gin.

Lummus stayed with the spiral pickers for quite some time. However, this arrangement was not of particular help in preventing the congestion in the top of the huller ribs. When the high-capacity gin stand was developed, they eliminated the double roller and installed a single picker roller in place of the top spiral roller. This roller, or cylinder, was located forward of the top spiral roller, and had large pins that projected into the space between the top of the ribs where the congestion occurred. The cotton fed on to this roller delivered it to the saw. The pins wiped the top of the ribs clean. Cotton that was knocked free of the saw was picked up by a reclaimer saw, then doffed by the gin saw (figure 32).

Other manufacturers did not use a reclaiming mechanism; to take into account the volume of hulls being rejected, they merely adjusted the picker roller to and from the saw. If a heavy volume of hulls reached the huller breast, the picker

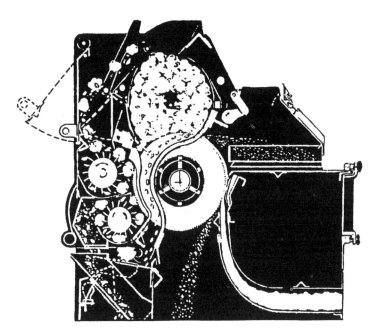

Figure 31. Lummus double-spiral picker roller huller breast

roller was backed off from the saw, allowing the hulls to escape between the picker roller and the saws.

Before an adequate drying system was developed, there was congestion in the huller ribs because the cotton was pulled between them into the roll box. This congestion caused choking and fiber damage. To avoid this congestion, the Hardwicke Etter Company picked up an old idea and adapted it to their gin stand: the huller rib came in two parts with an opening at the point where the saw passed through the rib (figure 33). This eliminated the congestion, but it also greatly reduced the effectiveness of the huller breast in removing hulls. The design is similar to the open-end huller rib used by Contentinental Gin Co. described previously.

Today, huller ribs are becoming obsolete. With harvesting and extraction methods becoming more efficient, and the gin stand itself approaching the twenty bales-per-hour level, huller ribs, seen as a hindrance to capacity, are being removed. In the mid-1970s at the J. G. Boswell Company, I was the first to remove the huller-rib arrangement. On my 164 saw gin stand currently manufactured by Consolidated, huller ribs are also eliminated. Other manufacturers of gin stands are following this lead. This is the same, in principle, as the single-rib gin used in the 1800s. However, we are now processing up to fifty pounds per saw per hour,

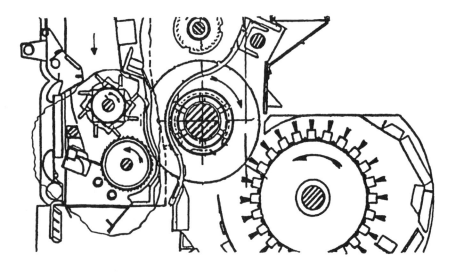

Figure 32. Lummus high-capacity huller breast

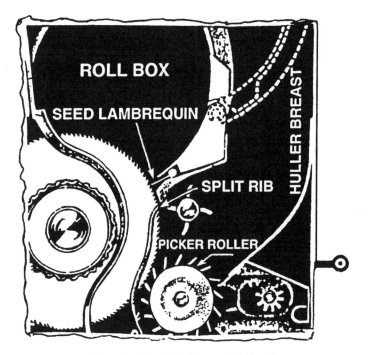

Figure 33. Hardwicke Etter split huller rib

compared with five to seven pounds per saw in the early 1900s. Some of the old single-rib gins were manufactured well into the twentieth century.

Doffing Systems

Another basic component of the gin is the gin saw doffing system. The most common method of doffing is by a rotating brush cylinder similar to that used by Whitney and Holmes. This method of doffing is clearly illustrated by the sketches of the Whitney and Holmes gins (figures 18 and 19). Although the design of the brush cylinder has been improved in modern gins, the principle is the same. The wind board located above and between the brush and saw is important in directing the air, generated by the brush rotation, across the saw teeth. Doffing is done primarily by this air, which must be directed toward the mote board to prevent fibers from escaping or bypassing the inlet of the lint duct.

Just how much doffing is done by the air is difficult to determine. The air, however, is all-important in getting the lint into the lint duct. After the brushes of the cylinder have passed the doffing point, they drag an air current along with them as they rotate. This causes air to flow toward the surface of the cylinder and it is this induced air that drags the lint into the duct and conveys it out of the gin.

Tests have established that the bristles do not have to touch the saw teeth for the brush to doff the saw. In fact, in operation, the bristles that contact the saw teeth soon wear off. However, the centrifugal action of the saw-blade rotation causes the fibers to stand out from the teeth; thus, the fibers—which are the object of the doffing—are contacted by the bristles. As far as discussions about the merits of brush doffing versus air-blast doffing are concerned, it is sometimes noted that, because the brush bristles do not touch the saw, both methods are really air-doffing systems. It has been proven that the brush doffing is more positive and therefore more trouble free.

The brush-doffing cylinder is usually fifteen to sixteen inches in diameter and rotates at fifteen hundred to sixteen hundred revolutions per minute. An old rule of thumb is for the surface speed of the brush to be about three times that of the saw. The bristles are set in three-quarter-inch square wooden sticks; they project out of the stick about three quarters of an inch. Good wood for brush sticks has become difficult to obtain: in any lot of replacement sticks, some have to be rejected because they are warped. In the last few years, a brush called the Poly Stick has been popular—a plastic stick seems to be straighter and easier to balance.

All of the gins being built today use the brush-doffing system, although many gins still in operation use an air-blast system (figure 34). I have worked extensively

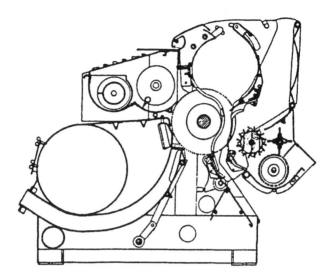

Figure 34. Commonly used air-blast doffing arrangement

on variations for air-blast doffing systems and in my early days at Lummus was granted two patents in this area. One incorporated a novel and successful method of using the doffing system as a trash-removing device.

The Vandergriff air-blast system shown in figure 35 consists of an air chamber mounted in the gin frame behind the saw cylinder. This air chamber has an air nozzle built into the section adjacent the saw blades. The nozzle opening is about one-quarter inch (some systems use three-sixteenths). Air discharges from the nozzle across a curved metal section, the upper end forms the back of the nozzle opening.

As the air passes over this surface, it crosses the saw teeth at high velocity—in the range of twelve thousand to fifteen thousand feet per minute. The high-velocity air strips the lint from the saw teeth and there is sufficient induced air moving toward the high-velocity stream to cause the lint to follow the stream into the lint duct. I have always been fascinated to observe how the high-velocity air stream hugs the surface of the metal: there is a vacuum behind the stream, and atmospheric pressure forces the outside of the stream back against the metal surface. The lint does not penetrate the high-velocity air current but moves along with the induced air—without the induced air, the fibers would escape the lint-duct inlet.

The patented feature of the Vandergriff arrangement is demonstrated by the initial direction of the air leaving the air chamber outside the lint-duct opening. As the air contacts the lint held by the saw teeth, it initially propels loose trash in this direction. As the air makes the first turn it loosens the lint; the denser particles

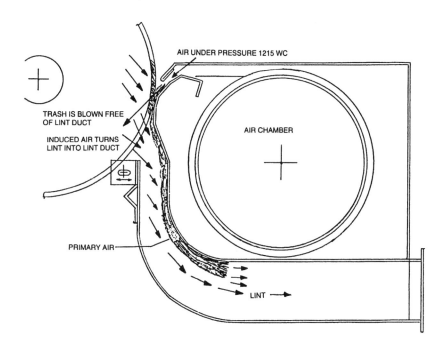

Figure 35. Vandergriff air-blast doffing system

are thrown through the induced air current and propelled out of the lint stream. The velocity and mass of much of the trash is great enough to permit it to pass through the induced air currents without being deflected into the lint stream. This method of removing foreign matter is known as *moting*. The amount of trash removed when using this method is startling, and I still have misgivings about giving it up in favor of the more trouble-free brush doffing.

Most problems with air-blast systems arise from sticky material in the lint. This material gathers on the upper edge of the lint-duct opening (usually referred to as the *mote board*). Sticky material, which comes from crushed immature seed and green plant material, collects fibers and starts spinning a thread in the turbulent air entering the lint duct. The spinning thread collects a mass of fiber from the flow in the lint duct. If the mass breaks loose it does not cause a problem, otherwise it will build until it eventually blocks the flow of lint into the duct. The fibers that should be going into the lint duct will escape into the open area under the saw. The saw picks up some of them and deposits them into the spaces between the bottom of the gin ribs. In time, these fibers will build up enough to block the seed passage. An alert operator will discover that seeds are not falling from the seed roll at the point of this blockage and will remove it. Removing the sticky material on the mote board will put the gin back into normal operation. Operator failure to discover that seeds are not falling may produce a buildup in the bottom of the ribs. This could become so tight as to cause a friction fire—a serious matter.

A variation of this air-blast doffing—and another of my patents—was the multijet nozzle. Basically, this consisted of a separate nozzle for each saw. This doffing system was designed so that it could be installed in place of the existing air-blast system in the Lummus gin. The advantage to the system was that the individual jets would induce less air than the full nozzle, and as a result more of the foreign matter released by the initial impact of the air against the saw would escape the induced air and find its way into the trash conveyor. This multijet nozzle, in conjunction with top moting, was highly effective at trash removal. It was introduced in the late 1940s when machine-picked cotton was causing cleaning problems. It did the most complete job of cleaning I have ever witnessed from a single unit.

Many multijet units went into use even though the individual jets did not provide enough induced air to keep the mote board clean. The situation required more attention than most operators were willing to undertake. Today, some of the newcomers to cotton ginning research are showing renewed interest in improving the cleaning by the gin stand. I think this multijet approach warrants further exploration.

A variation that I think has good possibilities—one that would restore the advantages of air-blast doffing systems—is to put a secondary nozzle below the lint-duct opening, as shown in figure 36. I have not tested such a system, but the primary nozzle opening could be reduced to one-eighth inch, and the secondary nozzle the same. This would induce a stronger pull of air into the lint duct, making it possible to move the mote board down, out of the path of the sticky material. Such a variation would enable the doffing system to operate against a higher back pressure, thus assisting and improving the performance of the air-jet cleaners that often are used following the gin stand.

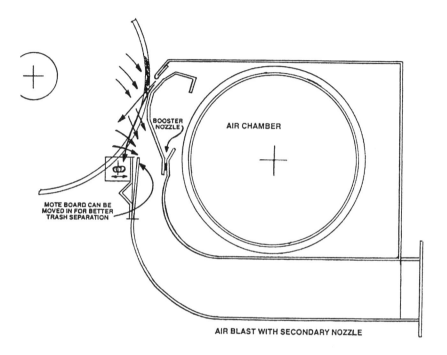

BOOSTER NOZZLE

AIR CHAMBER

MOTE BOARD CAN BE MOVED IN FOR BETTER TRASH SEPARATION

AIR BLAST WITH SECONDARY NOZZLE

Figure 36. Air-blast arrangement with a secondary nozzle

Gin Stand Moting

Prior to the general use of lint cleaners, considerable emphasis was placed on gin stand moting. In fact, from the beginning of saw ginning, trash removal by moting in the gin stand has been emphasized, each company claiming advantages over its competitors.

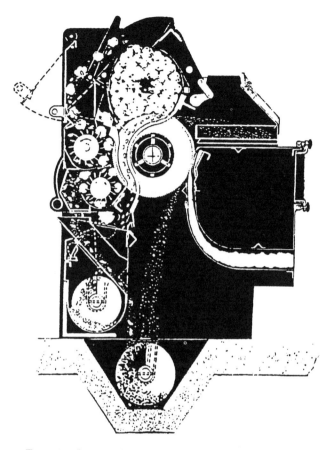

Figure 37. Lummus double moting gin with two sources of moting

The top moting system is extremely effective when the trash being thrown off the saw as it comes through the ribs is allowed to collect in a semisealed chamber. The top moting system of the Lummus gin shown in figure 37 effectively accomplished this. The trash, and a small amount of lint, was deposited on a moving belt that ran close to the saw as it moved through the sealed chamber. Some lint was deposited on the edge of the belt next to the saw. If the belt was not adjusted to run to the rear side of the trough, this lint might hang on the edge of the trough as it exited the chamber. If this buildup was not removed, the entire mote chamber soon built up with trash.

This system was worthwhile until the gin was modified to operate at a higher capacity. The trash thrown off from the saw was then so heavy that this moting system had to be abandoned. This system is of particular significance in light of the new efforts by researchers to emphasize trash removal by the gin stand.

Other manufacturers used various devices next to the saw to aid in delivering the trash into the moting chamber. Some used a sharp edge as a mote board, but without some means of wiping this edge, the buildup of sticky material often became so great as to interfere with the doffing, with a resulting backlash in the bottom of the gin ribs. Some tried knife-edged bars next to the saw, moving them laterally slightly, back and forth, so the lint on the saw would wipe them. The sticky material almost always was between the saws only, thus the reciprocating movement was calculated to prevent the buildup. Some used a rotating shaft, some a shaft with a wiper. This sticky mote problem was so prevalent that we often joked about installing a wiper to wipe the wiper. Lummus became so discouraged with the situation that, at the time of their switch from air-blast doffing to brush, they stopped supplying top moting systems. This policy lasted a number of years.

The moting system introduced in the late 1950s (figure 38) has proven to be the most efficient; it and the reciprocating or rotating shaft are the only approaches currently used. This moting system consists of a knife edge next to the saw, with the knife edge being the upper section of a trough. A rotating blade is mounted on arms on a shaft to wipe the knife edge and sweep the bottom of the trough. Back of the trough is a screw conveyor in a trough. The wiper moves the trash into the conveyor, whence it moves to end of the gin and falls by gravity into a trash conveyor under the gin.

The cover of the mote chamber has louvers to allow air to enter, thus reducing the vacuum at the end of the conveyor and allowing the trash to discharge. It is significant that in this system the motes do not discharge into a sealed chamber. The doffing brush attempts to get some of its air out of this chamber; were it sealed except at the discharge end, the brush would create enough vacuum to prevent the trash from discharging against this incoming air. The discharge end of the conveyor could be sealed with a rotating seal. The louvers then could be eliminated and the amount of trash removed would be significant. The rotating seal should be designed so that material containing some fiber can be accepted. An effort to solve this problem of sealing the mote chamber could be productive. The Lummus Double Moting Gin had the ends of the chamber sealed by floating rollers that rode the belt, with covers fitting snugly against them.

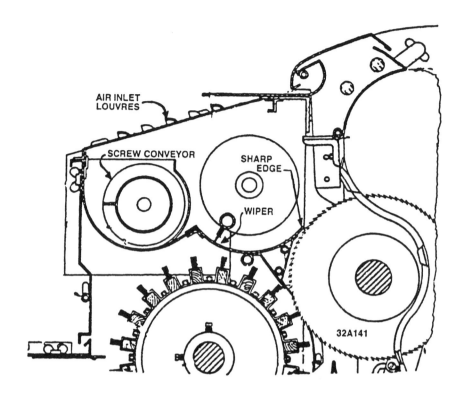

Figure 38. Modern moting system

Seed Rolls

Seed roll operation—how the roll turns and the factors influencing the seed discharge rate are critical. These factors are the least understood of any in the gin stand.

When Eli Whitney invented the cotton gin, he settled for a roll box with a simple seed-discharge arrangement. A hinged bottom kept the seed contained. An operator filled the roll box cavity with seed cotton and, when all the lint was ginned from the seed, a stick holding the hinged bottom in place was removed, allowing the seed to fall out. The hinged section was then pushed back up, secured by the stick, and the procedure was repeated. It was not a continuous gin, but it had no seed discharge problems.

A couple of years later, in 1796, Holmes patented his gin with an opening in the bottom of the roll box cavity to permit the seed to discharge continuously (figure 19). This was a great improvement over Whitney's hinged door and use of this crude "little engine" spread rapidly. The fuzziness of the cotton seed permitted the Holmes gin to perform magic. When the lint was removed from the seed, the remaining fuzz and short fiber caused the seeds to adhere to each other. This resulted in a mass in the seed roll that clung together to such an extent that a sizable opening could be left at the bottom without all the seed dropping out. The natural tendency of the seed to hang together greatly aided the rotation of the seed roll.

However, Holmes had a problem—and it has dogged the industry for almost two hundred years: how to determine the size and location of the opening in the bottom of the seed roll cavity to permit the seed to discharge with the ideal amount of residual lint? Moreover, at the same time this discharge rate had to match the rate of feed, to ensure that the lint had a smooth texture acceptable to the classer. The seed discharge opening must have an adjustment that ensures that all the lint is removed from the various sizes of seed, and under a variety of moisture conditions. This adjustment was made by means of a movable seed board that controlled the sag in the roll as it approached the saw (figure 39).

This is sometimes referred to as *seed lambrequin; seed board* is commonly used, but I usually refer to it as *seed fingers*. It usually consists of a small shaft about five-eighths-inch in diameter, with pins about one-eighth-inch to three-sixteenths-inch in diameter and two inches long projecting in a row from the shaft. The pins are spaced the same as the saw blades to project between the saws when desired. The shaft projects through the ends of the gin head plates and a handle is placed on the shaft on one end so that the fingers may be adjusted up and down. Moving the fingers up reduces the amount the seed roll sags into the seed passage. This causes the seed to stay in the seed roll longer and discharge with less residual lint. Lowering the seed fingers has the opposite effect. In the early days of ginning, when there was no seed-cotton drying and very little cleaning, the seed finger adjustment played an important part in both amount of residual lint and lint grade. The ginner often walked a tightrope between grade and turnout.

When starting a gin without any roll, the roll begins to turn as the cotton is fed to the saws. The ginning process starts, but little seed is discharged for some time. This is interesting. The reason is that the ginned seed starts accumulating in the center of the roll and this core builds until it reaches the surface; then the seed starts discharging. Practically all of the seed in the roll are fully ginned.

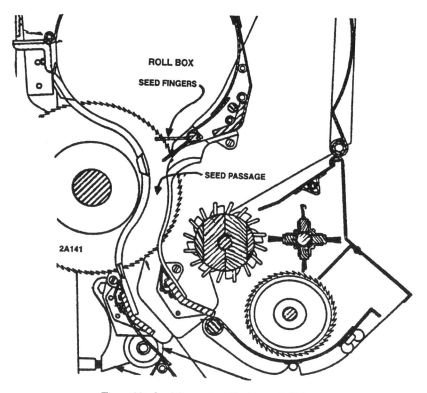

Figure 39. Seed fingers for adjusting seed discharge

The gins with essentially round roll boxes operated with tight rolls were referred to as *tight-roll gins*. The surface of the roll was seedy and hard. The operator had to decide how far to go in holding the seed for maximum turnout; a lesser density would produce a smoother sample. In some cases the operator ran loose roll at the beginning and end of the bales so that the outer surface of the bale from which the sample was cut would be clean and smooth.

With these gins, there was not much the operator could do to improve the rate of ginning per saw, except be alert to the moisture content of the cotton, the size of the seed, and the trash content. Thus, it became necessary to be able to adjust the rate of feed and the seed board. Dry cotton could be ginned with a tighter seed roll and still make a smooth sample, the fiber remaining smooth under more pressure than it would with more moisture present. Moreover, it is normal for more trash to be present in damp cotton.

These tight-roll gins prevailed until the 1930s. The loose-roll gin resulted from a change in the roll box shape—from essentially round to a vertical oval. The back scroll of the roll box was raised (using a longer radius on the scroll), but the important change was to the front, which was given a longer radius. The size of the opening in the bottom of the seed roll was not always changed. The longer radius of the front caused the roll to approach the opening at a steeper angle and this resulted in the roll sagging deeper in the opening, rupturing the surface more drastically. With this roll box shape, the seed would start discharging before the core built all the way to the surface. This left a thin layer of unginned cotton on the surface. That the seed would discharge with a looser roll made it easier to make a smooth sample. Under comparable conditions and with comparable results, this type of gin would gin a little more cotton per saw.

If too much cotton was fed any of these gins, the seed roll would tighten and stop turning. This was assumed to be caused by the increased feed rate. The problem actually was more one of not getting the seed out fast enough. Further improvement could have been made with these loose-roll gins by further increasing the sag angle and leaving the back scroll curvature only slightly more than that of the gin rib.

The Departure from Loose-Roll Ginning and Development of High-Capacity Gin Stands

The loose-roll gin was the standard well into the 1950s and the intervening period saw little change in per-saw capacity (figure 40). But with the increased rate of harvest from the use of mechanical pickers, there arose great demand to address the capacity issue. Manufacturers attempted to meet this need by increasing the number of saws in a stand, first from eighty saws to ninety saws, then to 120 saws. But no significant changes were made in the actual design of the stands. Some companies were trying larger-diameter saws before the end of the 1950s, but there was still no significant improvement in the per-saw capacity.

During this time, *combing lint cleaners* had made their appearance; the roll density could be increased without fear of a rough sample. The old, persistent problem of getting the seed out fast enough to permit an increase in ginning rate defied the efforts of the gin manufacturers.

In the middle 1950s, the Hardwicke Etter Company had experimented with additional saws in a stand by placing one hundred saws in the ninety-saw frame. They concluded that this was not the improvement they wanted and abandoned the idea. The increased saws might have proved a major advance if they had

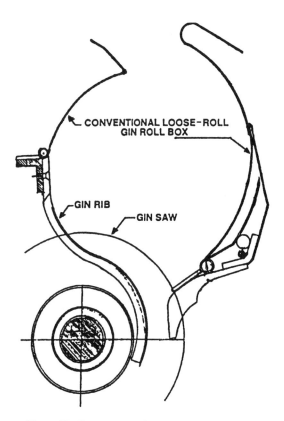

Figure 40. Cross section of a typical loose-roll gin box

changed the roll box shape, allowing seed to discharge at the increased rate required by increased lint production (figure 41).

At this time I was in charge of engineering at Lummus. We had not done much gin stand research until then, except with the doffing system. We had, however, given the machine a good face-lift in the early 1950s when we went to the 90 saw gin. Now we decided to find a way to increase the per-saw capacity rather than going to a larger unit with more saws or larger-diameter saws. We experimented with different roll box shapes and discovered that making the front of the roll box steeper and changing the contour of the ribs would significantly increase the seed-discharge rate.

In the meantime, W. C. Pease III came up with the idea of an agitating cylinder in the seed roll. We had a cylinder made consisting of 4.5-inch-diameter

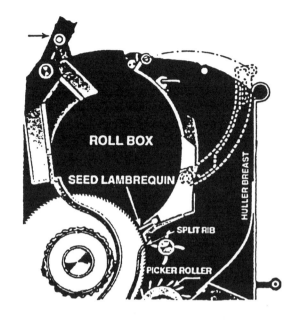

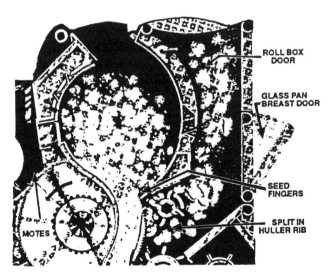

Figure 41. Hardwicke Etter Company roll boxes

disks with serrated edges, mounted on a shaft about 1.5 inches apart and set at angle so that, as they rotated, they would wobble. This wobble was designed to move the seed roll back and forth across the saws to expose the unginned lint to the saws. The loose-roll gin operated with white streaks of lint between the saws. It was our idea to shift these bands of lint into the path of the saw. This disk assembly was located slightly to the back of the center of the roll box, about 0.75 inch off the saw. Initially, we powered it from the shaft of one of the picker rollers.

We continued to experiment with locations, speeds, and roll box shapes and learned one important fact: that the front side of the roll box had to be almost vertical as it approached the turn at the bottom. This made the roll sag enough to release the seed at the rate comparable to the rate at which the saws would remove the lint. The added pressure from the agitator cylinder expedited this process, and the discharge rate increased to about three times the previous rate.

As others increased the number of saws in their gin stands, they tried to adapt the agitator concept to them. They failed because the front side of the roll box must be modified as well, allowing greater sag in the seed roll and thus increasing the seed discharge. Simply removing the lint at a faster rate will not do it. The seed must be let out at a rate comparable to the increased lint-removal rate. This development would have been a relatively inexpensive conversion for our existing gins, but we chose to redesign the entire gin stand around these new features. This new design became the Lummus Super 88 saw gin, the first gin stand on the market with a significant increase in the per-saw capacity (figure 42).

It will be useful to summarize the key reasons for this tremendous increase in per-saw capacity. The agitator cylinder compressed the mass tightly against the teeth of the saws; as the saw passed through this compressed mass, the seed could not run from the saw teeth; the lint was pressed into the teeth of the saw. The steep angle of the front side of the roll box (or a steep sag angle, to use my description) allowed efficient seed discharge, moving the seed out at the necessary rate. With this improved discharge rate, we increased the saw speed from 650 rpm to 1000 rpm (we later dropped the speed back to the 900-950 rpm range).

Although I realized that the contour of the gin rib also could play an important part in rupturing the seed roll, promoting even better seed discharge, I was not able to implement this change at this point. Gin rib contour had been mostly untampered with by Lummus and the other companies for at least half a century. On later designs I was able to change rib contours and seed discharge markedly improved (see "Gin Rib Design," this chapter). An additional feature is the contour of the huller rib at the top. Figure 43 compares the Lummus huller rib with that of the Continental twelve-inch huller rib. Note that the Lummus rib

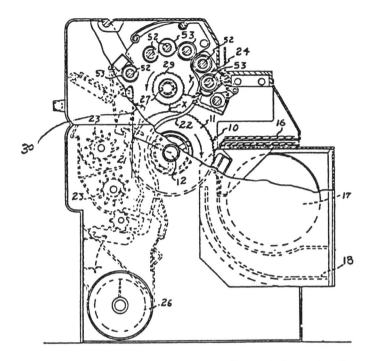

Figure 42. Lummus Super 88 high-capacity gin from original patent issued to
Vandergriff and Pease

does not project into the seed passage nearly as much as the Continental. Note
also that the front side of the seed roll scroll approaches the saw much higher than
does the Continental. Looking at the gin rib contour as it forms part of the seed
passage, it can be noted that the dotted line representing the Lummus rib leaves
a wider seed passage than the Continental. These are significant differences,
especially when closer saw spacings are used.

This gin was our most important development and added significantly to
the growing prestige of Lummus. A patent on the gin was issued to Bill Pease and
me jointly. This work was done in 1958, and the first sales were made in 1959.

I continued my work in this delicate area of the roll box shape during my
time at the J. G. Boswell Company, where I designed the capacity booster
discussed in Chapter 5 (figure 44). The principal change I made at this time was
in the front side, along the same line as with the Lummus Super 88. The lower
front of the roll box approached the saw at an angle twenty degrees off vertical.

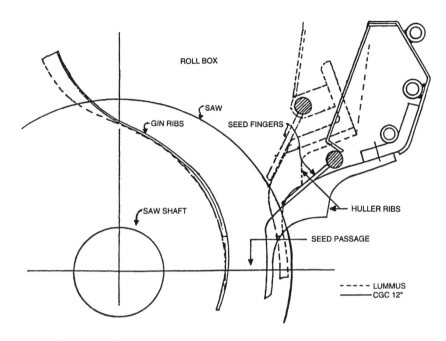

Figure 43. Comparison of the Lummus and Continental twelve-inch saw gin
seed-discharge passages

Later, when these were made for the Murray gins, the approach angle was only
ten degrees, because the Murray saw spacing was considerably less than the
Continental (0.71875-inch instead of 0.787-inch). The steeper angle on the
wider spacing would let the seed out too fast and leave an unacceptable amount
of residual lint on them. The entire front of the roll box was moved in so that the
bottom scroll, approaching at twenty degrees, would end at the proper place above
the seed fingers. The radius of the back of the roll box scroll was also shortened.
This held the mass of the seed roll tighter against the saws and provided increased
capacity. A loose seed roll permits the seed with its lint to run from the saw teeth
and it takes longer to remove all the lint. The steeper approach angle caused the
bottom of the seed roll to rupture more drastically as it turned over the seed passage,
which is the primary reason for the improved seed discharge. This, along with a
higher density seed roll, accounted for the greatly improved capacity.

Operators of capacity-booster conversions, using them in conjunction with
combing lint cleaners to smooth out the sample discovered over time that more

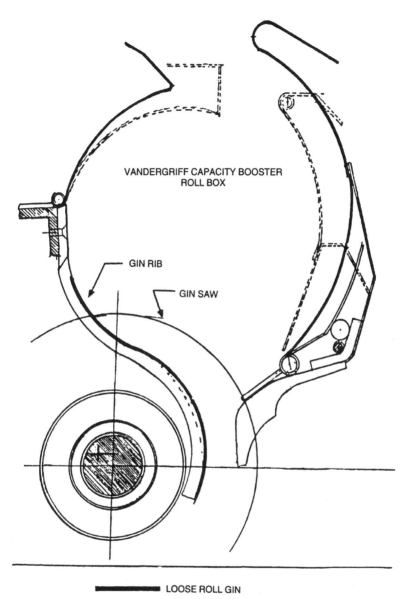

VANDERGRIFF CAPACITY BOOSTER
ROLL BOX

GIN RIB

GIN SAW

LOOSE ROLL GIN

CAPACITY BOOSTER

Figure 44. The Vandergriff Capacity Booster, 1964

horsepower could be used on the saw shaft, doubling the capacity. Ginners not using the capacity-booster conversions were increasing their capacity somewhat by adding horsepower, feeding more cotton to the gin stand, and operating with higher-density seed rolls. This approach had severe limitations, because no steps were taken to increase seed-discharge capabilities. Other methods of improving the capacity of the gin stand have evolved in the intervening years. The most successful methods have all involved rupturing the seed roll at the turn as it approaches the saw, removing some seed from the core of the seed roll, or both.

The Industry Moves to Narrower Saw Spacings

The 141 Saw Gin Stand

When I took over at Continental in 1959, they had been doing some experimental work with the sixteen-inch saw gin. They had increased the size of the roll box in proportion to the increase in the diameter of the saw, which was a mistake, and they had allowed the saw spacing to remain at 0.787-inch, which was not a good choice. This not only limited capacity, it also left too much lint on the seed. This spacing was a holdover from the early Pratt and Munger gins. Although it was satisfactory at the low production rates necessary before combing lint cleaners, at higher capacities the results would not be acceptable. When we attempted to operate this gin at its expected capacity of about six bales per hour, we found it impossible to prevent the discharge of some seeds with lint tags on them.

Excessive residual lint on the seed is usually thought of as being governed by roll box shape. This gin, however, operated with dense seed rolls for the desired capacity, producing some only-partially ginned seed that would be pushed out between the saws. For this gin to be completely successful the saws would have to be spaced closer together.

From other standpoints, the gin was successful. In contrast to all the gins made by Continental up to this time, the frame of this gin was entirely fabricated from steel plate, not the earlier cast-iron construction. It had a good brush doffing system, which allowed it to operate trouble free. The rib-saw relationship was such that the seed roll was aggressive and turned freely, except for an occasional stoppage on the ends. This problem was caused by too much space between the end saw and the roll box head. The space was almost a full rib wide. It should have been less than one-half the gin saw spacing, or one half rib. At that time the field of saw spacing, rib contours, and roll box shapes was not well researched. And most information was determined empirically. Over the years, this one error

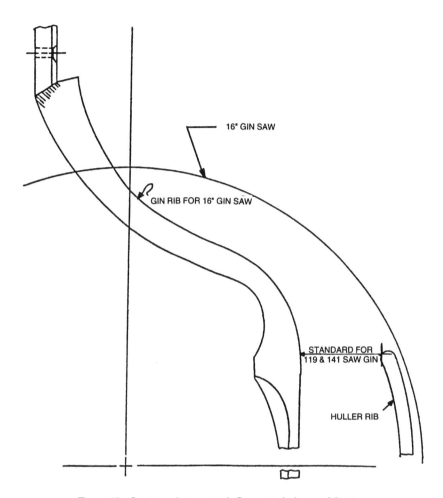

16" GIN SAW

GIN RIB FOR 16" GIN SAW

STANDARD FOR
119 & 141 SAW GIN

HULLER RIB

Figure 45. Continental sixteen-inch Comet gin before modification

has cost customers thousands of dollars to replace end saws ruined by roll chokes on the ends.

Figure 45 shows the seed passage on the Continental Comet Gin before modification. The contour of the rib permitted the seed roll to sag too deeply into the passage. With the wide saw spacing of 0.787-inch, seed was released prematurely. Early in my work at Boswell I asked Continental's engineering department to make some test ribs as specified in my drawings—a design that would reduce this sag. They had a short gin with twenty-one saws that would

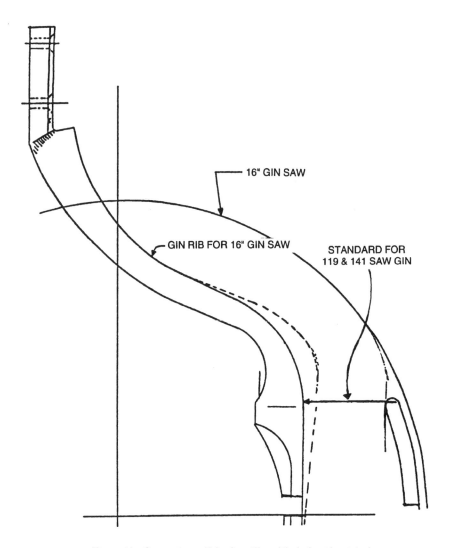

Figure 46. Comparison of Vandergriff modified rib with original

require only a few ribs for testing. For test purposes, the ribs were cast from a single pattern and installed. To obtain comparative data, a number of tests were conducted: the residual lint was less and more uniform on my modified rib design. A comparison of the old rib and the modified one is shown in figure 46.

With such encouraging test results, I had a set of these ribs made and ran them for a season. They performed up to my expectations and I placed them in the rest of Boswell's 119 saw stands. At this point, Continental began to equip their future stands in California and Arizona with this same rib. They called it the Western Rib. I knew, however, that my improved rib was only a partial answer to the problem. The saw spacing of 0.787-inch remained and would soon have to be addressed.

When the super-high-capacity plant was built for Boswell in 1968, we installed six 119 saw gin stands to obtain the forty bales-per-hour capacity that was my goal. These stands contained my improved gin rib, but when running at the desired capacity, the amount of residual lint on the seeds was unacceptable. However, I was unable to address this problem until later.

With the 1970 season approaching, I again contacted Continental's engineering department wanting to narrow the saw spacing on our 119 saw stands. Although they did not believe this would be a change for the better, they produced a 141 saw cylinder spaced at 0.663-inch, as per my request, along with gin ribs and huller ribs.

As the 1970 season wound down, I had this arrangement installed in one gin stand late in the season. The results were outstanding: low residual lint and almost a 20 percent increase in capacity. Boswell changed all of their 119 saw gins to 141 saw gins. Everyone else soon began to experiment with narrower saw spacing. Continental began to promote their new 141 saw gin stand. As far as the industry was concerned, no more 119 saw gins were sold, and in a matter of a few years most of the gins in the field were converted. The 119 saw gin, for all practical purposes, had become extinct.

The Murray Company then introduced an eighteen-inch saw gin. It was made with eighty saws, a few with ninety saws, and the more popular one, 120 saws. The saw spacing they chose was the same as the Continental sixteen-inch saw gin—0.787-inch and they encountered the same problems as Continental did with their sixteen-inch Comet gins.

Joe Laney, a long-time friend, former associate, and acting head of the Murray Company (1971-72), called to seek my opinion of the closer saw spacing of the 141 saw gins. I recommended it highly. He indicated that Murray would try it on a test basis. During the next season, a customer who had a four-stand 120 eighteen-inch saw Murray plant called me. He had converted from the 120 to 142 saws at Laney's suggestion and was pleased with the results. The 142 saw gin has been Murray's standard ever since.

Concurrently, Lummus was making a 128 saw gin with a saw spacing of about 0.750-inch. They were reluctant to change to the narrow spacings, but soon joined Murray and Continental, introducing the 158 saw gin—saw spacing 0.6171 inch.

Today, the industry continues to narrow saw spacings even further. Continental coverted from 141 saws to 161 with a spacing of 0.580 inches and Lummus converted from 158 saws to 170 with a spacing of 0.574 inches. I am convinced that saw spacings can be made even narrower. Currently, we are working at Elbow gin to convert their 152 model to 182 saws. This will leave a saw spacing of 0.5175, the closest in the industry. However, with an increase in per-saw capacity, seed discharge must be considered to prevent an overly tight seed roll. The Elbow gin stand will have a Vandergriff seed tube arrangement in it, plus the improvements to seed removal from the roll that were made to the Consolidated 164 Gin Stand (patent # 4,974,294).

The Murray Eighteen-Inch Saw Gin Conversions

Since introducing the eighteen-inch saw gin, Murray went through a change of ownership, a liquidation, and a rebirth of sorts. As a result of the work I was doing in California, I was approached in 1979 by the reorganized and renamed Murray Carver Company: would I consider a project to adapt my seed tube to their eighteen-inch saw gin? I learned that most of the machinery they were selling was being made in Brazil, and, on agreeing to negotiate with them, found myself negotiating with a Dallas corporation acting as the U.S. agent for the Brazilian-made machinery. This corporation, the Murray Piratininga Machinery Corporation, was also responsible for the machinery improvement. It was headed by Vitally Veyslip and Joe Neitzel—former executives of the old Murray company—and I found them easy to deal with. In the spring of 1979 we reached an agreement for me to adapt my seed tube to their 142 eighteen-inch saw gin.

They shipped one of these gins to Corcoran, California, for modification. The roll box in this gin was unconventional and the modification proved to be an exasperating experience. As the sketch in figure 47 shows, the roll box had an almost normal front and back scroll, but it was sixteen to seventeen inches from front to back, compared with eleven to twelve inches on other gins. My experience with the seed tube had indicated that the tube should go near the center of the seed roll—but determining the center of this long oval configuration would have to be accomplished empirically. I chose a position about concentric with the gin rib curvature and the back scroll.

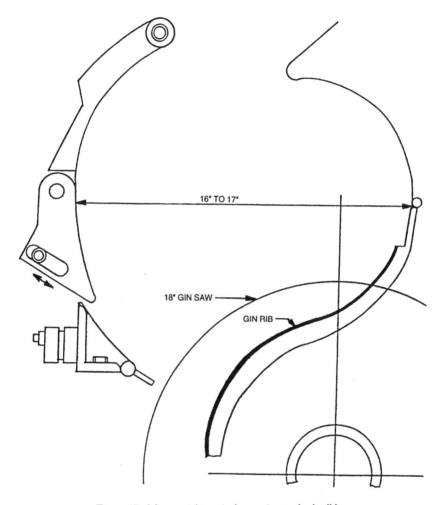

Figure 47. Murray eighteen-inch saw gin standard roll box

To remove the seed from the tube, we used the blower arrangement that was chosen for the conversions at Elbow Gin discussed further in the 152 saw gin section. We also used the same tube-drive arrangement, but mounting the tube bearings satisfactorily was much more difficult. It was necessary to cut out a large chunk of the gin leg casting to clear the tube.

Once this modification was complete, the complete gin stand with tube installation was shipped back to a stripper-cotton area in the Coastal Bend region

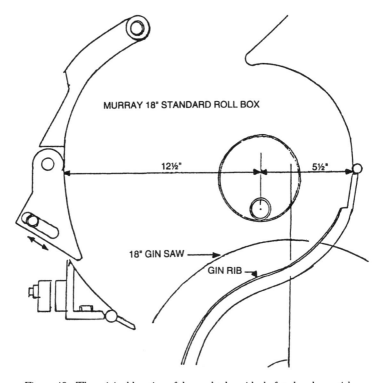

MURRAY 18" STANDARD ROLL BOX

12½"   5½"

18" GIN SAW

GIN RIB

Figure 48. The original location of the seed tube with shaft to break up sticks.

of Texas. It was installed in a plant that left much to be desired and—to add to the problems—it was a rainy harvest season. We quickly encountered a problem with the wet sticks from the stripper cotton projecting into the tube and blocking the flow of seed. In the gin yard, I saw a piece of rusty one-inch pipe, about five or six feet long. It occurred to me that such a pipe, rolling inside the tube, might be the solution. It was. That old piece of pipe broke the sticks off as they projected into the tube. The next day, I obtained a new one-inch shaft and fitted it inside a piece of one-inch PVC Schedule 40 pipe; not only was it a good fit, it eliminated the noise of the metal-to-metal contact—and the stick problems ceased (see figure 48).

From the beginning, it was obvious that the tube location in relation to the front and back scroll would not be successful. The power requirements needed to turn the saw shaft demonstrated this. The initial effort to correct this was to move the front of the roll box and lower front scroll in by three inches, thus reducing the horizontal dimension to thirteen inches. This placed the five-inch tube in the center of this

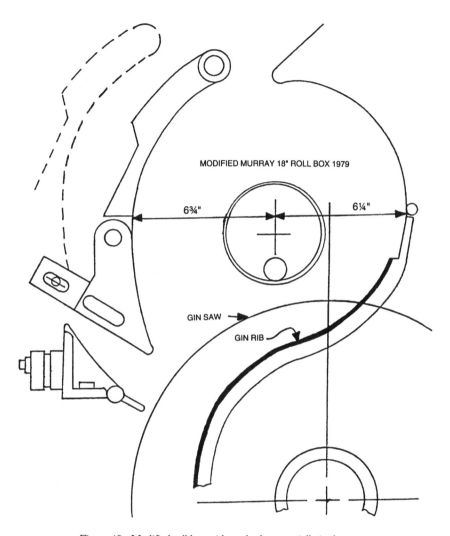

MODIFIED MURRAY 18" ROLL BOX 1979

6¾"   6¼"

GIN SAW →

GIN RIB

Figure 49. Modified roll box with seed tube essentially in the center

dimension. Other details, such as bearings, rotating joints for the air connections to the tube, and discharge chutes needed to be worked out (see figure 49).

When these modifications were completed, Murray Carver started having new fronts made for their existing gins. A shop in Corcoran was chosen because Murray Carver had no manufacturing facilities and I wanted to oversee construction. These new fronts were sold as a field conversion for existing gins. They were

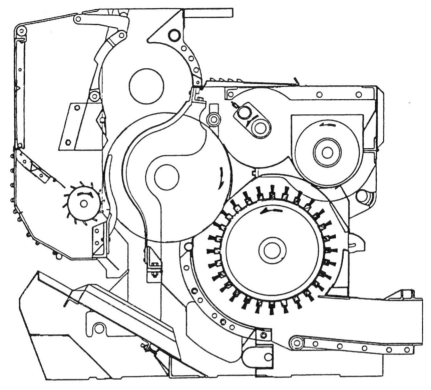

Figure 50. The Murray Triple Crown Gin

also made as part of the new gins being sold under the name of Murray Triple Crown Gin (see figure 50).

Despite the changes in the roll box, the capacity did not reach the level we thought it should. There was a good flow of seed from the seed tube, but the seed roll was dense, seedy, and sensitive to any unevenness in the end-to-end feed from the feeder. A slightly uneven feed would move most of the seed to the end opposite the heaviest feed. It was a constant challenge to try to keep the feed even with deflectors. This problem was aggravated by the larger than normal roll box. However, the real problem was the contour of the gin rib. The seed discharging through the tube reduced the roll density. This reduced density resulted in less seed discharging through the normal seed passage. The remaining seeds, even though they were ginned, rode the top surface of the gin rib. The slightest uneven feed would cause this mass of ginned seed to shift to the end with the light feed and sometimes, rather than discharge through the normal seed passage, even spill

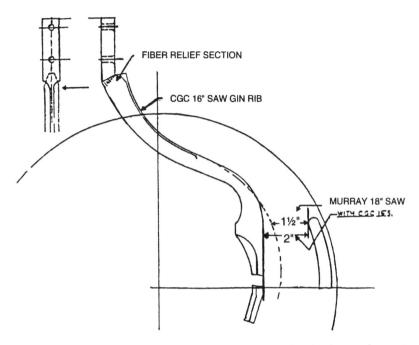

Figure 51. Comparison of seed passages between the sixteen-inch and eighteen-inch saw gin

over the top of the roll box. Figure 51 compares the seed passage between the ginning rib and the huller rib with that of the Continental sixteen-inch saw gin. It may be noted that the gin rib does not break down sharply enough to prevent the seed roll from riding its top surface.

Figure 52 illustrates how this rib contour should be changed, both to open the seed passage and to increase the sag into the passage. A substantial improvement could be made by making this change in the rib. Changing the rib contour involves changing the pattern for the casting, or fabricating the rib as shown in the figure.

Another serious weakness in this gin stand is the radius of the rib curvature of the ginning section—6 3/8 inches; whereas the radius of the curvature of the scroll above the rib is only 5.5 inches (figure 53). The seed roll is compressed into this smaller curve as it leaves the rib curvature. This increases the density of the roll, which in turn increases the power required to turn the saw cylinder. This could be easily corrected by the use of a fabricated rib with a 4.5-inch radius (figure 53).

The suggested change for the standard cast-iron rib is offered for information only. It is assumed that anyone wishing to change the rib curvatures would use the

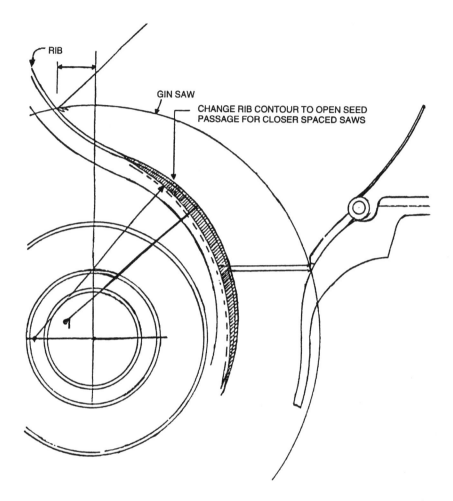

RIB

GIN SAW

CHANGE RIB CONTOUR TO OPEN SEED
PASSAGE FOR CLOSER SPACED SAWS

Figure 52. Illustration of changes needed in the eighteen-inch saw gin rib
to improve seed discharge.

fabricated rib with the replaceable reversible wearplate, which would incorporate the change in both curvatures.

The safety covers for the ends of this gin, as supplied by Murray, are expensive and difficult to manufacture. To keep the modifications of these to a minimum, we designed a tube-supporting weldment that placed the tube bearings (120 mm ball bearings) against the heads of the roll box. This lacked a good seal to protect the bearing as dirt worked its way out of the roll box. There was an

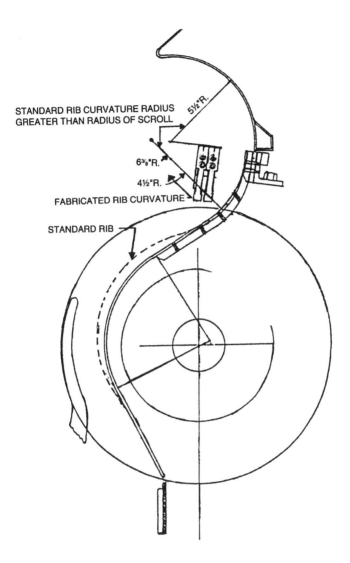

Figure 53. Fabricated rib with a 4¹/₂-inch radius instead of the standard 6³/₈-inch radius
at the ginning section of the eighteen-inch saw gin.

occasional loss of seal when dirt got into the bearings, causing them to freeze up.
When this happened, sometimes the tube was damaged to the extent that it had
to be replaced. In working with other gins, I have redesigned the weldment to place
the bearing outside the head of the roll box, where the seals are not exposed to the
dirt. This however, requires modification of the end covers.

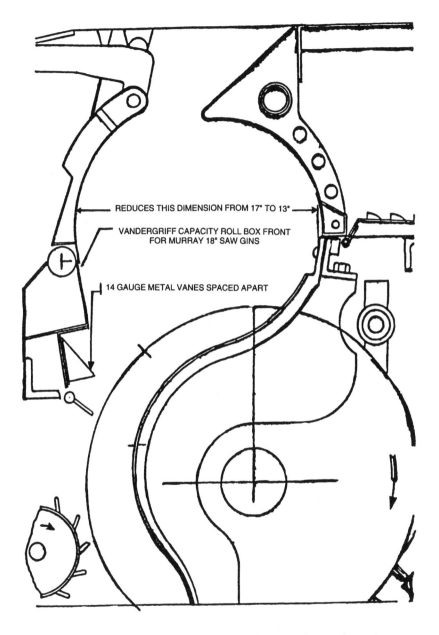

REDUCES THIS DIMENSION FROM 17" TO 13"

VANDERGRIFF CAPACITY ROLL BOX FRONT
FOR MURRAY 18" SAW GINS

14 GAUGE METAL VANES SPACED APART

Figure 54. Complete conversion for standard Murray eighteen-inch saw gin

With the changes that I have suggested, this gin could be competitive: it is ruggedly built and reasonably free of troubles. A negative factor not easily removed is the large disk-brake area of the saws. Sudden stalling of the saw shaft can occur when the seed roll becomes too dense—a condition that produces more saw damage than is generally acceptable. The proposed modifications would provide substantial relief from these problems.

In redesigning this gin into the Triple Crown Gin, it was necessary to redesign the entire ginning front—both the ginning breast and the huller breast. The new huller ribs were cast-aluminum and open at the top. This open-top rib does little in the way of removing foreign matter. At the higher capacities of present-day gins, it is not possible get the cotton through the standard huller ribs. This is especially true if a significant amount foreign matter reaches this point. If there is not a significant amount of foreign material, its removal by the huller ribs is not important. My design for a new type of huller rib is discussed in both the 152 saw gin and 164 saw gin sections later in this chapter.

For several years, I have had some of these Murray eighteen-inch saw gins operating with a modified roll box front, as shown in figure 54. This type of front eventually will be standard on all gins with the closer saw spacing. It permits the seed roll to bulge at the lower edge of the front scroll, which has a 1.5-inch offset at a point 2.5 inches from the saw. The scroll has an approach angle of ten to twenty degrees off vertical, depending on the saw spacing, and the approach line would intersect the saw at a point thirty degrees above the horizontal centerline. The metal vanes, spaced 1.5 inches apart, project inward at the bottom for 1.5 inches. They help prevent the release of partially ginned seed. This offset is sufficient to allow the roll to rupture as it passes, thus releasing the ginned seed into the seed-discharge passage. This does more to free up the seed-roll density and increase the capacity of this big-saw-big-roll-box gin than anything else (except the seed tube) that I have tried.

The Murray gin has a solid reputation built up over a long period and their Triple Crown Gin has been well received by their customers. However, it has a weakness in not getting the ginned seed out of the roll box.

All of these modifications can be applied to the standard Murray eighteen-inch 142 and 94 saw gins at reasonable cost. The complete set of conversions for the standard Murray eighteen-inch saw gin is shown in figure 54. In earlier redesigning of the Triple Crown, the huller breast picker roller was moved up, thus simplifying the design of the cast-aluminum open-end huller rib. It is possible to use a simple huller rib fabricated from a straight piece of flat bar. Conversion of the Triple Crown gin is shown in figure 55. Figure 56 shows the seed-tube

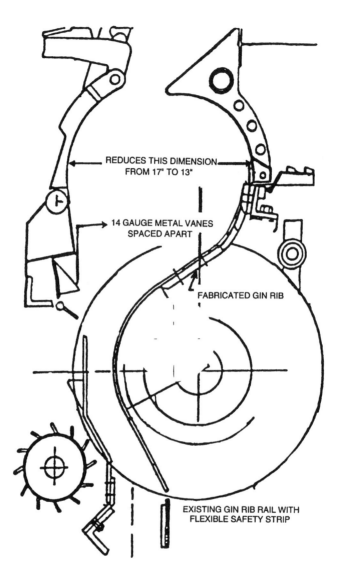

REDUCES THIS DIMENSION
FROM 17" TO 13"

14 GAUGE METAL VANES
SPACED APART

FABRICATED GIN RIB

EXISTING GIN RIB RAIL WITH
FLEXIBLE SAFETY STRIP

VANDERGRIFF CAPACITY ROLL BOX FRONT
FOR MURRAY 18" SAW GINS

Figure 55. Complete conversion for Triple Crown eighteen-inch saw gin

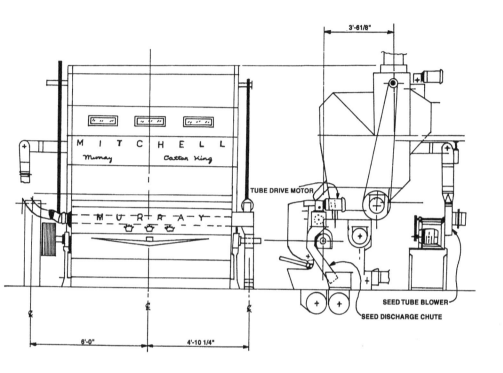

Figure 56. Seed tube and blower arrangement for Triple Crown Gin

blower and tube discharge chute that can be used on either the standard eighteen-inch saw gin or the Triple Crown.

The Continental Sixteen-Inch Saw Gin

There have been differing claims as to "who did what and when" in the area of removing seed from the core of the seed roll. I believe I was way ahead of the field in both research and development and successful implementation of this concept. My research on this project was done both with Continental Gin

Company during the mid to late 1970s and as an independent researcher, mostly at Elbow Gin in Visalia, California.

I entered into an agreement with Continental Gin Company on 1 September 1975, whereby I would submit to them my inventions. One of our mutual interests was improvement of their gin stand. Discussions centered around what I referred to as a "third-generation gin stand." The main components were to be an improved gin rib contour, a closer saw spacing, and—importantly—a means to remove seed from the core of the seed roll. If they chose to manufacture any of my inventions, I was to be compensated on a royalty basis. There was a time limit on how long they had to accept or reject them. If and when inventions were released back to me, I was free to do whatever I desired to do or could do with them. A number of inventions were submitted to them, one of note being the hot-shelf dryer.

In early 1976 shortly after this agreement, I began to get involved in more research with the gin stand. Most of the experimentation would be with older Continental 120 saw stands and would take place at Elbow Gin. I also did experimental work on the tube and ribs at both Westlake Farms near Stratford, California, and J. G. Boswell Company. Much of this work involved the use of a seed tube to aid in the removal of seed from the core of the seed roll.

The closer saw spacing of the 141 saw gin, (0.663 vs. 0.787 on the 119 saw gin) yielded a greater lint-removal capacity than seed-discharge capacity. The residual lint situation was good, but the production rate per saw had the potential for improvement. The whole front of the 141 roll box configuration was not the best from the beginning, and with the closer saw spacing, the weakness in this design was evident. While I was still at Boswell in 1973 I had worked to improve this situation on our 141 saw stands. My first effort involved making a longer radius curve in the front side of the roll box, which would make the seed roll approach the turn at a steeper angle. This was a follow-up to my approach with the Lummus Super 88 saw gin in 1959, and my 1964 capacity booster roll box. Any positive effect this might produce, however, was negated by the location of the seed fingers and the large support bar under them. The bar was necessary to support and protect the seed fingers from the inflow of cotton. A major change was needed to correct this problem, and I lacked the resources to accomplish this at that time.

My next effort was to open a slot in the front side of the roll box, above the seed fingers, wide enough to permit the seed roll to extrude, or bulge, into it enough to rupture the surface. This rupture allowed the ginned seed near the surface of the roll to pop out through the slot. The seed would fall into the huller breast and from there into the seed conveyor under the gin. This particular gin had a slide instead of the picker roller to deliver the cotton to the saw. This arrangement appeared to have potential, but a problem remained with controlling the residual lint on the seed, which was and still is an age-old problem.

It appeared that this residual lint situation might be improved by installing some tapered vanes on two-inch centers above the opening (figure 57). As the roll turned past the vanes, they would project into the surface of the roll, break the seed loose, and cause it to discharge through the slot. This showed promise, but if the seed was restricted enough to control the residual lint properly, not enough seed was discharged to make a significant difference in the capacity.

A sequel to my experimental work with this method of removing seed occurred three years later. I was experimenting with a seed tube in a Murray eighteen-inch saw gin at Duncan Gin, Inverness, Mississippi. The gin superintendent, Randy Williams, had removed the top huller rib rail and the lower front section of the roll box. This left a rather wide gap between the surface of the saw and the lower edge of the roll box front. He welded a 5/8-inch shaft in the end of a 1.5-inch pipe. The shaft extended through the holes in the head plates that previously held the seed-finger shaft. By rotating this shaft on this eccentric mounting, the gap could be closed or opened to help control the seed discharge. In operation, the seed roll extruded through the gap, rupturing the surface of the roll and permitting seed to spill out through the gap (figure 58). This arrangement operated well, but it failed to control the residual lint on the seed sufficiently. As the history of the discovery shows, he had duplicated my efforts to remove seed through a slot above the seed fingers. More recently, a company has advertised this modification on a Murray gin as producing the highest capacity of any gin.

After the 1976 efforts my notes indicate: "After experimenting with a number of these various methods of more efficiently rupturing the surface of the seed roll, there was increasing evidence that removing the ginned seed from the core of the roll would be a better approach." A sketch made 4 June 1976, illustrates an idea as to how this might be done (figure 59).

Another sketch (figure 60) illustrates another idea. This concept, later experimented with to some success, utilized a stationary PVC tube with slots. It was found that the rate of seed discharge could be varied by different placements of the slot in relation to the saw. A heavier flow of seed would result when the slot was rotated toward the saw. I encountered no problem with the roll turning around the tube, but this was only a four-inch tube, and leaf stems had a tendency to collect in the slot. The air would move the stems to the discharge end; there, they would build up and block the seed flow. I also experimented with using compressed air and a small nozzle in the end of the tube to convey the seed out.

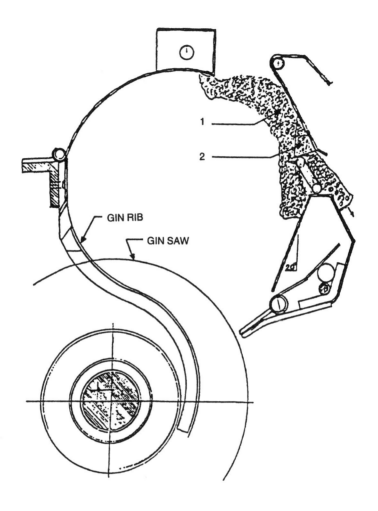

GIN RIB

GIN SAW

1   OUTSIDE LAYER OF GINNED AND UNGINNED SEED, INTERIOR
    OF ROLL CONTAINS GINNED SEED

2   VANES RUPTURE SURFACE OF SEED ROLL, GINNED SEED
    RELEASED INTO THE INCOMING COTTON

Figure 57. Method of discharging seed above the seed fingers

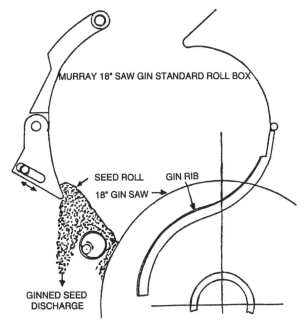

Figure 58. Seed tube
arrangement tested
at Duncan Gin, Inverness,
Mississippi.

The stick problem most likely could be resolved by the use of a stationary perforated metal tube with a "no hole" section over the saws. Such an arrangement (figure 61) would simplify the tube installation, for no bearings or drive would be necessary.

In 1976 I suggested to Continental that changing the rib contour for closer spaced saws might expedite seed discharge (figure 62) but they chose not to pursue it at the time. I started work on closer-spaced gin saws and gin ribs with replaceable wear plates at Elbow Gin in 1977. This fabricated rib was chosen because this was simpler than making patterns for cast-iron ribs. Ribs were made up with 0.5625-inch (9/16-inch) spacing and installed for testing. In the same gin stand, variations on the seed tube were also being tested. This introduced more variables than we could deal with and maintain the production of the gin plant. At this point, Robert Faris suggested we concentrate our efforts on using a seed tube for removing the seed from the core of the seed roll in a gin with standard ribs.

We completed a limited test before the end of the 1977 season. This test included a five-inch OD aluminum tube with one-inch by six-inch slots. The slots were covered with light rubber flashing, mounted in a way we hoped would allow the seed to depress them and enter the tube. The seed did not do this. We removed

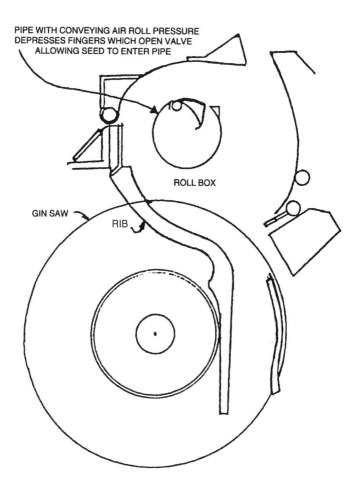

PIPE WITH CONVEYING AIR ROLL PRESSURE
DEPRESSES FINGERS WHICH OPEN VALVE
ALLOWING SEED TO ENTER PIPE

ROLL BOX

GIN SAW

RIB

Figure 59. Method of removing ginned seed from the core of the seed roll

the flashing and had some success in moving the seed into the tube. Air from a small centrifugal fan was used to convey the seed out of the tube.

We attempted to have the seed roll turn the tube, which we had supported on casters mounted outside the roll box heads. This method of supporting the tube offered too much resistance to the free turning of the tube.

One of my concerns about using air to convey the seed out of the tube was whether the commingled mass of the seed roll surrounding the tube would form a sufficient seal to maintain the necessary air flow through the tube. I set up a test

Figure 60. Stationary
four-inch PVC tube

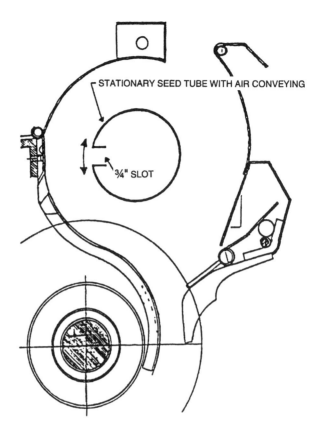

to move the seed with a vacuum. This resulted in practically no flow at the opposite
end of the tube. Approach abandoned. However, the 1977 testing convinced us
that air-conveying of the seed was practical. The design challenges then became
a matter of determining the best hole pattern for the tube, and whether to power
it or not. If powered, we would need to ascertain what type of bearings were
available, investigate tube speeds, and so on. The 1978 season was spent trying
to resolve these problems. Considerable experimenting was done using PVC pipe
for a tube, because we could cut slots and drill holes easily.

All this experimental work had to be done with the plant in full operation.
Although my friends at Elbow Gin were patient and helpful, the down time that
could be spared for this work was limited. Nevertheless, by the end of the 1978
season, we had satisfactorily determined we could design and construct a successful
system for removing seed from the core of the seed roll by means of air and a
perforated metal tube.

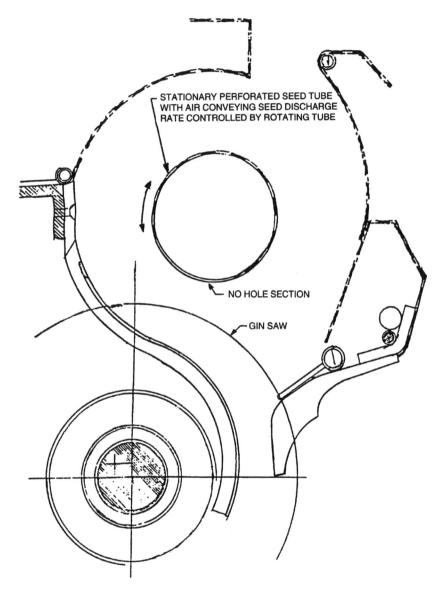

STATIONARY PERFORATED SEED TUBE
WITH AIR CONVEYING SEED DISCHARGE
RATE CONTROLLED BY ROTATING TUBE

NO HOLE SECTION

GIN SAW

Figure 61. Stationary perforated metal tube in a seed roll

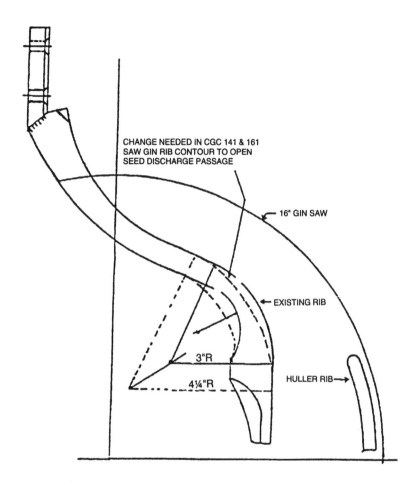

Figure 62. Suggested change in rib contour for closer spaced saws

For the metal tube, I chose stock stainless steel perforated metal with a staggered pattern of 3/8-inch holes. Working with local shops, we cut the metal between the line of holes to the proper width, to the nearest hole spacing, to roll into a tube with a dimension nearest to five inches. This worked out to give us a 4.84-inch diameter tube. We devised a means of rolling, seaming, and straightening that produced a satisfactory tube. I chose a 120 mm extra-light-duty bearing that had an inside diameter of 4.7244 inches. The remaining parts had to vary with each make of gin. Although there were many complications in fitting them to the various makes, it was not too difficult for an experienced shop man. We chose to drive the tube with a one horsepower gearhead motor with an output speed of 350 rpm. The first installation involved converting two stands. We used a small centrifugal fan to supply air to both units, an arrangement that, although it did not permit stopping the fan when the gin breast was in the "out" position, did not prove to be a big problem.

These first two conversions went into the Elbow Gin plant for a portion of the 1979 season. The plant was equipped with two presses that, for test purposes, allowed us to direct the output of these two converted stands into one press. During the seventy-day period of this 1979 season, these two gins produced 19,941 bales (an average of 278 bales per day). These original seed tubes, along with the bearings, blowers, and other components continued to perform well. In 1981, tubes were added to two more of Elbow Gin's six gin stands. Individual blowers were used on each of the four stands. The addition of Vandergriff hot-shelf dryers and other improvements made it possible for the plant to handle the increased capacity of the six stands. By 1984, the plant capacity had reached a spectacular one thousand bales per day, with a season average of about 850 bales per day.

This research convinced me that most older gins could be modified to about the same efficiency as the industry's new stands. These modifications were accomplished comparatively easily and at a reasonable cost. I continued to experiment at Elbow Gin.

While I was working with Continental on other projects, we had numerous discussions about the gin-stand improvement. In early 1977 I was disappointed to learn that Continental was pursuing on their own a modification I thought we would be working on together—closer-spaced saws. I was also advised that Continental had checked out the seed tube idea and found that it was not patentable. At that point I canceled my formal agreement with them (21 March 1977). It was agreed, at their request, that the door be left open to work with them on future projects, and that I would continue to give them a chance to look at any developments I had available.

They went ahead with the closer-spaced saws—part of the development of what I had termed the third-generation gin stand. They installed a modification containing 161 saws in one of the stands at Farmers Co-op Gin for the 1977 season. With the closer saw spacing and no auxiliary means of getting the seed out, extreme pressure was placed on the saws—so much so that either the saw cylinders would have to be changed frequently or the capacity would have to be cut back for them to run at all. Continental asked me to look at this installation and offer suggestions.

My suggestion was that the third phase of the plan for the new generation of gin stands be implemented. This would cover the rapid removal of seed from the core of the seed roll via a seed-tube arrangement. (I had earlier suggested that they modify the 161 saw gin rib by taking some of the hump out of it to let the seed roll sag deeper into the seed passage for a better seed discharge. My suggestion was ignored and they proceeded with the closer-spaced saws, which made a bad situation worse.) Without changes to improve seed discharge, the 161 saw modification had no chance of success. The seed roll became seedy and the seed was badly damaged from staying in the seed roll too long. I advised them that I was involved in experimentation with a seed-tube arrangement and invited them to look at what I was doing. They did, but made no comment.

During the 1978 season, I had made considerable progress with the seed tube at Elbow Gin. I called Charles Merkel, then president of Continental Gin Company, to advise him of my progress. He told me they were, at that time, installing a version of the seed tube in a 141 saw gin stand at Farmers Co-op Gin and suggested I take a look at it, and, in view of the progress I had made at Elbow Gin in this area, he said he would have his people look at what I was doing.

In my discussions with them regarding the seed tube, I made the request that they not use my ideas without my permission. I do not believe this request was honored. They had developed some minor modifications on the tube arrangement that they thought might be patentable and chose to pursue the matter on their own. We both made patent applications assuming they would be thrown into interference at some point in the patent process. However, neither of us was allowed a claim due to the contention by the patent office of prior art—citing an old patent showing a seed tube in a gin stand roll box for removing trash.

Ironically, Joe Salmon, a capable engineer who had followed the developments, retired from Continental Gin and made his own patent application on a seed tube with a conveyor in it. This device was what Continental was using. He acted as his own attorney and got a patent strong enough that Continental elected to buy, in order to continue manufacturing the tube. I have a copy of his patent and it is a masterpiece.

Continental Gin Company went ahead and installed their version of a seed-tube arrangement in a 141 saw stand in Buttonwillow late in the 1978 season. After installation, serious problems were encountered, the most obvious being the mislocation of the tube. It was only three-fourths of an inch off the saw. Figure 63 clearly depicts a wedging action as the seed roll passes between the tube

Figure 63. Continental Gin Company's first effort with a tube in a sixteen-inch 141 saw gin.

and the gin rib. This pressure was so great that the teeth were ripped off the saw blades. The power required to turn the saw shaft was extreme.

When the Lummus gin with the agitator in the seed roll was designed (part of my patent), we located it three-fourths of an inch off the saws. When I participated in the development of the sixteen-inch saw gin at Continental Gin in 1960, following my work at Lummus, we tested a solid five-inch diameter tube in the seed roll. I located it three-fourths of an inch off the saw, the same as the Lummus agitator, but the tube was not powered. Our hope to improve the capacity by holding the seed roll down on the saw was not realized, so the tube idea was abandoned.

Changing the location of the tube in the Continental stand would be a major operation. Instead they changed from a five-inch diameter tube to a four-inch diameter tube, which would leave the tube 1.25 inches off the saw. This was the same location used for the tubes in the conversions I had installed at Elbow Gin. This made a significant improvement in the power requirements and the stress on the saws. However, it still could be improved: the tube could be located so that it is more concentric with the gin rib contour.

The holes in the Continental seed tube are upset; that is, the leading edge is expanded outward, making a rough outer surface on the tube. In order for this roughness not to interfere with the turning of the seed roll, it is necessary to turn the tube at a speed high enough to avoid this interference. This seems to be in the range of 400 rpm with the four-inch tube. At this speed, the amount of seed entering the tube is limited, although the flow increases some as the seed roll density increases. The primary benefit of this tube is found in increasing the pressure of the seed roll mass against the saws, thus removing the lint more rapidly. This pressure is significant, but by comparison, the tube I use has a smooth surface and can turn at a slower rate. This produces a greater seed flow into the tube at a lower roll density.

Continental continued to pursue the concept of using a seed tube to remove ginned seed from the core of the seed roll with their 141 saw stand, enjoying better results. Today, the Continental 161 Golden Eagle is an example of their success in this area.

The 152 Saw Gin

The seed tube conversions begun at Elbow Gin in 1979 continued to operate well. We were aware that we were leaving more lint on the seed than was desirable, although tests of residual lint showed them to be competitive. In 1984, I undertook a serious study of the possibilities of improving this situation. The most logical approach seemed to be to find a practical way to use a closer saw spacing (we were still operating the 120 saw gins with the 0.787-inch saw spacing).

After considerable effort, I found a way to mount an already available rib (the Lummus 158 model) and provide for a spacing of 0.6171 inch. This would enable the use of 152 saws in these old 120 saw frames. The rib was mounted so that the surface adjacent to the seed passage permitted a wider passage and a steeper sag. This made it necessary to move the top straight section of the rib back seventeen degrees off vertical. The Continental twelve-inch saw gin rib is spaced three degrees off vertical and on the Lummus gin stand, the top is about twenty-two degrees off vertical. The angle is not critical, so long as the section forming the seed passage is properly designed. In addition to the new gin ribs and rails, we also required new huller ribs and rails and a saw shaft and space blocks. No change was made in the seed roll or seed tube components. A slight change was made in the top roll box scroll to accommodate the relocation of the upper surface of the ginning rib.

The location of this gin rib was such that the seed-discharge passage was opened up to permit a better discharge. The resulting contour is close to what I have suggested for other ribs when a closer saw spacing is used. Vanes were added to the lower front of the roll box where the seed fingers would normally be, although seed fingers could still be used if desired. These vanes served to aid in rupturing the bottom of the seed roll as it makes the turn, because the closer-spaced saws tend to hold the roll up as it makes contact with the saws. These vanes also aid in the control of the residual lint on the seed. In figure 64—a cross section of the conversion—note that the huller ribs are merely short pieces of 3/16-inch flat bars, with one forty-five degree break.

The conversion was installed on one stand late in the 1984 season. The gin was put into production with absolutely no problems. It produced ten bales per hour with a 75 hp motor on the saw shaft. These improvements provided residual lint at least 1.5 percent lower than before the conversion. The same seed tubes with all of their auxiliary equipment (installed in 1979) were used. We used the original Vandergriff capacity booster roll boxes, with the lower front twenty degrees off vertical and with this new saw spacing achieved even better results. No change was made in the Model 30 huller front of the gin.

This performance justified the conversion of the other five stands for the 1985 season. The ginning record for the season speaks for itself: in seventy-eight days, 67,600 bales were ginned—a daily average of 866.67 bales per day or 36.1 bales per hour. The best twenty-four-hour run was 1042 bales—an average of 43.4 bales per hour. And these gins are 1959 models. We believe that with the modifications we have made, they are competitive with any gins in use today, new or old.

Moreover, two of these six stands do not have seed tubes: conversion of four stands provided all the capacity the plant could handle. To convert the two stands without seed tubes to the narrow-spaced ribs the procedure is exactly the same as that for those with the tubes. The operating results are good, but there is lower capacity—probably two bales per hour less.

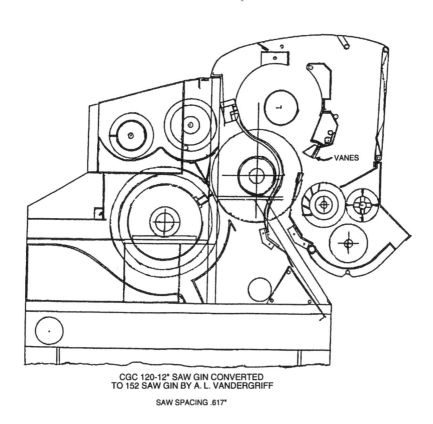

CGC 120-12" SAW GIN CONVERTED
TO 152 SAW GIN BY A. L. VANDERGRIFF

SAW SPACING .617"

Figure 64. Cross-sectional view of the 152 saw gin (see also figure 65).

The Continental 120 saw gins use a half rib at each end of the roll box. Lummus uses a full rib at each end and puts a filler plate in each end to cover about half of the rib. To use the Lummus rib, we also used a full rib on each end with a 0.25-inch filler plate. The plate has to be cut to fit the inside of the roll box. For smoothness, we chrome-plated these, as well as the roll box front and back scrolls. The fabricated rib discussed in the "Gin Rib Design" section is now available. It greatly simplifies conversion, and, beyond simplification, rib replacement problems are also greatly reduced.

The Elbow Gin plant does not gin modules. The cotton is unloaded by the use of two seventeen-inch telescopes, both delivering into one eight-foot-wide separator, then to a six-foot by twelve-foot hot-shelf dryer, to a ten-foot, six-cylinder cleaner, to another six-foot by twelve-foot hot-shelf dryer, and then it splits into

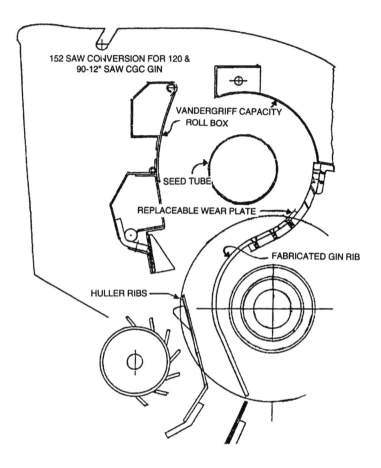

Figure 65. An enlarged view of the 152 saw gin roll box

two lines of cleaning. The original two sets of six-foot inclined and impact cleaners are still feeding the distributor. We helped make a number of other modifications to various parts of the gin to enable it to operate at these fantastic capacities. These changes are discussed in Chapter 9.

New gin stands are costly. Most old gin stands can be modified, at a reasonable cost, to gin about as much cotton as present-day lint cleaners can process successfully. The capacity of a gin plant is influenced by many factors other than gin stand capacity. Gin owners can watch with pleasure as beautiful, heavy flows of cotton feed into their new gin stands, and then purchase still more new gins and feeders—but without sufficient consideration of the potential bottlenecks in the rest of the plant, there will not be a substantial increase in total daily capacity.

The 164 Saw Gin Stand

The success of the gin stand conversions at Elbow Gin in Visalia, California, prompted James Horn, of Horn and Gladden Lint Cleaning, to ask me in 1986 to adapt these same principles to a new gin stand for his company. I accepted his offer, with the stipulation that I retain total control over all aspects of engineering that went into the stand.

This stand would be the first new complete gin stand built since Continental Gin Company introduced the sixteen-inch saw gin in 1961, a project I supervised during my tenure there as president. It would incorporate all of the key innovations that improved the capacity and fiber quality in existing gin stands over the years: improved roll box contour, modified gin rib contour, a change in the scroll shape forming the roll box cavity, and narrower saw spacings, to name only a few. These ingredients, incorporated into a totally new gin stand that would place 164 saws in the standard ninety-six-inch length stand, would have the potential to be the best high-capacity gin stand on the market.

We started work on the design and engineering of this stand in 1986. I received good cooperation from Horn and Gladden's engineering department, but toward the end of the project, I lost control over some key components of the design—mainly over fabrication of the gin ribs, leaving them too inaccurate to function, and a faulty seed-tube arrangement. Despite my protests, four stands were completed and and delivered to the P. A. Gin owned by J. L. Massey, near Robstown, Texas. The first season with these stands was a disaster. Horn and Gladden lost control of their company, and the new owners had serious financial problems to deal with. I was concerned: these gin stands had A *Product of Vandergriff Research* on their fronts, even though they did not meet my design specifications.

The restructured Horn and Gladden Company would be known as Consolidated HGM Company. The owners of the four stands turned to me for help, and I was glad to have the opportunity to modify the stands to make them functional for the 1987 season. To eliminate the problem with the ribs, I had new ones fabricated and installed. This enabled the stands to operate successfully but at a reduced capacity. I did not have the resources to reinstall the seed tubes correctly, but this would be a minor operational problem, because, even without them, the stand's capacity would be adequate for this particular plant. These four stands ran well during the 1987 season—a performance that helped me rebuild both my and the stand's credibility.

For the Vandergriff name to continue being associated with the 164 saw gin stand, I insisted on full cooperation in all aspects of the engineering process. The new ownership was receptive and the entire staff supported my efforts. We completed all the necessary adjustments during this season, and ended up with basically the unit that we have today (1996). In 1992 Consolidated HGM was bought by three key employees and became known as Consolidated Cotton Gin Company. The gin stand would be in good hands under this new ownership; they continue to be supportive of my ideas and efforts.

A key factor in the success of this stand, in addition to those already mentioned, is seed discharge. I have studied this area, as it relates to the capacity of the gin stand, my entire career, and I applied fifty years of experience to the 164. The importance of balancing seed discharge with lint-removal rate cannot be overemphasized. In spacing the saws closer for higher capacity, the seed-discharge rate becomes critical because the lint-removal rate is increased. Although the lint-removal per saw may or may not change significantly, more saws are removing lint from the seed roll, thus the ginned seed must be discharged at a higher rate.

One effective means of improving the seed discharge rate is the use of a rotating perforated metal tube in the core of the seed roll. Its action was described in the section on converting Continental's 120 saw gin to a 152 saw gin. The success of the modifications of the 152 at Elbow Gin led me to choose a saw spacing of 0.580 inch, the closest in the industry at the time. This made it possible to use larger holes in the perforated metal seed tube—yet still remove only fully ginned seed. This permitted the use of a more drastic slope in the contour of the gin rib to increase the seed-roll sag, which also led to better seed discharge.

The huller ribs in high-capacity gins are almost completely ineffective. Any effort to make them reject foreign matter usually results in troublesome operation. The open-top huller rib had become quite common on gins, but it rejects no foreign matter. I therefore chose not to use huller ribs in the 164 saw gin. This made it possible to locate the front scroll of the roll box cavity in such a way that it approaches the saw along a line outside the circumference of the saw. This is not possible with gins using huller ribs, because the saw projects through the huller ribs to pick up the cotton, and the seed passage is between the huller and ginning ribs (figure 66). With all other gins, the discharged seed has to pass between the saws. Even in cases where the huller ribs have been removed, the front side of the

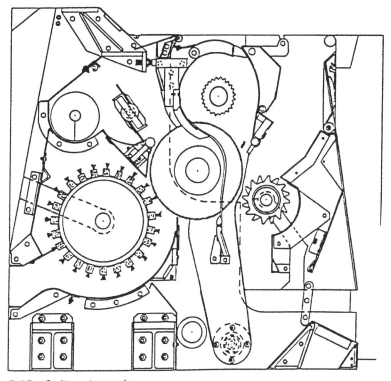

Roll Box Cavity on steep angle
to allow seed to discharge outside of the saws

Figure 66. Roll box cavity of the 164 saw gin

roll box still approaches the saw on a line inside the circumference of the saw and the seed must still discharge only between the saws. With my arrangement, the seed not only discharges between the saws but outside of them as well.

In order to take advantage of this unique feature, it is necessary to rupture the surface of the seed roll as it passes over the sag between the saw surface and the lower front side of the roll box. In the earlier discussion of the seed roll, it was explained that the ginned seeds work their way to the core of the roll; as the core builds, they approach the surface of the roll. However, the incoming cotton picked up by the saws is not all ginned on its first pass over the ginning point; there is a layer of partially ginned cotton formed on the surface of the roll. This layer must be ruptured to obtain an effective seed discharge. Just under this layer of partially ginned cotton is a mass of fully ginned seed; because this seed is coated with fuzz that causes it to adhere to the mass, the discharge rate is retarded.

The steep approach angle may provide enough rupture by the saws for the wider saw spacings, but with a lower potential capacity. This steep angle was the principal feature of the Vandergriff capacity booster roll box. For closer saw spacings, an additional means of rupturing the surface is necessary; otherwise the roll will become too tight. In the case of the Consolidated gin stands, the closer saw spacing tends to lift the seed roll as it makes contact with it, in much the same manner as the seed fingers do in standard gins. This lifting effect is present to some extent in gins with somewhat wider saw spacing, and it can be partially overcome by a high-density seed roll that forces the surface to snag between the saws. However, this density results in excessive and unacceptable power require- ments to turn the saws (the aforementioned disk-brake effect as the saws pass through the dense seed roll). The advantage of having the surface of the seed roll sag and be ruptured before being penetrated by the saws should now be obvious: the saws will not encounter nearly as much resistance from the roll, and the mass of ginned seed will be freer to discharge smoothly.

One method of rupturing the seed roll surface ahead of the saws is that of using a series of vanes over which the surface of the seed roll passes (figure 67). These vanes are spaced to permit the seed roll to sag between them. This allows the seed roll to rupture between the vanes as well as between the vanes and the saw blades, thus releasing the ginned seed from the surface. I have found an acceptable spacing for the vanes to be about three saw spacings (about 1.75 inches). It is important that this rupture take place so that the seed falls outside the perimeter of the saw.

Improved seed discharge outside the saws has permitted the use of the agitator cylinder instead of the perforated metal tube in the core of the seed roll. Although the tube is effective in removing seed from the seed roll, it is not as simple as the agitator; it requires some duct work and a blower. Further tests with the seed tube may show it to be effective in combination with the closer-spaced saws (and seed discharge outside the saws). The agitator developed by myself and W. C. Pease while I was at Lummus has also proven effective. Many efforts have been made to adapt this agitator to other makes or models of gins—but none of them have been successful. To operate efficiently, a special roll box arrangement with a changed rib contour is needed. The benefits of the agitator are negated if adjustments are not made to accommodate the increased lint removal.

Another unique feature of the 164 saw gin stand is the rib contour. I have explained the importance of having a rib contour that will permit the seed roll to sag more between the saws (figure 68); although the seed discharge outside the saws is important, so is the discharge between the saws. If the seed roll sets on top

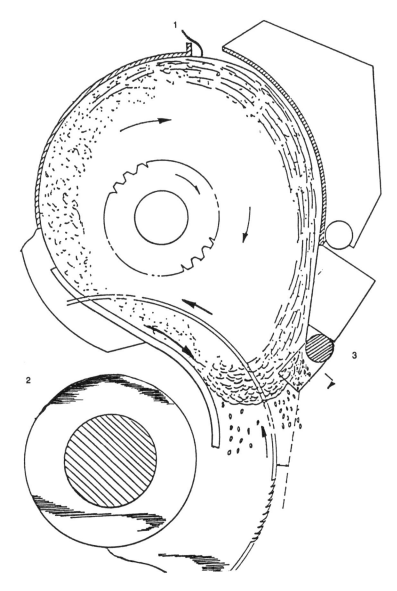

Standard roll box arrangements are unable to place the seed roll outside the circumference of the saw. Seed discarge outside the saw is impossible. Vandergriff patent #4,974,294

1　Seed roll sets at steeper angle, allowing for seed discharge outside the saws.

2　Gin rib contour is modified promoting greater sag. Reduces pressure at neck of rib and promotes more efficient seed discharge.

3　Vanes project into roll box and rupture seed roll prior to contact with the saws. This allows for discharge outside the saws, as well as between them.

Figure 67.　Consolidated 164 roll box arrangement

of the rib curvature (as is the case with standard rib contours) pressure increases in the top area of the rib at the ginning point, the roll becomes tighter, and the seed will not discharge freely. This leaves the roll seedy all the way to the surface, limiting capacity. Much of the hump is taken out of the curvature of my rib, compared with the standard rib, providing for a much steeper contour. This alleviates pressure at the top portion of the rib and expedites seed discharge between the saws, allowing the seed a steeper slope to slide down between the saws. This contour must vary with the saw spacings. To date, no one else has changed this curvature when narrowing their saw spacings—a critical error.

The 164 gin saws are of the finest quality steel, 0.45 inches thick and manufactured to the highest standards of heat treating and finishing. They are mounted on a solid steel 4 3/4-inch diameter mandrel supported by 3 7/16-inch diameter roller bearings, the largest in the industry, for longer life and less maintenance. Other gins use 0.36-inch and 0.037-inch thick saws. Switching to a thicker saw would require modifying all the spacers between the saws, which is expensive.

Another unique feature is the rib itself. First, it is a stainless steel investment casting, absolutely rust- and corrosion proof and unbreakable. Second, it has a replaceable super-hardened wear plate, making the gin rib itself almost permanent. The only part that has to be replaced is the 1 1/2-inch long by 3/16-inch wearplate. This wearplate is also reversible. When the initial ginning point of the rib is sufficiently worn to need replacing, the wear plate can be turned end for end by removing and replacing one screw, presenting a new wear surface. Once the wearplate itself wears out, it can be replaced with a new one without disturbing the placement of the rib.

A dynamically balanced brush doffer cylinder and stainless steel brush chamber doffs gin saws positively at all capacities and cotton conditions. It has the heaviest construction in the industry and features one-inch-thick steel plates end heads and massive rib rails to provide strength and rigidity to maintain gin stand settings. Saw and brush cylinder shafts are large diameter turned, ground and polished shafting supported by heavy duty, double roller-bearing pillow blocks.

A load-sensing, automatic, electric gin stand control allows easy adjustment of feed rate and seed roll density, while providing overload protection. All surfaces exposed to the flow of cotton are stainless steel for smooth flow and permanent life.

The 198 Saw Gin

With the 164 firmly established (figure 69), I began to think about the possibility of designing an even bigger stand, one that would incorporate all the

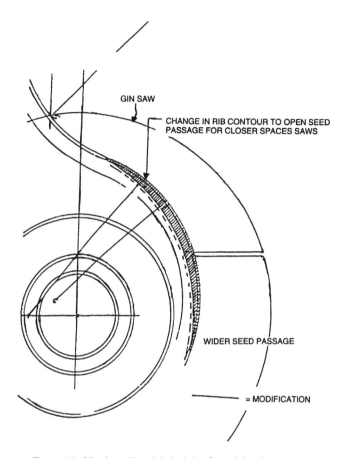

GIN SAW

CHANGE IN RIB CONTOUR TO OPEN SEED
PASSAGE FOR CLOSER SPACES SAWS

WIDER SEED PASSAGE

= MODIFICATION

Figure 68. Vandergriff modified rib for Consolidated 164 saw gin

key concepts of the 164. I was not sure about the feasibility of marketing it, but
the effects of being first with this type of stand would make the effort worthwhile.

How did we arrive at 198 saws? Why not 200? We arrived at 198 due to
the interchangeability of the feeder cylinders with those of the ten-foot incline
cleaners and stick machines used overhead. These ten-foot machines were 116
inches inside. When we applied the saw spacing of 0.580 of an inch to these inside
dimensions, 198 saws was the result.

This arrangement is not much longer than that of the 164 saw gin. It resulted
in a ratio of 1:2 between the two (198 divided by 164 saws). This 1:2 ratio times
the fifteen-bales-per-hour capacity of the 164 indicated the 198 had the potential
capacity of eighteen bales per hour. Given stands of consistent design, capacity

Figure 69. The Consolidated 164 saw gin

does not increase in a straight line with the number of saws, nor with the length of the gin stand. This is because roll box friction is less with the longer stands. The roll box heads offer a certain amount of friction. With a longer roll box, the friction of the heads is a smaller proportion of total friction; therefore, the longer the roll box, the less the total friction per unit of length.

Conceptually, the 198 saw gin is an extension of the 112 and 164 gins manufactured by Consolidated Cotton Gin. The structural elements of these gins were strong enough to allow them to be extended, and we made only minor changes. We changed the air flow to the brush chamber slightly, to eliminate some of the air being drawn into the front of the gin. We also relocated the picker roller to assure better control of the cotton into the saw and cleaned up a rough spot or two in the surface of the roll box. The 198 has the same seed discharge arrangement as the 164; as with the 164 and 112, the rib contour is modified; the ribs also have a wearplate. These minor changes increased the 198's capacity beyond our expectations. One of these units in operation at Dunn, North Carolina, for the 1994 season operated at a capacity of twenty bales per hour with less than a 150 hp requirement. Given ideal conditions of cotton preparation, consistent twenty-one bales-per-hour capacity can be achieved.

7

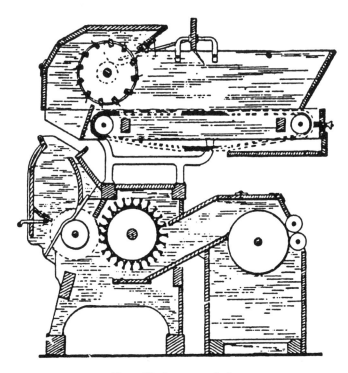

Feeders

The primary function of a gin stand feeder is to feed the cotton into the stand at a controlled rate. Figure 70 shows an early version of a feeder called an apron feeder. The cotton was hand fed from the wicker baskets that were used to transport cotton to the gins. These gins were usually single units on a plantation and generally were operated by slave labor. Figures 71, 72, and 73 illustrate other stages in the sequence of event in the development of the gin stand feeder.

Figure 71 shows a version used after Munger's development of system ginning. The belt distributor (a part of system ginning) over the feeder could be used to distribute cotton to feed more than one gin stand. Figure 73 shows the

Figure 70. Apron-type feeder

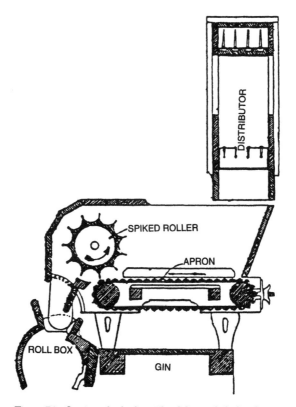

Figure 71. Section of a feeder with a Munger belt distributor

next step in feeder evolution: the apron is eliminated and replaced by a hopper and a pair of feed rollers under the belt distributor. These feed rollers fed the cotton to a large drum cleaning cylinder with a screen surface around part of the drum over which the cotton is scrubbed for removing trash. The cylinders with pins took the cotton from the feed rollers, carried it around the screening surface, scrubbed out trash, and delivered the cotton onto an apron. The speed of the feed rollers could be varied to control the rate of flow to the gin stand. The apron feeder shown in figure 72 is also equipped with a cleaning cylinder and a screening surface. The rate of flow from the apron feeder was controlled by the speed of the belt on the apron.

For a number of years, the feeder cleaners were small drum (cylinder) units. Around 1920, a feeder-cleaner with a large drum came into use. This was known as a big drum feeder and it was to this unit that Streun's Burrs Out was attached.

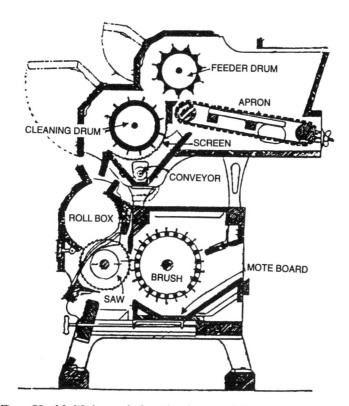

Figure 72 . Modified apron feeder with a cleaning cylinder and screening surface

The rate of flow from the feeder to the gin is still controlled by the speed of the star-shaped rollers above the feeder. Many mechanical arrangements have been tried to permit the operator to set the feed rate according to existing conditions. In the early feeders and well into the 1940s, the speed of the feed rollers was controlled by mechanical means and manually adjusted. When I designed the Thermex Feeder at Lummus, I used a small hydraulic pump driving a hydraulic motor. A valve controlling the flow was actuated by a spring-loaded scroll over the back of the seed roll in the gin stand. A higher feed rate would result in the seed roll pushing the scroll up. This movement would, through linkage, reduce the flow of oil to the hydraulic motor driving the feed rollers, thus reducing the feed rate to the gin stand. The feed rate could be increased by tightening the spring tension on the scroll. As far as I know, this was the first arrangement not to employ a purely mechanical means of driving the feed rollers.

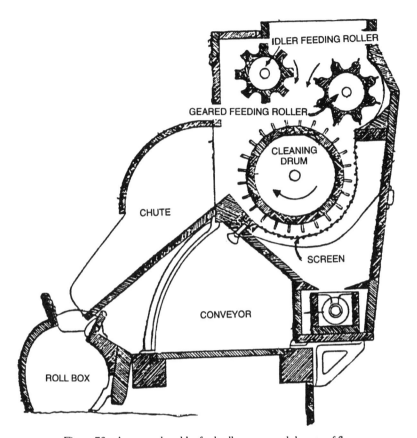

Figure 73. Apron replaced by feed rollers to control the rate of flow.

The hydraulic driving arrangement was soon replaced by small DC motors, the speed of which could easily be varied by altering the electrical current to the motor. This was done by taking a signal from the motor load driving the gin stand. When the load reached a preset level of feed, the control current to the feed roller motor was reduced, thus lowering the feed rates. As load was reduced, the signal called for an increase in feed rate. This electric feed control opened a number of possibilities for other controls. At a Lummus brainstorming session, we listed a number of conditions it would be advantageous to control. We then applied for and received a patent covering these controls. I believe the patent was issued to Don Van Doorn and Bill Pease of my engineering department. This patent covered gin breast throw-outs activated by a pressure switch in the flue behind the gin stand to detect a blockage downstream, or from a choke in the lint cleaner, condenser, or other downstream chokes that might put too much back pressure on the gin stand. Also, the gin breast throw-out mechanism could be actuated by limit switches in the hopper above the feeder to move the gin breast into ginning position when the cotton reached the hopper, and move it out when the cotton ran out. Forty years later, these features are commonplace in the industry. Lummus licensed their competitors to use these features and thus enhanced their prestige in the industry.

An early (1912) Mitchell feeder is in shown in figure 82 (Chapter 8). These feeders—called extractor feeders because they were designed primarily for removing hulls—came into use slowly, but by the 1930s they were in extensive use. The Mitchell extractor feeders were heated by air passing through a steam radiator and into the feeder—a valuable asset, especially in high humidity areas (see Chapter 3). By the late 1940s, all major gin machinery manufacturers were making extractor feeders, but the Mitchell feeder dominated the field.

Not much emphasis was placed on the combination of cylinder cleaners and extractors as feeders. In the late 1940s at Lummus, I designed a feeder that had three cleaner cylinders with perforated metal screening surfaces under them preceded by an extractor section for removing larger particles. The contour of these screening surfaces was different from standard cleaning surfaces (see figure 106, Chapter 9). This feeder—designed for adding hot air, similar to the Mitchell feeder—proved helpful in drying the cotton. These were soon made in multiple units. First, a second extractor section was stacked on top of the basic unit (referred to as the Dual Thermex or Super Thermex) with heat in both of the extractor sections. This was followed by a feeder with three sections (the Triple Thermex). Forcing the hot air through the cotton as it was held by the extractor teeth was effective. Prior to my leaving Lummus in 1959, almost fourteen hundred of these feeders, using various arrangements, were sold. The Murray Company, a major manufacturer of the time, never developed a successful feeder; they sold Mitchell feeders exclusively with their gin stands.

Sometime in the 1960s Lummus changed the Thermex, placing the cylinder cleaner section above the extractor section instead of under it (figure 74). An additional cleaner cylinder was added making it a four cylinder arrangement. The high-profile screening arrangement shown in figure 106 was retained. This proved valuable; it separated the cotton into single seed locks (a single seed with its fiber) and fluffed it nicely. Separating the cotton into single seed locks aids both the cleaning and ginning capacity. This cleaner was followed by a two-saw stick machine to complete the feeder.

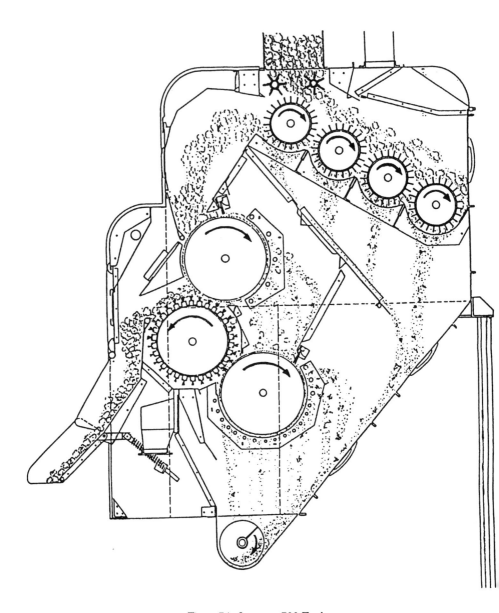

Figure 74. Lummus 700 Feeder

This type of seed cotton preparation adds significantly to the potential capacity of the gin stand. Once combining lint cleaners came into general use, it was not necessary to limit the gin stand capacity to a loose roll to make a smooth sample. More cotton could be fed to the gin stand and the stand could operate with tighter seed rolls. In the days of loose seed rolls, pre-ginning of the cotton was a no-no. (Many ginners today may not even know what *pre-ginning* is: it is the process of separating the lint from the seed before the seed cotton reaches the gin stand.) It was thought that any action drastic enough to tear the lint from the seed would damage the fibers—a foolish assumption, because no action could be more drastic than that of the gin saw in removing the lint from the seed. Pre-ginning of damp cotton tended to string out the seed locks tying them in knots, a condition referred to as *roping*. This was not good and emphasized the importance of drying.

The effort now is to increase the pre-ginning, more commonly referred to as "single locking," in every possible way. The obvious way to do this is with more cylinder cleaning and extractors (stick machines). In addition, my effort has been, and continues to be, to speed up the cylinder from the standard 450 rpm to 600 rpm and raise the screens higher between the cylinders; an extreme case is the roller gin feeder (Chapter 12) I can not overemphasize the importance of drying in properly preparing the cotton for ginning. Generally, machinery manufacturers nibble at the edges of this and most discussion centers around adding cylinder cleaners.

Horn and Gladden made a feeder similar to the Lummus 700 feeder in the mid 1980s (figure 75). All the cylinders—the cleaner cylinders and the stick-machine cylinders—are interchangeable with the precleaners over the distributor. This interchangeability is practical and popular. When this type of feeder replaces older feeders over old gin stands, the capacity may be increased by more than a bale per hour.

The Lummus 700 feeder may not have the interchangeable cylinders feature, but its performance is excellent. It was plagued in its early days with some of the components being too light (e.g., cylinder pins coming out) but this has been corrected. Continental Gin Company, now Continental Eagle, has gone through more changes in basic design of their feeders than Lummus. While at Continental in the early 1960s, I participated in the design of a couple of extractor feeders with no cylinder cleaners. It was thought then that extractor cylinders did a good job of preparing the cotton for ginning. A version still in use—but only by good operators who are capable of maintaining them—is the Comet Feeder. They were replaced by another extractor design after I left—the version originally in the superplant at Boswell in 1968 that proved to be a big maintenance problem. I had replaced these feeders at Boswell with a version of the impact cleaner. This unit had a large cylinder with pins, and around this were twelve-inch impact

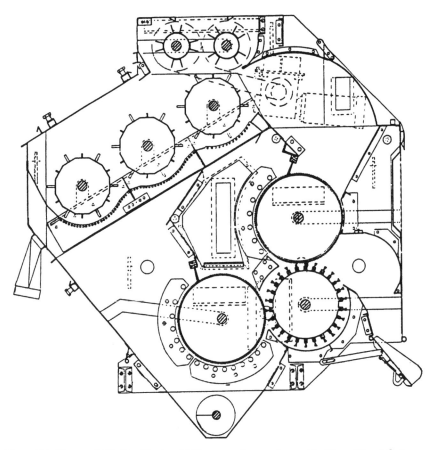

Figure 75. Horn and Gladden Feeder, 1980s, currently manufactured by Consolidated Cotton
Gin Company Inc. of Lubbock, Texas.

cleaner cylinders. As I remember, there were four or five of these cylinders, the
large cylinder scrubbing the cotton over the rotating disks. This was a good feeder,
but it did not meet with the approval of my successor.

At another Boswell plant, I used a feeder made up from a three-saw stick
machine that I had designed at Continental (figure 76). This feeder was built by
adding feed rollers and a breaker cylinder at the top of the stick machine, with a feeder
apron to direct the cotton into the gin stand. Continental adopted this as their
standard production model and used it for about twenty years. In the last two or
three years, they have basically gone back to the Comet feeder, adding a small

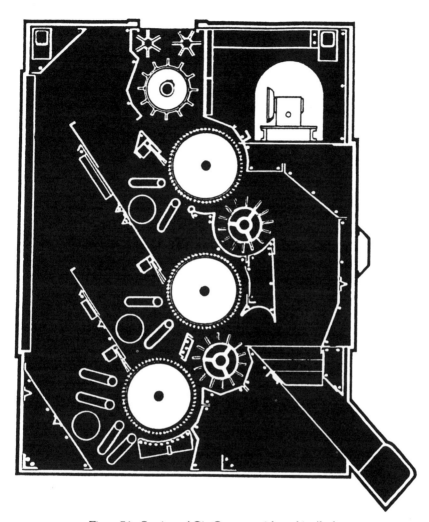

Figure 76. Continental Gin Company stick machine/feeder

four-cylinder cleaner under the feed rollers like Consolidated and Lummus (figure 77).

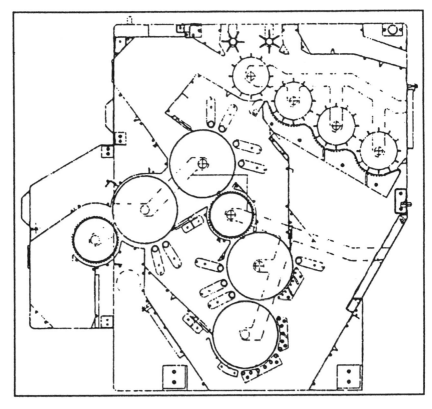

Figure 77. Contemporary Continental Gin Company feeder

8   Hull Extractors

Attempts to find a way to remove hulls date back a long way. Ginners noted that under some harvesting conditions (for example, early frost or damp weather), bolls frequently would rot while still on the stalk and these would be removed with the cotton. When the bolls were fed into the gin, they would be broken up by the saw and carried along with the lint. This trash in the lint lowered the grade, and thus, the price. Naturally, attempts were made to find a way to remove these pieces of boll, more commonly called hulls, or burrs.

The first attempt to remove these hulls was done in the gin stand. One of the first efforts to show promise—patented by B. G. Beadle in 1859—involved a knee projecting from the ginning rib. The cotton, as it was picked up by the saws, passed between these projections on its way into the ginning chamber (roll box) and the pieces of boll were stripped back and discharged with the seed. This simple device (figure 78) was quite effective and its use continued for many years.

When the huller gin was developed, the seeds were considered to be of no value, so the mixing of the hulls with seed was of no significance. Years later, when the seeds were found to be of value (primarily for animal feed) there was an incentive to find a way to separate the hulls. In 1882 or 1883, the Daniel Pratt Gin Company developed a double-rib huller gin (figure 79). It was patented by W. L. Ellis in 1889 and the patent was apparently owned by the Daniel Pratt company at the time of their merger with Continental Gin.

Bollies and the Double-Rib Hulling Era

Because of the shortage of labor following World War I, a new method of harvesting—pulling bolls—was begun about 1918, which brought new problems for the gins. How could the large volume of burrs be extracted from the seed cotton during the ginning process? The double-rib huller gin of the Continental Gin Company was by then in common use, providing a makeshift method of extracting the burrs, but ginning capacity was limited.

My first experience with the bollie cotton, commonly referred to at that time as *bollies*, was in my father's gin. The gin had a Continental plant equipped with three 80 saw Munger brush gin stands, with double-picker rollers in the double-rib

B. G. BEADLE.
COTTON GIN.

No. 25,943.   Patented Nov. 1, 1859.

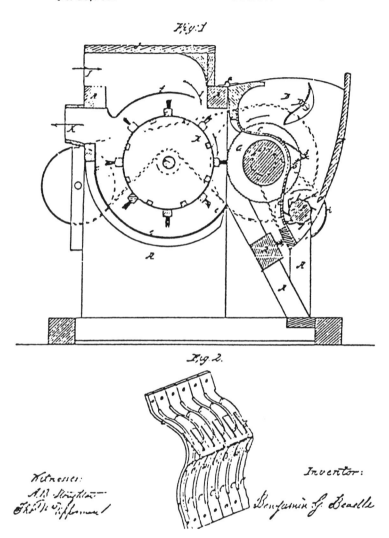

Fig. 1

Fig. 2.

Witnesses:
A.B. Stoughton
Thos. W. Tippman

Inventor:
Benjamin G. Beadle

Figure 78. Single-rib huller gin

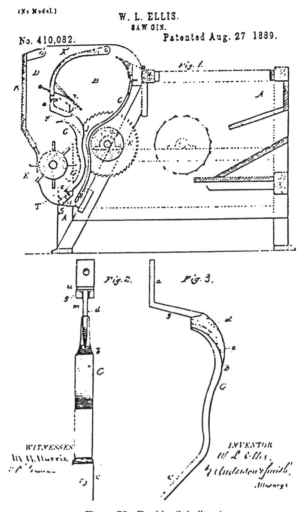

Figure 79. Double-rib huller gin

huller breasts. All the cotton we ginned in the year 1919 was bollie. The gin was fed until the huller breast was completely filled with cotton and burrs. The feed was then cut off while the saws picked the cotton out of the burrs. Next, the bottom of the huller breast was pulled open, allowing the clean burrs to fall on the floor. The process was repeated until the burrs were piled so high there was no passageway in front of the gin stands. The burrs were raked to the back of the building, scooped up, and thrown out of the window. They were then hauled to the boiler room and burned for fuel for the boiler. These ginning conditions reduced our capacity by 50 percent. We rigged belts and other conveyors to get the burrs to the furnace, but we still were faced with the slow process of extracting cotton from the bolls. This problem prevailed over a wide area of the cotton belt. Some farmers in eastern sections of Texas and Oklahoma returned to the previous practice of hand picking the cotton, because of the difficulty in getting the bollie cotton ginned. In more arid sections of these states, the cotton plants were smaller, the bolls easier to remove, and the new method of harvesting continued.

The need for equipment to handle the bollie cotton led to many efforts to solve the problem. This is where John Streun made his mark. In the early 1920s, he developed a unit called a Burrs Out machine in the form of an attachment to hang on the front of the feeder to process the cotton before it entered the huller breast of the gin stand. The unit was made up of a small-diameter cylinder with aggressive, hooked teeth to engage the fibers as it rotated. Today this cylinder is commonly called an extractor cylinder (see figure 91). The fibers of the cotton are picked up on the up-going side of the cylinder and carried, along with attached hulls, over the top of the cylinder. At this position, another cylinder with vanes or blades, rotates in the opposite direction to the surface of the extractor cylinder and the vanes strip back the hulls, where they are reapplied to the extractor cylinder by a rotating cylinder with spikes, or pins, in a spiral pattern. This spiral cylinder conveys the rejected hulls to the ends of the machine, where they drop through an opening in the scroll surrounding the cylinder. The partially cleaned hulls fall onto a second conveying cylinder with pins, or lugs, which reapply them to the extractor cylinder as they move spirally toward the center of the machine. Here, free of cotton, they are discharged from the machine. The cotton, having been engaged by the teeth on the extractor cylinder, is doffed from the cylinder by a rotating brush cylinder into the declining chute (slide) and into the gin stand (figure 80). This unit proved to be popular and was sold to be attached to all feeders in use at that time. It was a small unit and had limitations, but it was certainly better than anything else available.

The success with this unit led directly to the development of a larger, master unit that also became popular. The master unit operated in the same manner as the small attachment and was manufactured in two sizes, one ten feet long, the other fourteen feet long. The ten-foot units were usually used in pairs, with the cotton flow split into the two machines. The larger, fourteen-foot machines were fed by a cylinder cleaner usually composed of seven, sixteen-inch-diameter cylinders. Under the cylinders were screens around approximately sixty degrees of the cylinder to sift out the trash (see figure 107, Chapter 9). The cotton was fed onto

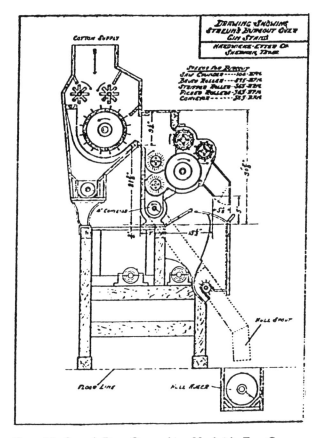

Figure 80. Streun's Burrs-Out machine, Hardwicke Etter Company

the top of the cylinders and carried under them, where it was scrubbed, the screening surfaces shaking out the dirt and small trash, and discharged into a screw conveyor. From this point, it discharged into one end of the extractor—an extractor that became known as Streun's Big Burr Machine. It was introduced in the mid-1920s, following quickly on the burrs-out attachment.

The cotton fed into the end of the extractor dropped onto a spiral conveying cylinder, which applied the cotton to the main extractor cylinder. This extractor cylinder, thirty inches in diameter, usually rotated at a speed of 105 rpm. As in the little burrs-out unit, the hulls were conveyed to the end of the machine while being applied to the surface of the extractor cylinder. At the end, they dropped to a second spiral cylinder that conveyed them again the full length of the machine, knocking them against the extractor cylinder. One reason for the long travel was that, on occasion, an early frost would kill the bolls before they were fully opened. When they were harvested in this condition, the beating against the surface of the extractor cylinder would open and extract the cotton from them.

The Big Burr machine usually discharged into a screw conveyor on the back of the machine; the conveyor moved the cotton across another cleaner, and this second cleaner discharged into the distributor feeding the battery of gins through a feeder over each gin. At that time, cleaning machines with rotating cylinders for scrubbing cotton over screening surfaces were in limited use.

In almost all areas except the Texas-Oklahoma area, cotton continued to be picked comparatively free of trash. The need to clean the cotton in the gin was not considered to be of particular importance; in fact, few farmers or ginners had heard of such machines. But in the Texas area, where bollies were the rule, all gins were soon equipped with at least two seven-cylinder cleaners and Big Burr machines.

Others entered this field rapidly, but the Hardwicke Etter system dominated for many years. Almost all gin plants in the bollie-cotton area, whether new or old, were equipped with Hardwicke Etter hull extracting systems. The systems were called Single Type I and Double Type I systems, depending on whether one or two machines were used. A Type I system is shown in figure 81.

Many of the plants built in the bollie area in the 1920s and early 1930s were either Murray or Continental. Lummus and others had most of their success in the South. Prior to the Hardwicke Etter development, John E. Mitchell, Sr. had developed and patented an extractor feeder for removing burrs from the cotton *before* it entered the gin stand. The early extraction was in the gin feeders, no doubt because the rate of flow was low and at a controlled rate. The early Mitchell extractor feeder, which appeared around 1912, made use of a toothed cylinder similar to that used today. It also had a unique feature: the hull board.

Like all extractors, the cotton was applied to the up-going side of the extractor cylinder. The difference was that above the cylinder was a rotating stripper roller for rejecting the burrs, while the cotton, engaged by the teeth of the cylinder, passed under the roller. The rejected mass fell back on a slide, commonly referred to as a hull board, which reapplied it to the cylinder. As it was reapplied, the hulls were free to kick back over the hull board and discharge from the machine. Some of the commingled mass could fall between the board and the cylinder on to a second board, where the application process was repeated. Again, the hulls could kick over the board and out of the machine.

Almost forty years later, I designed an extractor feeder incorporating essentially the same hull-board arrangement. At the time I was not aware of the

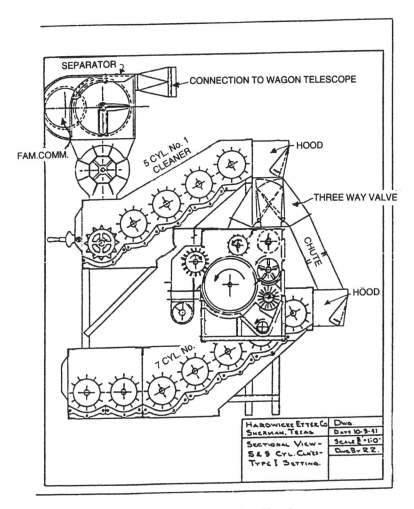

Figure 81. Big Burr machine Type I

early Mitchell machine and applied for a patent for my design; prior art was cited against me and I was not able to patent it. I was, however, able to use it, because the Mitchell patent had expired long since. My feeder incorporating this feature is shown in figure 82 (also shown are early Mitchell feeders). In my feeder, a spiral picker roller is placed under the kick board, instead of a second hull board, to reapply the rejected material until all of the cotton that might have kicked over the board was reclaimed.

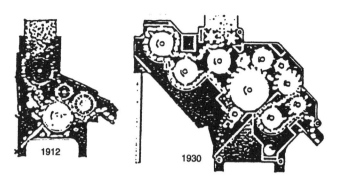

EARLY MITCHELL FEEDERS

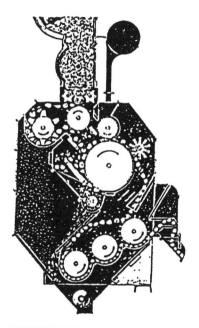

VANDERGRIFF THERMEX FEEDER

Figure 82. Vandergriff Thermex Feeder and early Mitchell feeders

When I was at Lummus in the early 1950s, the Big Burr Machine was still the best master extractor available in West Texas and Western Oklahoma. By this time, pulling the bolls by hand was rapidly being replaced by machines (called strippers). Bolls, stems, and leaves—all were stripped. Although various versions of the master extractor were in use, Streun's machine generally was recognized as the most successful unit.

The burr machines were designed for hand-snapped or bollie cotton, which was relatively clean except for burrs. Stripper cotton, which was fast becoming standard, contained a large amount of sticks and stems on which the burr machine was not efficient. To increase its efficiency, I experimented with an attachment that would utilize the sling-off principle (figure 83). The doffing cylinder was relocated to a position under the saw cylinder. This exposed a large segment of the saw cylinder between the rotating stripper and the doffing brush. The sling-off components were applied to this section of the cylinder, permitting the sticks and other foreign matter (which had passed under the rotating stripper) to sling off the cylinder, while the cotton that stayed on the saw was doffed into a conveyor. The sling-off material from the main saw cylinder went into a second stage of sling off—one more suited to removing sticks and stems (figure 84). The normal extraction of the burr machine remained intact and handled the bulk of the foreign matter. (With this type of harvesting, trash was generally about one thousand pounds per bale.)

By the late 1950s, manufacturers were using a close approximation of the Hardwicke Etter Big Burr as their extractor. The reclaimer attachment they used was based on the USDA-designed principle of placing a grid screening section around a segment of a small-diameter extractor cylinder and passing the entire flow of material through this section. Two extractor cylinders were used and the grids were spaced far enough apart to permit some cotton to pass between them. This is not the sling-off arrangement as shown in figure 83. These companies were copying the principles used in the USDA's stick remover, introduced in the mid-1950s. Cross sections of these two machines are shown in figures 85 and 86. Note that the doffing cylinder of the primary extraction is not relocated, so there is no sling off from the main extractor cylinder. All the flow is doffed into the attachment. The rod grids around the small-diameter extractor cylinder had to be close together to prevent the loss of cotton—loss due to the heavy flow of material going to the attachment. This grid spacing did not permit much separation of the sticks and other large material. The net result was that these machines were short lived, as was the USDA-designed stick remover.

The stick machines using the sling-off attachments shown in figures 83 and 84 were introduced in 1953. Because this arrangement has proven to be more efficient, most plants in the stripper cotton areas still use them.

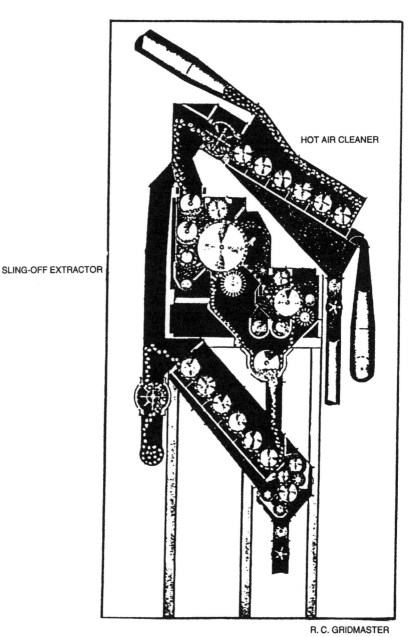

HOT AIR CLEANER

SLING-OFF EXTRACTOR

R. C. GRIDMASTER

Figure 83. An early Vandergriff version of a Big Burr machine with a stick machine attachment. (Patent # 2,898,635, filed 10 September 1953)

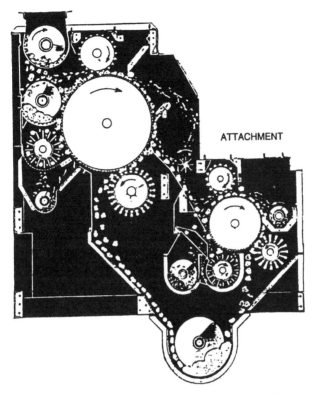

Figure 84. Cross section of the arrangement shown in figure 83, introduced into West Texas in the early 50s.

The Development of the Stick Machine

The experimental work done in 1949 with the sling-off principle later led to the development of a unit separate from the Big Burr Machine called a stick machine. A method of removing sticks, stems, and larger pieces of green leaf that extractors and cleaners in common use were not efficient in removing needed to be developed. (Stick machines are sometimes referred to as a green-leaf machines; however, because cotton plants generally are defoliated before harvesting, few green leaves are present.) This machine has been as popular as any cleaning machine of modern times.

The initial experiments were done using the extractor cylinder section of my Thermex Extractor Feeder. The cotton was fed to the up-going side of the toothed

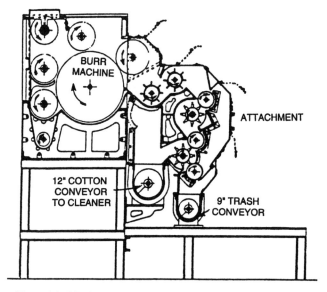

Figure 85. Hardwicke Etter version of the burr machine attachment

ATTACHMENT

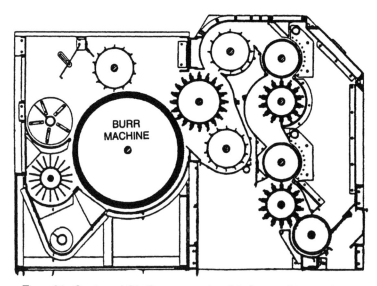

Figure 86. Continental Gin Company version of the burr machine attachment

cylinder, similar to that used in the burr machine. Engaged by the teeth, it was carried over the top, to be passed under a flexible steel-wire brush with bristles about four to five inches long, the tips of the bristles just clearing the saw teeth. The brush redistributed any wads, engaged by the aggressive action of the teeth, more evenly over the surface of the cylinder and allowed the trash to separate. Practically all of the larger foreign matter would sling-off the extractor cylinder, along with some cotton. Initially, no reclaimer was used to reclaim the cotton.

After applying this development to the Big Burr Machine as an attachment, I began to develop the stick machine as a separate unit. A second extractor cylinder was added to the arrangement used in our 1949 experiments. A single doffing cylinder was used to doff both extractor cylinders. The second cylinder was exactly the same as the first: it received the material slung off the first cylinder and reclaimed the cotton; the trash was discharged into a screw conveyor for removal.

In this early machine, a stationary board, located about three-fourths of an inch off the teeth of the cylinder was used as the initial restraining member to prevent large wads from going over the top. Following this board, or rod, were three flexible steel-wire brushes on the down-going side of the cylinder. They served both to redistribute the cotton and to comb the trash loose. As the trash was loosened, much of it was deflected over the wire-brush supports and down to the next extractor cylinder. The cotton combed loose from the teeth was reapplied by the next brush. At a rate dependent on the rate of flow, a limited amount of cotton passed to the next cylinder, where three restraining brushes kept the cotton on the saw and permitted the trash to discharge. The tips of the bristles on both cylinders just cleared the tips of the saw teeth. As the cotton passed by the tips of the bristles, it was further redistributed over the surface of the cylinder, releasing the foreign matter. Some of the larger pieces—hulls and sticks—that passed under the bristles of the first brush were thrown over the top of next brush holder into the trash conveyor. The cotton and other material followed the surface of the first extractor cylinder past the second brush, which was located above the horizontal center of the cylinder. As the mass passed under this second brush, most of the cotton was applied to the cylinder teeth, then around to the next brush. As it passed under the bristles, the foreign matter was loosened from the cotton and the cylinder teeth. Centrifugal force then forced the material to be released at a tangent, on a line just outside the upper end of the divider board, allowing the separated material to be delivered to the next process.

The location of the divider board is critical, because almost all of the separation of the machine takes place at this point. Some of the cotton will separate from the cylinder with the foreign material. This makes it necessary to reclaim this

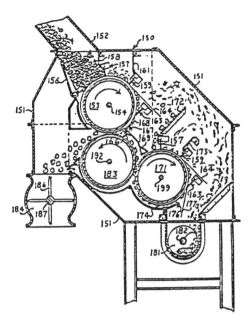

Figure 87. Cross section of the original Vandergriff stick machine (patent application filed 24 November 1953).

cotton from the foreign material, downstream. In the case of the first stick machine, this material was passed to a second extractor cylinder and repeated the separation process. Here, the location of the divider board under the last flexible brush was even more critical, because any foreign matter staying with the path of the cylinder will have no other chance to be separated. When the commingled trash and cotton are well distributed on the saw cylinder and pass the tips of the brush bristles, the particles of trash having a greater mass will separate in the direction of a tangent from the cylinder at that point. The top of the divider board should be located slightly inside this tangent so that these particles will pass outside it. This top edge of the divider board should be about one-half inch from the tips of the saw teeth and the exposed edge should not be sharp. All of the cotton may not be attached to the saw teeth, but its light density permits it to pass inside the divider board.

When only two separations are made, the rate of flow must be limited to what can be retained by the cylinder teeth and still permit a high percentage of the foreign matter to be released. As the rate of flow is increased and there is more cotton than can be handled by the two extractor cylinders, the material leaving the first cylinder may be applied to two or more additional cylinders. (I later built such

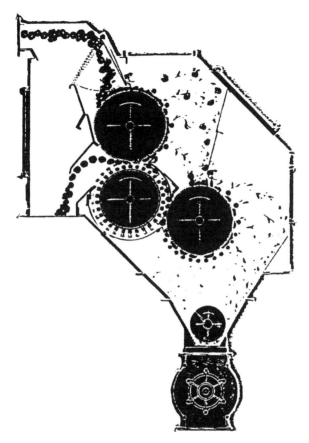

Figure 88. An early air-fed Vandergriff stick machine

machines.) However, at some point it will be necessary to split the flow into two streams because the first extractor cylinder has to process the entire flow. As the flow increases, the separation efficiency decreases. Limiting the rate of flow is not practical because of the many variables involved.

The original machine was designed either to be fed by gravity from a cylinder cleaner (or other processing unit) or to be inserted in an air line (such as that between a dryer and a cylinder cleaner). (See figures 87 and 88.) Many of these early units were sold to be air fed—a process that permitted them to be installed in almost any location—air and cotton being routed to them on its way to the hot-air cleaner. The cotton would be applied to the saw and the air would bypass into a chute down the front of the machine. The cotton was then doffed back into the air stream and continued to the cleaner. Although the air delivered the mass to the saw unevenly and in clumps, it did a good job and was a popular arrangement. However, the adjustment of the divider board in relation to the tangent from the tips of the brushes was so critical on both machines that many operators would merely move the divider board up far enough to be sure there was no cotton loss and leave it there. This impeded efficiency. Years later, I found much more efficient ways to feed the cotton by air to the machines.

Over the years, most manufacturers have replaced the lower steel-wire brushes with a grid screening surface, with the grids rods spaced far enough apart to permit the trash to pass between them—an arrangement that is similar to the USDA design and requires less attention and maintenance. However, it is not nearly as efficient in removing sticks and stems. It is quite effective in removing burrs; however, the burrs have to be broken up to escape through the grids. With my first units—those using the flexible wire bristles—if the burrs were not broken when they entered the machine, they came out unbroken. However, if the cotton was harvested with only partially opened bolls, they had to be opened by cylinder cleaners before entering the machine; otherwise, they might be discharged with cotton in them.

The USDA's *Cotton Ginner's Handbook* (Agricultural Handbook no. 503, page 25, 1977) discusses a USDA-developed stick remover (shown in cross section in figure 89). A specific date is not given for the origin of this machine. The original stick machine I developed also appears in the USDA handbook (figure 3-24, page 27). I see no resemblance between the USDA design and the stick machine I developed that was the first to incorporate the sling-off principle. However, the handbook states "the basic principle [sling-off] introduced by the USDA was being rapidly adopted, and further developed by gin machinery manufacturers." The engineer in charge of the USDA ginning laboratory at Stoneville, Mississippi, had visited our plant in 1949 and I showed him the machine I was working on that incorporated the sling-off principle of separation. A satisfactory method of reclaiming the cotton from the separated material had not been completed for the unit at that time. He asked and was granted permission to do some work on this aspect of the unit. I was permitted to follow the work on the stick remover shown in figure 89. This design was not commercially successful and by 1953 they began to experiment with designs using the sling-off principle.

A good patent was not obtained on this method of extraction. Before the first action by the patent office on the application, I left Lummus to become president of Continental Gin Company. I was not notified of any patent office

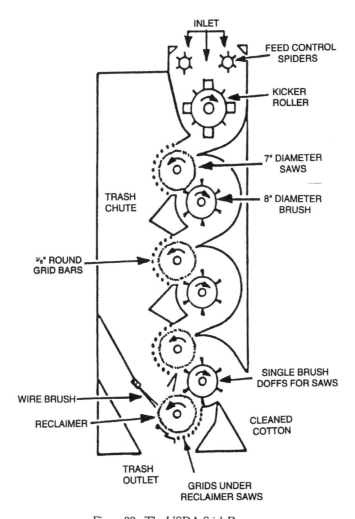

Figure 89. The USDA Stick Remover

action on the application and had no opportunity to participate in amending the action. The resulting patent was limited, making it easy for a competitor to build a machine that was similar but would not infringe my patent.

At Continental in late 1959, we built the first three-saw machine (figure 90). By that time, the capacity of some gin plants had been increased and I thought the third saw was needed to obtain a good separation. This new machine became

Figure 90. Vandergriff-designed three-saw
stick machine, Continental Gin Company

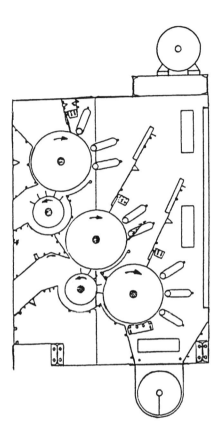

popular, and most of our competitors copied it. Within six years of their introduction, hundreds of these machines were sold.

The first two extractor cylinders of this three-saw machine were arranged as
in the original machine. One difference was that I used a smaller-diameter cylinder
than the Lummus (13³/8 inches compared with 17³/8 inches). Much of the
circumference of the cylinder was not used and I could not—and still am unable
to—see the logic in taking up space with the larger cylinders. Figure 90 shows the
location of the third cylinder. It was doffed by a separate doffer.

This machine had a combination of pipe and flexible brushes. For the final
separation, flexible brushes and an adjustable divider board were used, as in the
two-saw Lummus machine. This provides better separation of sticks and stem,
but requires adjustment of the brush position or the divider board or both, as the

brush wears and the teeth on the cylinder become dull. The flexible bristles were later replaced by round rod or pipe grids, making a reasonably good separation of burrs and other small trash but not as efficient at stick separation.

In this type of extraction, each extractor cylinder makes a separation, leaving less cotton in the sling-off material. This is an important point. The process must be repeated until all the cotton is separated from the slung-off material. The number of separations required varies with a number of conditions: the restrictions around the first cylinder must be such that a maximum amount of foreign matter will be released and the amount of cotton released must be limited to what can be reclaimed by the succeeding units. My preference was to arrange the restrictions around the first extracting cylinder so that the cotton could be reclaimed from the sling-off mass with two reclaimer sections. The reclaimed cotton from each reclaimer section will still include some foreign matter; the number of reclaimer sections is a compromise. It is best to make two or more separations from the main stream and process the sling-off material through cylinder cleaning to remove the small foreign matter first, then reclaim the cotton from the larger foreign matter. Another approach is to keep the reclaimed cotton separate from the main stream and send it back upstream for reprocessing.

Splitting the Cotton into Two Streams

Over the years, I designed and used many different arrangements of stick machines. One arrangement used one section, a saw cylinder and a doffing cylinder, as a unit to split the flow of cotton in two streams (figure 91). The basic stick machine as originally designed split the cotton in two streams and the main stream and the reclaimed stream were mixed together after each process. In the three-saw stick machine, the good cotton doffed from the first extractor cylinder discharges into a common duct with the cotton from the two reclaimer cylinders; that is, the two streams are mixed together. The cotton doffed from the first extractor cylinder, or cylinders, contains less foreign matter than that from the reclaimer cylinders and could be treated separately with less cleaning than the other stream. Later in the 1960s at Boswell, I built a three-saw stick machine with three cylinder cleaners to clean the sling-off material from the first saw. A cross section of this unit is shown in figure 92. It is still in use in some plants today.

A feature of the machine shown in figure 92 deserves particular mention. The grids around the extractor saw are made up of a pipe with a triangular metal strip welded to it. This makes a triangular grid bar with a small point toward the saw. The pipe can be rotated from the outside of the machine to move the point

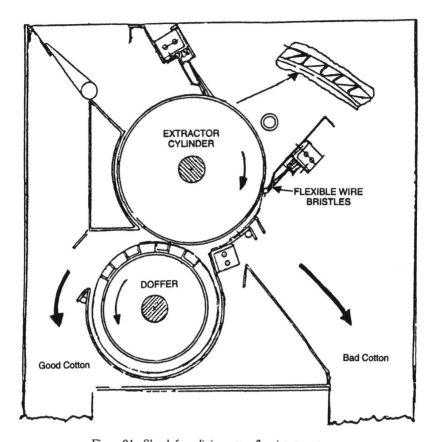

Figure 91. Sketch for splitting cotton flow into two streams

to and away from the saw. All of the pipes extend through the head of the machine and are tied together with a linkage so they can be quickly adjusted.

While at Continental, I had worked with a single-saw and doffer unit as a means of splitting the flow into two streams. Most of the trash and about one-third of the cotton would sling-off the extractor cylinder. Cotton that stayed on the cylinder was doffed separately, requiring less additional processing. The Big Burr Machine was still in common use at that time and I had one of the single-saw doffer units installed between the cylinder cleaner and the burr machine. The sling-off material entered the burr machine; the material that stayed on the extractor cylinder was doffed to the next process. The cotton doffed from the cylinder was as clean as the cotton at the feeder apron. With this modification the Big Burr

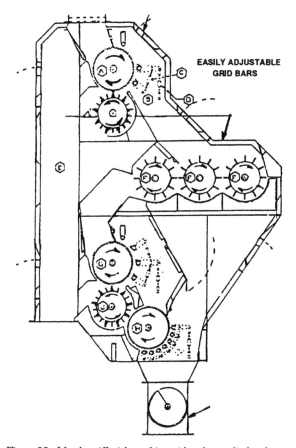

Figure 92. Vandergriff stick machine with a three-cylinder cleaner

Machine, although it still handled the same amount of trash, had to handle only about one-third of the cotton (figure 93). The same results would not be obtained under all conditions, but this arrangement had much potential and I made limited use of it later.

Although they were successful with most cotton, stick machines did not do well on stripper-harvested cotton with partially opened bolls. Once the stick machines as separate units had received wide acceptance in the industry, my attention again turned to the stick-machine attachment for the Big Burr Machine.

Lummus modified my 1953 sling-off machine in the mid 1960s to use as an attachment, a standard stick machine. Although a general improvement over the original machine, in modifying my burr machine for the sling-off attachment,

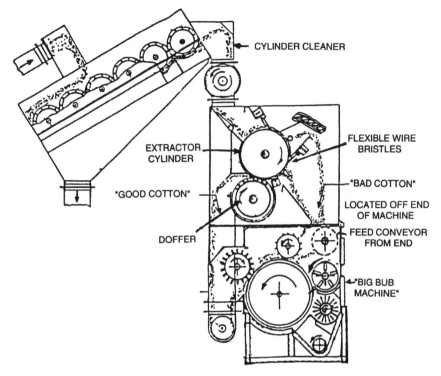

Figure 93. Single-saw separating unit over a burr machine

the rotating stripper in the machine section was eliminated and replaced by a stationary bar. This was not a good change: it did not reject the foreign matter as effectively as the rotating member. Also, as the mass was forced under the stationary restraining member, much of the larger foreign material was crushed and broken into small pieces, becoming difficult to separate in downstream processing. All the companies are now making such a machine and this crushing effect is still a common fault.

Lummus referred to this modified machine as a stripper machine: it was primarily designed for stripper-harvested cotton containing partially opened bolls. Both Horn and Continental soon copied this stripper machine. The cross section shown in figure 94 represents the Horn version of a unit made by Horn and Gladden Company, now Consolidated Cotton Gin Machinery Co. This unit uses a two-saw stick machine attachment of the same configuration as my original machine. Consolidated also made a unit using a three-saw stick machine attachment,

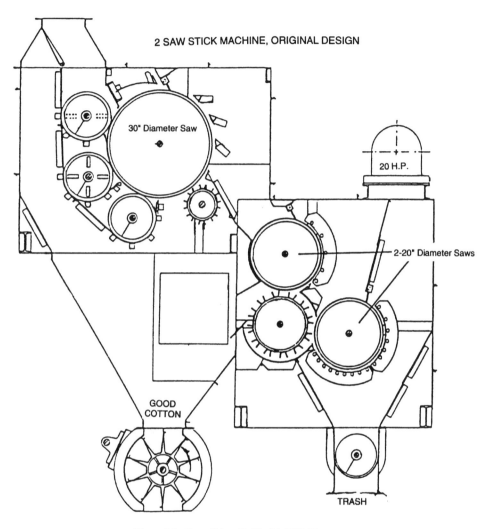

Figure 94. Consolidated's Model 4000 Extractor

with a bypass between the two-saw unit and the third saw. This is the unit on which I show the trash-rejection feature (figure 98), where the reclaimed material can be rejected and sent back upstream for further cleaning.

This group of extractors with sling-off attachment is now manufactured by all the companies, with only minor differences between the models. Each consists basically of the Big Burr Machine section, using a thirty-inch-diameter saw with the doffing brush moved to a lower position, as I had done in 1953. The large segment of the extractor cylinder exposed by moving the doffing brush to a position near the bottom of the cylinder permits foreign matter, which has passed under a stationary stripper along with the cotton, to sling off freely and pass to the stick-machine section. The time is ripe for improvements to this group of anti-quated machines such as the use of the scattered tooth pattern (figure 97) and the simplified multistage extraction shown in figure 101.

At a Boswell plant in California, I continued to work on splitting the cotton into two streams (figure 95). In developing equipment for the high-capacity plant there (Chapter 5), I set up two systems, one in 1967 and the other in 1968, in which the flow was split, following the tower dryers, by the single-saw extractor cylinder. Two stages of separation are shown in figures 95 and 96 of these systems. The cotton is conveyed by the drying air up a vertical duct, at the top of which the cotton follows the curved section of the duct into the extractor cylinder. In the Boswell plant, only one separating unit was used; however, experience has shown that more than one unit for an additional "cut," using two single-saw extractors unit, is preferable in most situations. The cotton remaining on the extractor cylinder is doffed back into the air that made the turn at the top. It then travels down the duct. The cotton and foreign matter that slings off the extractor cylinder enters a cylinder cleaner. It discharges from the first cleaner into a second cleaner, which then discharges it into the air duct to join the other stream. The air conveys it to the next process, which was another set up similar to the first one.

The cleaning arrangement in the Boswell plant also included two stages of stick machines, composed of these single-saw and doffer units stacked and fed by the drying air in the manner just described. The system essentially separated the cotton into a "good" stream and a "bad" stream. The good stream bypassed the cleaning units; the bad stream contained less that half the cotton—the amount depending on a number of factors but primarily the number of separating units used. Most of the trash was in the bad stream. With a reduced amount of cotton, the cleaning units were more efficient, but most importantly, less than half the cotton received anything more than minimum treatment. This was the most efficient cleaning and drying system I have ever seen, for both fiber quality and trash removal.

With this large volume of cotton, air feeding to these single-saw separating units did not deliver a uniform flow: the cotton reached the extractor cylinder in wads, as is usually the case when feeding by air, unless the flow is at a high velocity. The uneven flow both reduced efficiency and increased the maintenance needs of

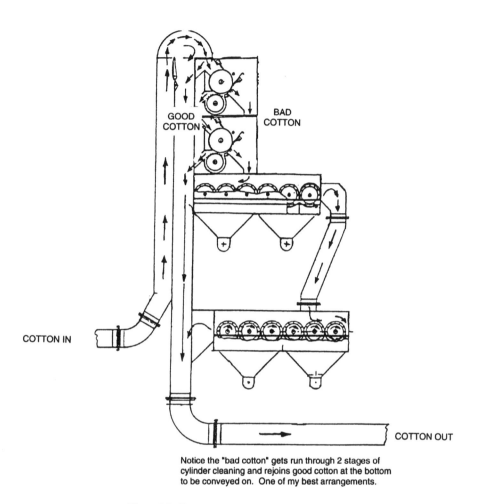

Figure 95. Boswell stack arrangement, 1967-68

the extractor saw segments. I later found ways to make such a system more efficient. Figure 96 shows a means of breaking up the wads.

In figure 96, the cotton is delivered to the top of the duct work, but it is applied to a spiked cylinder and then to a second one. A directing shield between them allows for a pulling action as the cotton passes from one cylinder to the next. This action will separate the cotton into a uniform mass that is then fed by the second cylinder to the extractor cylinder. This arrangement is probably worthwhile in feeding any extractor cylinder, regardless of the origin of the flow.

Figure 96. Means to break up
wads that form in air feed

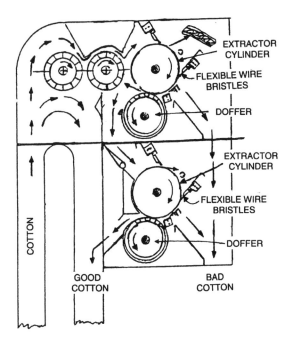

The other method of preventing the wads from damaging the cylinder and interfering with separation is to use the scattered-tooth pattern of saw teeth (an example is shown in figure 97). A properly designed pattern will not pick up the cotton in wads; it pulls the wads apart and redistributes them and thoroughly separates the trash. My experiments with this scattered-tooth pattern show it to be the most effective extracting method I have tested. If the cotton is applied to the cylinder in wads, as is usual, the scattered teeth pluck small clumps of cotton from the wads and allow the entrapped trash to be released.

As to the question of capacity with this scattered tooth cylinder, let us consider a twenty-inch-diameter extractor cylinder, 120 inches long, at 300 rpm and with a flow rate of 30 bph (800 lbs. per minute). Such a cylinder has a surface area of 15,708 square feet exposed per minute. Eight hundred pounds per minute, or 12,800 ounces, spread over this area is $80/100$ths (0.81) of an ounce per square foot. At two thousand seed locks per pound, or 125 per ounce, there would be less than one seed lock per square inch of saw-cylinder surface. Then the problem is not one of having enough saw teeth but of distributing the cotton evenly over surface of the cylinder.

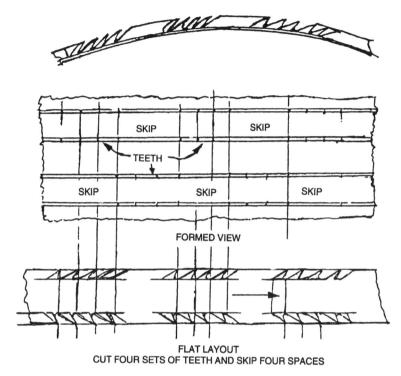

Figure 97. Extractor saw segment with a skip- or scattered-tooth pattern

It is possible to have a more uniform reduction in the tooth pattern by cutting the teeth on the saw segment in the flat, before it is formed, in the pattern desired. Figure 97 shows a flat layout with four teeth cut and skipping four spaces. On an eighteen-inch diameter cylinder, ninety-degree segments would align in such a way that when the segments were placed side by side a section of teeth would be opposite a blank section. Many combinations are possible, but the less aggressive tooth patterns are better and would also reduce the aggressive action of the master extractor cylinders—a problem today in the stripper-cotton areas; they break the foreign matter into small pieces that are not removed before reaching the roll box.

Another interesting possibility for improving overall extractor efficiency is the trash-rejection system shown in figure 98. The main flow of cotton can be subjected to multistages of extraction to separate the flow into two streams, the trash being concentrated in one of the streams. (This is the concept used in the Boswell plant, except that there the two streams were mixed back together after each stage of cleaning.) The clean stream requires minimal additional processing;

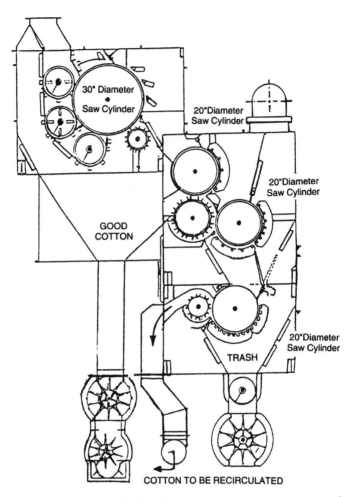

Figure 98. Stripper machine modified to reject trash from the last reclaimer saws and return it for reprocessing.

the sling-off stream requires additional processing. This rejection idea can be applied to the usual extractors (figure 98).

As the amount of cotton in the trash is reduced, the cotton reclaimed from the concentration of trash will have a higher percentage of trash reclaimed with it. So the cotton reclaimed from the last cylinder in the machines shown in figure 98 has a high concentration of trash in it. Although this is a small percentage of the total volume, it is best to return it upstream for more cleaning rather than allow

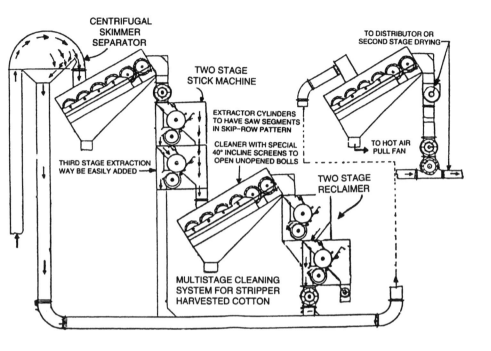

Figure 99. Splitting the cotton into good and bad streams

reentry into the main stream. Figure 98 illustrates the modifications used to reject the mixture from the last reclaimer cylinder. This mixture could easily be conveyed to a hot-air cleaner through a small line tapped into the line going to the cleaner. This rejection method can be applied in a number of ways to extractors (figure 99). A logical place to do so would be at the extractor feeder, thus keeping this ground-up material out of the seed roll.

In the proposal illustrated in figure 99, the cotton to be processed is conveyed by the air from the dryer; cotton is separated from the conveying air by the centrifugal separator. The cotton enters the cleaner and the air bypasses into the continuing duct and picks up the cotton again later. After passing through the cleaner and the rotary seal, the cotton enters the first stage of extraction; there, foreign material is separated by the sling-off principle. The cotton that stays on the saw is doffed into a second stage of extraction, which makes another foreign-matter separation—"taking a second cut" of foreign matter from the main stream. Each cut reduces the volume of the main stream and increases that in the sling-off stream. In some cases, it might be desirable to make a third cut. With use of the scattered-tooth pattern, this action would be relatively gentle on the cotton.

The cleaned cotton stream is now dropped back into the drying air, which conveys it to the next stage. The sling-off material, which contains almost all of the foreign matter (especially if a third stage was used) flows by gravity into a cylinder cleaner, the amount of cotton in this stream varies with the rate of flow and number of cuts. Generally, about 30 to 40 percent of the total flow of cotton will be in this stream. This makes it unnecessary for the cleaner processing this material to be as wide as the primary cleaner. If the primary device is eight or ten feet wide, the reclaimer cleaner and extraction can be six feet wide. In addition to removing trash, this cleaner will open any unopened bolls. It is recommended that this cleaner be equipped with special screening surfaces (figure 106, Chapter 9) to provide a more drastic action on the bolls and more efficiently remove the trash.

The cleaner discharges into two-stage extractor reclaiming units that can be the same as the primary units, except for width, but are arranged to process only the bad cotton stream material slung off from the first stage. The reclaimed cotton rejoins the primary stream in the drying air going to the next stage, which would normally be a cylinder cleaner. The drying air is now separated from the cotton and the cleaning process is continued. (To make use of the trash-rejection idea, the cotton doffed from last reclaimer section could be picked up and handled separately; not, perhaps, the most convenient point to incorporate the idea, but mentioning it here illustrates the point.)

In the stripper-cotton areas, practically all gin plants have two or more stages of extraction. This proposed system provides multiple-stage extraction in one system, a more compact and more economical arrangement, and provides for greater efficiency. Usually, all the material is commingled after each stage and has to be reseparated. With this proposed system, the commingled mass is reduced after each stage, allowing each succeeding stage to handle a lower volume. Under most circumstances, at least 50 to 60 percent of the foreign matter will be separated by the first extractor cylinder, along with 10 to 20 percent of the cotton. The volume going to the second stage of primary extraction is so reduced as to make it an efficient separation.

This type of separation, or extraction, is not as sensitive to moisture-content as cylinder cleaning. First, foreign matter is entangled and trapped in the seed locks, and this process pulls the locks apart or untangles them, releasing the foreign matter. Second, the foreign matter has larger openings through which to escape, compared with the screening surfaces of cylinder cleaning, and this is especially effective in releasing the larger particles. When moisture is present, there may be a better separation because the particles do not break up easily into pieces too small to be removed by the centrifugal action of the extractor cylinder. The scattered-tooth pattern of extractor saw segments will add to the effectiveness of this type of separation under conditions of higher moisture. Possibly, it could be used in the hot-air line ahead of the drying system to remove a lot of larger foreign matter and better prepare the cotton for drying. A stack of single-saw and doffer units could be used, with multiple stages of primary separation and two stages of reclaiming. This arrangement was used in Boswell's El Rico plant in the late 1960s.

Around the extracting cylinder, flexible wire brushes are preferable to round rod grids. The round grid bars around the first cylinder are acceptable for releasing foreign matter, but considerably more cotton is released to be reclaimed by the next cylinder. Flexible bristles reapply and seat the cotton into the teeth of the cylinder; thus, less of it is delivered to the next cylinder. A close examination will reveal that a tangential line from the surface of the cylinder opposite the grid rod, downward toward the next grid, will be inside that rod. Hence, any material escaping (e.g., a stick) does not have much chance of being thrown free by centrifugal force; it must be pushed between the grids. With flexible brushes, the larger foreign matter will flex the bristles enough to be thrown outside the tangent and outside the divider bar. Even light leaf trash will be released by the bristles and stay outside the divider board.

The multistage stick machine arrangement consists of a two-saw stick machine as the first unit; the cotton flow from this unit goes to a single-saw extractor cylinder and doffer (as in figure 91); the cotton is doffed to a second standard two-saw extractor and the sling-off material from the single-saw unit goes to the reclaimer section of the two-saw unit. (Essentially, this makes the two bottom units a three-saw stick machine; the arrangement is basically a combination of a two-saw machine and a three-saw machine in series.) The top and bottom sections are similar to the two-saw stick machine shown in figure 87.

I have proposed, for a number of years, a multistage stick machine as shown in figure 99. Several of my proposals precede the USDA multistage unit used by Consolidated (figure 100). Figure 101 shows a Vandergriff two-stage extractor followed by a two-stage reclaimer—a simple machine made up of single extractor cylinders that can be stacked in many different combinations. Figure 102 shows an interesting idea for a practical, complete cleaning and extracting system in one package.

Figure 103 shows another means of separating the larger foreign matter from the main flow of cotton—an idea I developed at Lummus in the mid-1950s. It proved to be popular, more than one hundred were sold even before the model

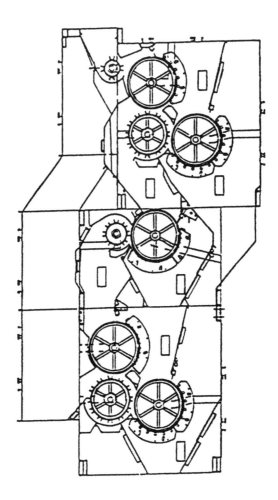

Figure 100. Consolidated multistage stick machine, licensed under U.S. patent no. 4,974, 293

was tested in the field. Practically every Lummus plant built since its introduction has contained this unit. The reclaimer section has been modified and the name changed from R. C. Gridmaster to Trashmaster.

This unit is a grid cleaner with the grids spaced so that larger particles of trash can pass through. The 3/8-inch grid rods were placed on 7/8-inch centers, leaving 1/2 inch between the rods. This spacing permitted some cotton to pass

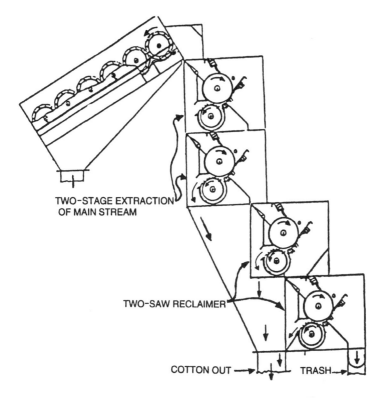

TWO-STAGE EXTRACTION
OF MAIN STREAM

TWO-SAW RECLAIMER

COTTON OUT ──►   TRASH──►

CLEANER FEEDING TWO-STAGE STICK MACHINE

Figure 101. A Vandergriff two-stage extractor

through with the foreign matter—the cotton was reclaimed at the bottom of the
unit and put back into the stream. The machine was installed on a forty-five-degree
incline so that both trash and cotton would slide by gravity to the reclaiming unit.

Developments in extraction methods will no doubt include use of the
scattered-tooth pattern to pick up cotton and leave the trash, instead of trying to
pick the trash out of the cotton. There are extractors operating now in which every
other one of the 180-degree extractor tooth segments is left off—a small step
toward better separation.

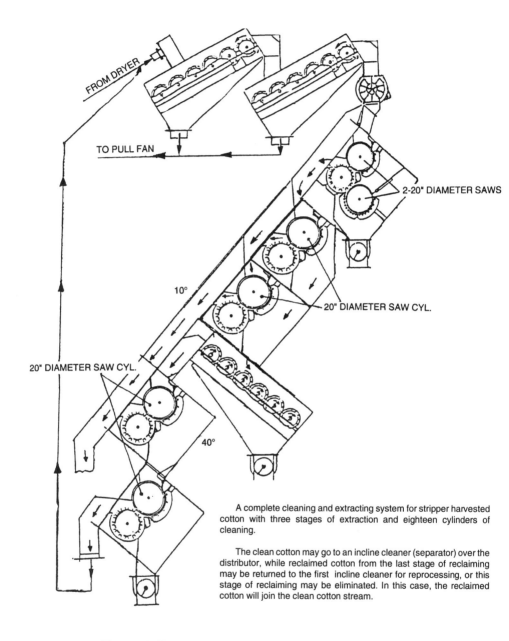

FROM DRYER

TO PULL FAN

2-20" DIAMETER SAWS

10°

20" DIAMETER SAW CYL.

20" DIAMETER SAW CYL.

40°

A complete cleaning and extracting system for stripper harvested cotton with three stages of extraction and eighteen cylinders of cleaning.

The clean cotton may go to an incline cleaner (separator) over the distributor, while reclaimed cotton from the last stage of reclaiming may be returned to the first incline cleaner for reprocessing, or this stage of reclaiming may be eliminated. In this case, the reclaimed cotton will join the clean cotton stream.

Figure 102. Whole plant cleaning and extractor system for stripper cotton.

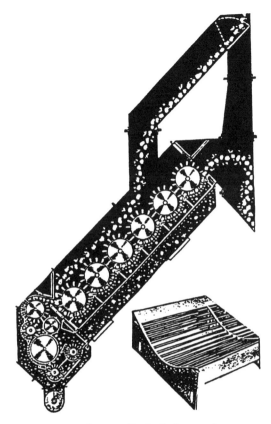

Figure 103. Lummus R. C. Gridmaster cleaner

9 Cylinder Cleaning

When methods of harvesting cotton changed and became more mechanized, trash in the cotton became more of an economic factor and a means to remove it became a necessity. There are two basic types of cylinders used to separate trash from seed cotton in the ginning process: extractor cylinders that use teeth to hold the fibers while the cylinder rotates to expose the cotton to various types of screening surfaces (discussed in Chapter 8), and cylinders with pins (this chapter). The most common type of pin is shown in figure 104, A and C. Cylinder cleaners as units were used to clean the cotton before it reached the distributor and delivered it to the gin stand feeder.

The earliest use of cylinder cleaners was in the gin stand feeders (figure 72, Chapter 7), which used rotating cylinders with pins, or spikes, to help shake and separate a mass of cotton from its trash. From the beginning of saw ginning, there was a demand for cleaner cotton, so screening surfaces were added around the cylinders to screen out the trash. There were cylinders with screening surfaces as far back as 1860, but their use was limited until Munger's introduction of system ginning in the 1880s.

For many years, the feeder cleaners were single-drum (cylinder) units. Later, perhaps in the 1920s, a feeder with a larger drum was introduced. One of the earliest cylinder cleaners to become a part of the Munger system was the Hart boll-breaker cleaner. To remove the hulls, the Ellis double-rib huller gin was developed.

In my early days in ginning in the mid 1930s, the most common cylinder cleaner used in West Texas contained five to seven cylinders, each about fifty inches long. This would accommodate a plant with a capacity in the six-to-eight bph range. The screening surfaces were heavy hardware cloth with 1/2-inch spacing.

There was not much emphasis on cylinder cleaners until the arid areas of Texas and Oklahoma started growing cotton, primarily after World War I. The cotton plant grown in this arid climate was smaller, had less foliage, and in most cases, harvest occurred after a killing frost. In addition, the moisture content of the harvested cotton was low. Unlike the method used in the more humid South, this cotton was harvested by pulling the bolls with the cotton, and the gin had to deal with a larger amount of trash, both leaves and burrs. Both cylinder cleaning for

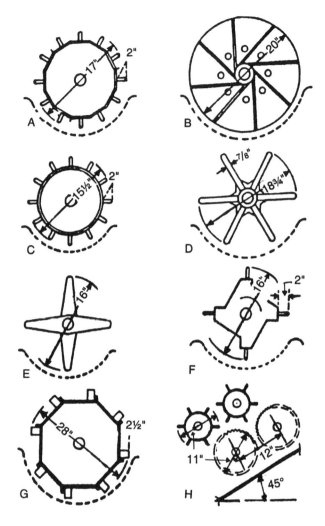

Figure 104. Types of cylinder pins

the leaf trash and extractors for the burrs would be needed. In the South, cotton was still hand picked and there was little interest in cylinder cleaning.

Some of the gins in this region tried cylinder cleaners because of the demand for cleaner cotton. However, this cotton could have a high moisture content (figure 105). With ambient conditions of eighty degrees Fahrenheit and a relative humidity of 80 percent (not uncommon for this region) the cotton fiber comes to equilibrium at 11.4 percent. Although such conditions were not ideal for the use of cylinder cleaners, they were used because of their potential to yield a cleaner cotton that would net a higher price.

An early problem caused by high-moisture situations was the production of rough samples. Cylinder cleaners did not help with this situation; in fact, they added significantly to it. The term used to describe the condition created by the cylinder cleaners was roping (Chapter 7). To avoid some of the kinks or naps forming in the sample, the rotation speed of the cylinders was reduced, in some cases to 250 or 200 rpm (in low-humidity areas the standard speed was 450 to 500 rpm). In addition, the screening surfaces were flattened to permit a less drastic transfer action of the cotton between the cylinders. Both of these actions reduced the roping, but the cleaning efficiency was also reduced.

Even before the introduction of cylinder cleaners to areas of high humidity, it was beginning to be recognized that there was a need to remove moisture prior to ginning. The high-moisture cotton in the seed roll of the gin could cause the fibers to be pressed into the saw teeth tightly enough to cause naps similar to that caused by the cylinder process. These tight groups of fibers were lost in the mill-cleaning process and considered waste. The buyer set a steep penalty for these naps—considerably more than the reduction in weight alone.

In the late 1920s, the USDA ginning laboratory started work in Louisiana, a high-humidity area, on a means to remove some of the moisture from the cotton before it reached the gin stand. Given the ambient conditions in the area (see Table 2), it is no surprise that work on drying started in that historic cotton-growing region. The research was under the capable direction of Charles A. Bennett. The most successful of the USDA efforts was the development of the parallel-flow tower dryer—the patent was issued to Bennett and the device became available to the public (Chapter 10).

The introduction of seed-cotton drying resulted in a rapid increase in the use of cylinder cleaners in the more humid areas. Many plant owners installed cylinder cleaners and a drying arrangement at the same time. These usually consisted of a short tower (stub) with eleven shelves, mounted on the cleaner itself so that the cotton would discharge directly from the tower into the cleaner. Another arrangement was the longer, seventeen-shelf USDA version that was installed in a number of gins prior to the installation of a cleaner. The stub tower (figure 105) became more popular when cleaners came into general use. Note the high-velocity blow box under the separator feeding cotton into the dryer air stream.

During the infant stage of cylinder cleaning in these areas, the thirty-degree (or less) contour of the screening surfaces was established. Even today, with the

Table 2. Moisture Regain Chart

Dry Bulb Temperature

Rel. Hum.	35°	40°	45°	50°	55°	60°	65°	70°	75°	80°	85°	90°	95°	100°	105°	110°
100%	22.1	21.8	21.6	21.4	21.2	21.0	20.8	20.6	20.4	20.2	20.0	19.8	19.7	19.5	19.3	19.1
98	19.0	18.8	18.6	18.4	18.3	18.1	17.9	17.7	17.6	17.4	17.3	17.1	16.9	16.8	16.7	16.6
96	17.7	17.6	17.4	17.2	17.0	16.9	16.7	16.6	16.4	16.3	16.2	16.0	15.8	15.7	15.6	15.5
94	16.8	16.6	16.5	16.3	16.2	16.0	15.9	15.7	15.6	15.4	15.3	15.1	15.0	14.9	14.8	14.7
92	15.9	15.8	15.6	15.5	15.3	15.2	15.0	14.9	14.8	14.6	14.5	14.4	14.2	14.1	144.0	13.9
90	15.2	15.1	14.9	14.8	14.6	14.5	14.4	14.2	14.1	14.0	13.8	13.7	13.6	13.5	13.3	13.2
88	14.6	14.4	14.3	14.1	14.0	13.9	13.7	13.6	13.5	13.4	13.2	13.1	13.0	12.9	12.8	12.7
86	14.0	13.8	12.7	13.6	13.4	13.3	13.2	13.0	12.9	12.8	12.7	12.6	12.5	12.3	12.2	12.1
84	13.4	13.3	13.2	13.0	12.9	12.8	12.7	12.5	12.4	12.3	12.2	12.1	12.0	11.9	11.8	11.7
82	12.9	12.8	12.6	12.5	12.4	12.3	12.2	12.0	11.9	11.8	11.7	11.6	11.5	11.4	11.3	11.2
80	12.4	12.3	12.2	12.1	11.9	11.8	11.7	11.6	11.5	11.4	11.3	11.2	11.1	11.0	10.9	10.8
79	12.2	12.1	11.9	11.8	11.7	11.6	11.5	11.4	11.3	11.2	11.1	11.0	10.9	10.8	10.7	10.6
78	12.0	11.8	11.7	11.6	11.5	11.4	11.3	11.2	11.1	11.0	10.9	10.8	10.7	10.6	10.5	10.4
77	11.7	11.6	11.5	11.4	11.3	11.2	11.1	11.0	10.9	10.8	10.7	10.6	10.5	10.4	10.3	10.2
76	11.5	11.4	11.3	11.2	11.1	11.0	10.9	10.8	10.7	10.6	10.5	10.4	10.3	10.2	10.1	10.0
75	11.3	11.2	11.1	11.0	10.9	10.8	10.7	10.6	10.5	10.4	10.3	10.2	10.1	10.0	9.9	9.8
74	11.	11.0	10.9	10.8	10.7	10.6	10.5	10.4	10.3	10.2	10.1	10.0	9.9	9.8	9.7	9.6
73	10.9	10.8	10.7	10.6	10.5	10.4	10.3	10.2	10.1	10.0	9.9	9.8	9.7	9.6	9.5	9.4
72	10.7	10.6	10.5	10.4	10.3	10.2	10.1	10.0	9.9	9.8	9.7	9.6	9.5	9.4	9.3	9.2
71	10.5	10.4	10.3	10.2	10.1	10.0	9.9	9.8	9.7	9.6	9.5	9.4	9.3	9.3	9.2	9.1
70	10.3	10.2	10.1	10.0	9.9	9.8	9.7	9.6	9.5	9.4	9.4	9.3	9.2	9.1	9.0	8.9
69	10.1	10.0	9.9	9.8	9.7	9.6	9.5	9.4	9.4	9.3	9.2	9.1	9.0	8.9	8.8	8.7
68	9.9	9.8	9.7	9.6	9.5	9.5	9.4	9.3	9.2	9.1	9.0	8.9	8.9	8.8	8.7	8.6
67	9.7	9.6	9.5	9.5	9.4	9.3	9.2	9.1	9.0	8.9	8.8	8.8	8.7	8.6	8.5	8.4
66	9.6	9.5	9.4	9.3	9.2	9.1	9.0	8.9	8.9	8.8	8.7	8.6	8.5	8.5	8.4	8.3
65	9.4	9.3	9.2	9.1	9.0	8.9	8.9	8.8	8.7	8.6	8.5	8.5	8.4	8.3	8.2	8.2
64	9.2	9.1	9.0	9.0	8.9	8.8	8.7	8.6	8.5	8.5	8.4	8.3	8.2	8.2	8.1	8.0
63	9.1	9.0	8.9	8.8	8.7	8.6	8.5	8.5	8.4	8.3	8.2	8.2	8.1	8.0	7.9	7.8
62	8.9	8.8	8.7	8.6	8.5	8.5	8.4	8.3	8.2	8.2	8.1	8.0	7.9	7.9	7.8	7.7
61	8.7	8.6	8.6	8.5	8.3	8.3	8.2	8.2	8.1	8.0	7.9	7.9	7.8	7.7	7.6	7.5

Table 2. Moisture Regain Chart (continued)

Dry Bulb Temperature

Rel. Hum.	35°	40°	45°	50°	55°	60°	65°	70°	75°	80°	85°	90°	95°	100°	105°	110°
60	8.6	8.5	8.4	8.3	8.2	8.1	8.1	8.0	7.9	7.8	7.8	7.7	7.6	7.6	7.5	7.4
58	8.3	8.2	8.1	8.0	8.0	7.9	7.8	7.7	7.7	7.6	7.5	7.4	7.4	7.3	7.3	7.2
56	8.0	7.9	7.8	7.7	7.7	7.6	7.5	7.5	7.4	7.3	7.3	7.2	7.1	7.1	7.0	7.0
54	7.7	7.6	7.5	7.5	7.4	7.3	7.2	7.2	7.1	7.0	7.0	6.9	6.8	6.8	6.7	6.7
52	7.4	7.3	7.3	7.2	7.1	7.0	7.0	6.9	6.9	6.8	6.7	6.6	6.6	6.5	6.5	6.3
50	7.2	7.1	7.0	6.9	6.9	6.8	6.7	6.7	6.6	6.6	6.5	6.4	6.4	6.3	6.3	6.2
48	6.9	6.8	6.8	6.7	6.6	6.6	6.5	6.5	6.4	6.3	6.3	6.2	6.2	6.1	6.1	6.0
46	6.7	6.6	6.5	6.5	6.4	6.3	6.3	6.2	6.2	6.1	6.1	6.0	5.9	5.9	5.8	5.8
44	6.4	6.4	6.3	6.2	6.2	6.1	6.1	6.0	5.9	5.9	5.8	5.8	5.7	5.7	5.6	5.6
42	6.2	6.1	6.1	6.0	6.0	5.9	5.9	5.8	5.7	5.7	5.6	5.6	5.5	5.5	5.4	5.4
40	6.0	5.9	5.9	5.8	5.8	5.7	5.7	5.6	5.5	5.5	5.4	5.4	5.3	5.3	5.3	5.2
38	5.8	5.7	5.7	5.6	5.6	5.5	5.5	5.4	5.4	5.3	5.3	5.2	5.2	5.1	5.1	5.0
36	5.6	5.5	5.5	5.4	5.4	5.3	5.3	5.2	5.2	5.1	5.1	5.0	5.0	4.9	4.9	4.8
34	5.4	5.3	5.3	5.2	5.2	5.1	5.1	5.0	5.0	4.9	4.9	4.8	4.8	4.7	4.7	4.6
32	5.2	5.1	5.1	5.0	5.0	4.9	4.9	4.8	4.8	4.7	4.7	4.6	4.6	4.6	4.5	4.4
30	5.0	4.9	4.9	4.8	4.7	4.7	4.6	4.6	4.6.	4.6	4.5	4.5	4.4	4.4	4.4	4.3
28	4.8	4.7	4.7	4.6	4.6	4.6	4.5	4.5	4.4	4.4	4.3	4.3	4.3	4.2	4.2	4.1
26	4.6	4.5	4.5	4.4	4.4	4.4	4.3	4.3	4.2	4.2	4.2	4.1	4.1	4.0	4.0	3.9
24	4.4	4.1	4.1	4.1	4.0	4.0	3.9	3.9	3.9	3.8	3.8	3.8	3.7	3.7	3.7	3.6
22	4.2	4.1	4.1	4.1	4.0	4.0	3.9	3.9	3.9	3.8	3.8	3.8	3.7	3.7	3.7	3.6
20	4.0	3.9	3.9	3.8	3.8	3.8	3.7	3.7	3.7	3.6	3.6	3.6	3.5	3.5	3.5	3.4
18	3.7	3.7	3.7	3.6	3.6	3.6	3.5	3.5	3.5	3.4	3.4	3.4	3.3	3.3	3.3	3.2
16	3.5	3.5	3.4	3.4	3.4	3.3	3.3	3.3	3.2	3.2	3.2	3.2	3.1	3.1	3.1	3.1
14	3.3	3.3	3.2	3.2	3.2	3.1	3.1	3.1	3.0	3.0	3.0	3.0	2.9	2.9	2.9	2.9
12	3.0	3.0	2.9	2.9	2.9	2.9	2.8	2.8	2.8	2.8	2.7	2.7	2.7	2.6	2.6	2.6
10	2.7	2.7	2.7	2.6	2.6	2.6	2.6	2.5	2.5	2.5	2.5	2.5	2.4	2.4	2.4	2.4
8	2.4	2.4	2.4	2.4	2.3	2.3	2.3	2.3	2.3	2.2	2.2	2.2	2.2	2.1	2.1	2.1
6	2.1	2.1	2.1	2.1	2.1	2.0	2.0	2.0	2.0	2.0	1.9	1.9	1.9	1.9	1.9	1.9
4	1.7	1.6	1.6	1.6	1.6	1.6	1.6	1.6	1.5	1.5	1.5	1.5	1.5	1.5	1.5	1.5
2	1.2	1.2	1.2	1.2	1.1	1.1	1.1	1.1	1.1	1.1	1.1	1.1	1.1	1.1	1.1	1.1

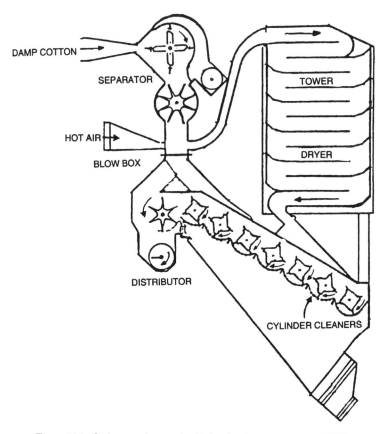

Figure 105. Stub tower dryer and cylinder cleaning arrangement, 1930s.

availability of good conditioning, the cleaner screens have not changed significantly. However, the efficiency of the cleaners can be improved by wrapping the
screening surfaces further around the cylinder, raising the transfer of the cotton
between cylinders to a higher point (figure 106). This results in more drastic action
on the cotton between the cylinders, pulling the seed locks apart and loosening the
trash. This can be accomplished efficiently only if the moisture is sufficiently
lowered by prior drying. High-moisture cotton will not separate in the cleaners as
efficiently and the trash will not shake out as well. For cylinder cleaning to work
at peak efficiency, the cotton must enter warm. Most drying systems today allow
too much of a temperature drop in the drying cycle, reducing efficiency.

   In 1949, I designed a feeder at Lummus with the cleaning cylinders
wrapped higher than standard. The feeder cleaning screens were inclined at forty

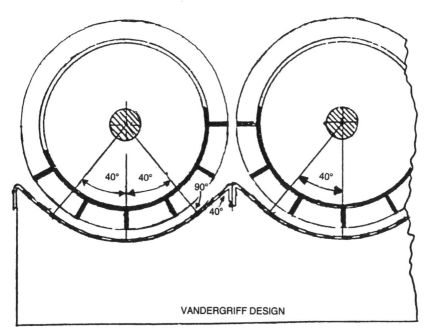

VANDERGRIFF DESIGN

1949 CLEANER SCREEN — 40° INCLINE

Figure 106. Arrangement with a forty-degree incline on cleaning screens

degrees, which resulted in the screen going higher between the cylinders (figure 106). This separated the cotton more thoroughly, providing more efficient trash removal and a more even flow of cotton through the cleaner into the gin stand (or the next machine).

I currently use some screens that have up to a forty-five-degree wrap. From the beginning, standard cleaner screens have had a thirty-degree incline between cylinders. This means the screening surface leaves the curvature of the screen at a point thirty degrees past the centerline of the cylinder, giving a surface incline of thirty degrees (figure 107).

A feeder of that time on a sixty-six-inch-wide machine would handle only about two bales per hour. With this low volume, there would be no problem at the transfer point. There was initial apprehension about how much this forty-degree arrangement would restrict capacity; however, capacity has been increased gradually over the intervening thirty-five years, and by the mid-1980s, the forty-degree screening surface with an eleven-inch-diameter cylinder was handling twelve bales

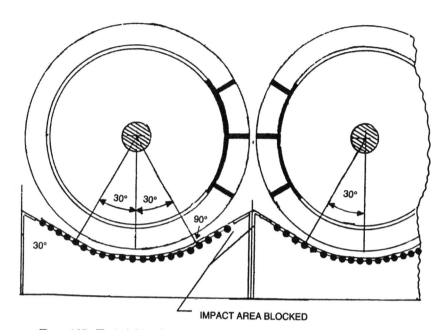

Figure 107. Typical thirty-degree screening surface with impact area blocked by joint between cylinders

per hour through a ninety-six-inch-wide machine. The industry as a whole has been slow to take advantage of the success of this arrangement.

Screen surfaces have gone through some changes over the years. The hardware cloth has been replaced with the rod grids running parallel to the axis of the cylinder, spaced about 5/16ths of an inch apart (figure 103, Chapter 8). This type of screening surface provides a better chance for larger particles to pass through, especially small sticks and stems. Other surfaces (e.g., perforated metal and flat expanded metal) have been used in a few machines.

With most cylinder cleaners, the screening surfaces are joined and overlapped at the apex of the surface between the cylinders. This practice continues today, even though other types of screening surfaces are used. This joint blocks the most efficient area of cleaning: the place where the cotton impacts against the screening surface (figure 107). Figure 108 shows a method of joining the surfaces directly under the cylinders leaving the section in between open for more efficient cleaning.

A novel arrangement I used on cleaners consists of a flat bar placed in the joint between the screening sections. This bar can be adjusted upward to get the maximum benefit from the action at the transfer point. With this point raised about

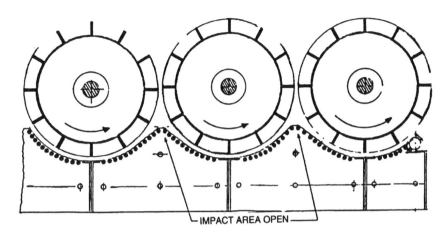

Figure 108. Method of joining screening surfaces to provide greater efficiency

one inch above the standard thirty-degree incline, the results are good (figure 109). The transfer of the cotton from one cylinder to the next over this bar pulls the cotton apart, resulting in the release of more trash and a flow of cotton that is even and smooth.

In the late 1940s and early 1950s, harvesting machines with rotating spindles that twisted the cotton from the bolls were introduced. Water was added to the spindles so the cotton would adhere to them, resulting in the harvest of a lot of wet leaves and stems. The added moisture presented the gin-machinery manufacturers with a real challenge—and opportunity. The first and logical approach was simply to add multiple stages of drying and cleaning. The tower dryers were removed from the cleaners and located so they could be made taller, with more shelves. The standard dryer had twenty-three or twenty-four shelves, depending on whether the cotton entered on the side it exited by or on the opposite side. The use of these taller towers was a mistake. A stub tower, mounted directly over the cleaner, has an obvious advantage: the temperature drop between units is low. When the cotton discharges into the cleaner, it is still hot enough to continue moisture removal. Hot cotton releases trash more readily, too. In the tall towers, for the cotton discharge to be at a good drying and cleaning temperature it must be exposed to extremely high temperatures at the mixing point, and this can cause damage to the cotton fiber.

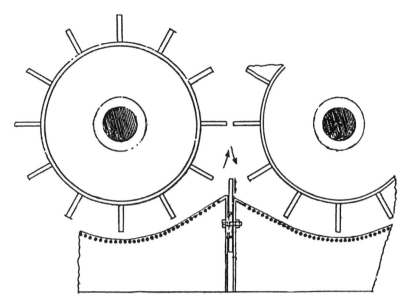

Figure 109. Use of a flat bar between screening sections to raise the transfer point

The first stage of drying is generally followed by six- or seven-cylinder cleaners—either one or two of them. The first set can act as the separator for the drying air. These cleaners are followed by another tall tower and two more cleaners. The last of these cleaners feeds into the distributor. Early on, all plants were equipped with extractor feeders, using the principle adopted in the bollie areas. In most cases, the feeder had both hull extraction and cylinder cleaning. Beyond running the cylinders faster and adding more machines, nothing was done to improve the efficiency of the cylinder cleaner.

If the ginners did not use a lot of cylinder cleaning and do a lot of drying, the grades would be so low as to result in severe economic losses for the farmer. Thus, although the cleaning process put a severe strain on the fibers, with spinning value significantly lowered, the ginners had no choice but to use everything available. At Lummus, where we had the first and only well-equipped, fiber laboratory in the manufacturing industry, we were aware of what was being done to the spinning quality. It was obvious then, as it is today, that the classer's grade does not go nearly far enough in measuring spinning value. We looked forward to the day when these quality factors could be quickly and accurately measured and price adjusted accordingly. Years have passed and not much has been accomplished in the field of quality measurement, but the mills, merchants, and ginners have a much better understanding of the problem. The mills realize that appearance may not be everything.

Gin plants still use a lot of cylinder cleaners—generally, a minimum of eighteen cylinders. Development of the ability to clean the lint after the gin stand has relieved the pressure on the seed-cotton cleaners; they are accepted, and it seems there is little effort to improve them. In the seventy five years since they came into use, the principal change has been the switch to the rod-grid screening surfaces, although there have been changes in the size of the machines and their arrangement in the plant. The improved cleaning screen shown in figure 108 has not been adopted by the industry.

The capacity of a cylinder cleaner is a subject of much controversy. A rule of thumb is two bales per hour per foot of cleaner width; thus, a six-foot-wide cleaner will handle twelve bales per hour. This is a safe figure; however some of my clients are using a six-foot-wide cleaner at twenty bales per hour with no mechanical problems and good cleaning efficency.

The question "How does the rate of flow affect cleaning efficiency?" has never been answered to my satisfaction. There are so many variables it is impossible to establish flow rates that would be optimum for all conditions. In my experience, when the cotton is properly conditioned, a ten-foot-wide machine will handle forty bales per hour if the cotton is dry and properly distributed over the width of the machine. Under some conditions, the moisture content may have to be lowered below the recommended level to get efficient cleaning at this high flow rate. I am convinced that the key to cylinder-cleaner efficiency and capacity is drying. This is discussed in detail in Chapter 10, but it is relevant here to emphasize that high moisture cotton (15-20 percent moisture) must be exposed throughout a drying cycle to a temperature of 200-220 degrees Fahrenheit and must be conveyed into a cylinder cleaner at this temperature, where the air is separated. Under these conditions, the exposure in the cleaner is an integral part of the drying.

Another important factor in cleaner capacity and efficiency is the distribution of the cotton. The cotton should be completely dispersed in a thin layer across the machine. This is probably the most overlooked factor in setting up cleaner installations. It is not uncommon to see cleaners in for repair with a large number of spikes gone from the cylinders, especially the back cylinder. This damage is almost entirely the result of the cotton not spreading across the cleaner. Often, this poor distribution causes the cleaner to choke or stall, resulting in serious delays. I advised a ginner on a problem with a ten-foot-wide cleaner handling about forty bales per hour, which is about double the recommended rate. Almost all of the

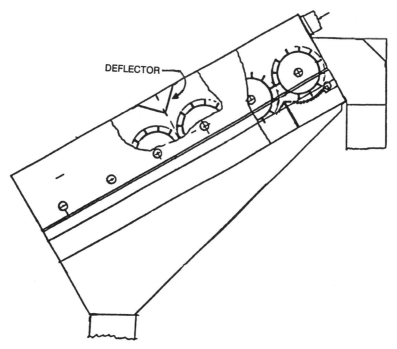

Figure 110. Deflector in the top of a cleaner to disperse cotton evenly

spikes had to be replaced on the back cylinder at the end of each season; the cleaner also often choked. Analysis indicated that the cotton was not spreading across the machine; it was reaching the back cylinder in wads too large to pass around the cylinder without excessive pressure against the spikes. The cotton was being conveyed into the front of the machine by the drying air and then blown back. I had deflectors, projecting down between the cylinders, attached to the top of the cleaner at two points (figure 110). Plenty of room was left between the cylinder and the deflector for a free flow of the cotton, but the flow was directed against the cylinders so that wads would be broken up and dispersed. With these modifications the cleaner was able to operate, trouble free, at a capacity of forty-five to fifty bales per hour.

With some cleaner installations, it is not practicable to use the deflector arrangement for entering the cleaner; in such cases, a splatter box may be used to spread and disperse the cotton across the machine. The conveying air moves the cotton against a flat surface, which breaks up wads and spreads the cotton to the sides of the box, where it impacts against the cleaner cylinders.

6-CYLINDER CLEANER

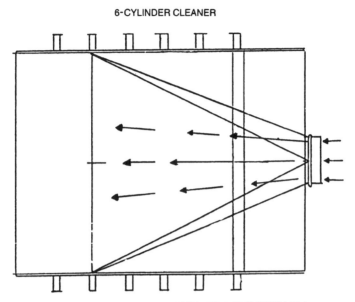

WITH THE CROSS SECTION OF THE RECTANGULAR SECTION 50%
MORE THAN THAT OF THE PIPE, THE VELOCITY DROPS AND THE
FLOW CONCENTRATES IN THE CENTER.

Figure 111. Top view of a typical cleaner with an inlet area that is too large

Figure 111 illustrates a typical cleaner inlet that delivers cotton to the machine by air. Delivery by air creates serious distribution problems. The desirable way to convey cotton from the drying system to the cleaner is through a round pipe at a velocity in the range of four thousand feet per minute. This pipe is connected to a transition section that changes the flow pipe from round to rectangular. The rectangular section width is the same width as the cylinder cleaner to which it is attached. The depth of the rectangular cross section should not be less than six inches to avoid bridging of the flow as it passes through it. The width of the cleaner varies from six to twelve feet. To illustrate the problem with this arrangement, consider a cleaner width of ninety-six inches. The rectangular section has a cross-sectional area of four square feet. Assume the volume of conveying air from the dryer is 12,000 cfm. At a velocity of four thousand feet per minute, the round pipe has a cross-sectional area of three feet. If the air and cotton spread across the width of the transition, the velocity will drop to three thousand feet per minute. In reality, the air and material will not spread to the width of the cleaner at this low velocity, but will spread only about three-fourths the width of the transition. A longer transition will permit better spread and more efficient air flow, but the velocity still would be too low for optimal spread of the cotton.

In most cases, the volume of air entering the cleaner is less than mentioned, so the spread problem is even greater. In thousands of such installations, the flow is heavy in the center of the cleaner and tails off toward the outside. This can be verified by checking the wear on the surfaces of the cleaning cylinders. The solution to this problem is to reduce the cross-sectional area of the rectangular inlet to that of the round pipe, which also will reduce the width of the inlet transition (figure 112). This results in the width being less than that of the cleaner. This change increases the velocity of air through the transition, forcing the air and cotton to spread to the outside of rectangular section. It is necessary to have a full width section long enough to permit the cotton to spread from the narrow section to the wider section. Once the cotton spreads to the outside of the initial rectangular section, it continues to travel along the line of the outer surface of the transition until it reaches the full width of the cleaner.

Figure 113 illustrates a cleaner inlet that I have encountered on a number of occasions. A number of these arrangements have been used with twelve-foot-wide cleaners. After passing through the tower dryer, the air and cotton are split into two streams, each delivered to one half of the cleaner. The flow in each line is between 5000-6000 cfm. As can be seen by the illustration, the flow can not spread beyond the width of the forty-two-inch inlet. Because each line only feeds six feet of the twelve-foot-wide cleaner, about 40 percent of the width of the cleaner is not being used!

I have replaced some of these arrangements with a "splatter box" inlet (figure 114), although this is not the only way a good spread can be accomplished. If the section attached to the cleaner and the elbow had been full width and the forty-two-inch transition attached to the center of this, there could be a good spread, provided the cross-sectional area of the rectangular section allowed for a velocity sufficient to force the cotton to spread across its width.

The spreading problem with cleaners that are fed through round to rectangular transitions can be improved by the use of V-shaped deflectors mounted in the transition to force some of the cotton to the outside. These deflectors reduce the effective cross-sectional area of the transition, thus preventing some of the decrease in velocity as the cotton passed through the transition. Although a more expensive method of improving spread, it is used frequently.

Another method to assist the spread of cotton when using the round to rectangular transition is to provide an air discharge at each side of the cleaner. It is assumed that moving air to the sides of the cleaner would also move the cotton.

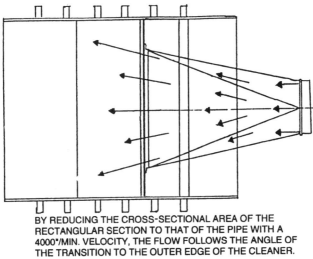

BY REDUCING THE CROSS-SECTIONAL AREA OF THE
RECTANGULAR SECTION TO THAT OF THE PIPE WITH A
4000"/MIN. VELOCITY, THE FLOW FOLLOWS THE ANGLE OF
THE TRANSITION TO THE OUTER EDGE OF THE CLEANER.

THIS CROSS-SECTIONAL AREA TO EQUAL
THAT OF THE ROUND PIPE

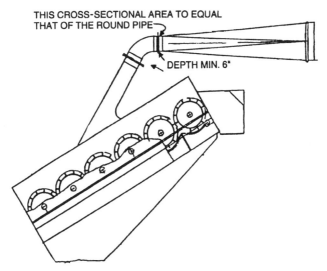

DEPTH MIN. 6"

Figure 112. Successful hot-air cleaner arrangement

Actually, this arrangement has little effect on the spread because the diversion of
the air flow is too far from the inlet transition.

In the San Joaquin Valley of California, cotton yields are high and the cotton
plant has dense foliage. When the plants are defoliated prior to harvest, the leaves
are prevented from falling to the ground by the dense growth and by the lack of

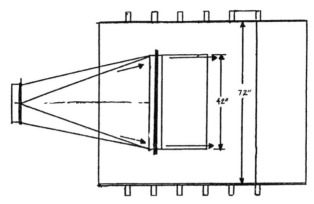

**IMPOSSIBLE FOR COTTON TO SPREAD MUCH WIDER THAN 42"
—LEAVING 40% OF CLEANER NOT USED**

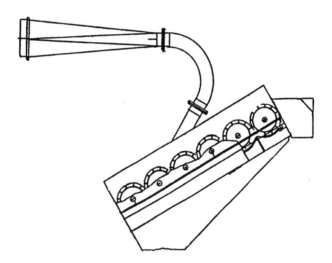

Figure 113. An inefficient cleaner inlet

enough rain after defoliation to "wash" the leaves to the ground. The leaves are ground up by the harvesting action and mixed with the cotton, which results in an excessive amount of leaf trash that must be removed by the cleaning process at the gin plant. Practically all of the gins in this area use more cylinder cleaners—in most cases three stages of cleaning versus two—than other regions of the country.

In the mid-South and southeastern part of the United States, where rains usually occur during harvest, cotton frequently is harvested with little leaf trash.

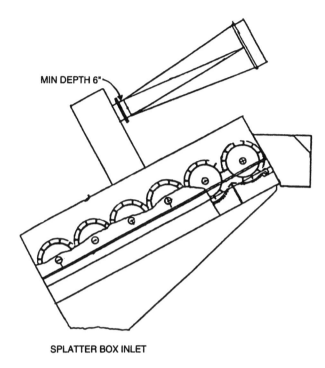

SPLATTER BOX INLET

RECTANGULAR CROSS SECTIONAL AREA TO EQUAL ROUND PIPE

Figure 114. Arrangement with a splatter box inlet

This makes quite a difference in the amount of cylinder cleaning needed. Some familiar only with the cotton grown in this region have concluded that cylinder cleaning plays only a minor part in total gin trash removal, that it only opens the cotton and prepares it for ginning and that in these areas lint cleaners do the majority of cleaning. This is hardly a valid conclusion for any area, but certainly not for the high yielding cotton grown and harvested with little or no rain.

Impact Cleaners

In the early days of machine-picked cotton, in an effort to find a more efficient method of cleaning this cotton, F. E. Deems, chief engineer of Continental Gin Company, copatented a machine that represented a major departure from the normal cylinder cleaners. The machine was called an impact cleaner—a readily understandable name (figure 115).

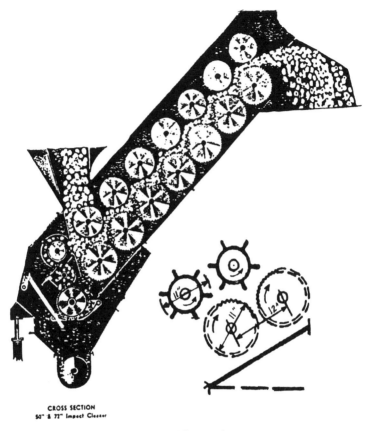

CROSS SECTION
50" & 72" Impact Cleaner

Figure 115. Impact cleaner

The screening surface was a series of rotating cylinders with disks spaced on a shaft far enough apart to permit trash to fall between them. Mounted above and between each pair of these rotating cylinders was a series of standard spiked cylinders. The cotton to be cleaned passed between the upper and lower cylinders and over the disks. The cotton was impacted against the disks by rotating spiked cylinders, and thus the name. As foreign matter passed between the disks, some cotton also fell through, and because of a forty-five-degree incline the commingled mass could slide down to the lower end of the machine. A reclaimer (consisting of a small-diameter extractor cylinder, a brush doffer, and a transfer roller) was located at the lower end to reclaim the cotton from the trash and return it to the main stream. This arrangement removed larger particles of trash than could be removed by the standard cleaning surfaces. The disks forming the screening surfaces were punched from twelve-inch gin saw stock with serrated edges to aid in propelling the cotton through the machine. These disks were stacked on a shaft with suitable spacers.

These machines are expensive to build and although they have been popular for many years, the extra cost may not always be justified. There is some evidence, however, that these machines may be less severe on the fibers than conventional cylinder cleaners, especially when a large number of cylinders is required to meet severe cleaning needs. Although the efficiency of these machines is affected by the moisture content of the cotton in much the same way as the standard cylinder cleaner, there is little roping of the cotton, compared with standard cylinder cleaners under the same conditions.

In the 1960s, I began to use the impact cleaner without the reclaimer. I respaced the disks closer to prevent the loss of cotton between them. These machines performed well in removing the large amount of leaf trash in cotton grown in the San Joaquin Valley. The principle advantage of this arrangement was the elimination of the reclaimer, which was usually a maintenance problem and added to the cost of the machines. Moreover, the machine could be set up without the steep incline, which provided for more flexibility in installation.

Although impact cleaners are usually considered more efficient than standard cleaners, their use alone rarely results in fewer machines being used. I suspect that the speed ratio between the disk cylinders and the spiked cylinders has not been fully explored. It seems logical that cleaning could be improved by having the spiked cylinders rotate at a higher surface speed than the disks. This would result in the cotton being drawn over the surfaces of the disks, providing a scrubbing action in addition to the normal impact action.

10   Seed-Cotton Conditioning

The science of seed-cotton drying is straightforward: the process involves nothing more than the exposure of the cotton fibers to air surrounding them at a temperature that will allow the moisture in the fibers to be transferred to the air. But the simplicity of this process is complicated by a number of variables that are always present in some degree. Among the variables are moisture content of the cotton; temperature of the drying air; rate of flow of the cotton; initial temperature of the surrounding, or conveying, air; volume of air in relation to the volume of cotton; the extent to which individual fibers are exposed to the air; and the length of the exposure time.

Efforts to dry cotton in the gin date back to the 1920s. By the 1930s, the John E. Mitchell Company of Dallas, Texas realized a smoother sample could be made if moisture reduction occurred prior to the seed cotton entering the gin stand and worked out one of the earliest successful methods of using heat in the machines. A small volume of heated air was introduced into the top of the gin-stand feeder, just under the feed rollers. The air was pulled out under a slight vacuum at the bottom of the feeder along with the trash. As in other early methods of drying, the heat was supplied by a small boiler/steam radiator system. These machines became popular; it was a method of drying that could be had for only a small investment, if reckoned apart from the cost of the feeders.

In the late 1930s, I had considerable experience with the Mitchell feeders and this method of drying. I knew that by putting more air in than was being pulled out at the bottom and letting some of it spill out with the cotton, the drying was much improved. This allowed the feeder to get hot; the cotton, too, coming out of the feeder was hot. On entering the gin stand, this hot cotton soon heated the machine, and even though the cotton moisture might be above that which would normally gin smoothly, the hot cotton, combined with the hot gin stand, produced a smooth sample. When no other drying was available, this system worked well, and I still have misgivings about abandoning it in favor of other systems. It was not a complete system because, as precleaners came into use, drying was needed earlier in the process. But having heat in the feeders could still be an advantage as a supplemental system.

The Mitchell company tried to use heat both during precleaning and drying in the feeders, but they were not successful: their precleaners roped the cotton. Much of the problem was caused by a lack of sufficient drying ahead their precleaning equipment. Heat in the cleaners can improve their efficiency, but drying ahead of the cleaners is almost always a necessity.

The Thermex feeder designed at Lummus in 1949 (figure 9, Chapter 3), provided for heated air to be introduced around the stripper roller over the extractor cylinder. The idea was for the air to blow back some of the trash entangled in the cotton, as well as to condition the cotton. The heated air found its way through the machine to the trash discharge in the same manner as in the Mitchell feeder. This feature was so attractive that a second extractor section was added and finally a third, with heated air in each section. These were highly successful machines for the two-bales-per-hour gin stands of that time, but when the capacity was significantly increased, modifications had to be made. This eliminated the stack of multiple sections and the hot-air feature. However, I still recommend that under severe moisture conditions some hot air be piped into the feeders.

Early Tower Dryers

In an effort to make the highest grade possible from machine-picked cotton with a high moisture content, all manufacturers turned to the tower dryer. Some used them to supplement their proprietary units (e.g., see figure 116) and some used the tower exclusively in multiple stages. There was little, if any, research into the selection of the proper size, shelf spacing, air volume, or temperature. In many cases, the ginner used as much heat as was available, whether it was needed or not. It was common practice to place the temperature control in the air discharge of the cleaner that separated the air from the cotton. The heater control modulated the gas valve to maintain a preset temperature at this control point—and that was a long way from the cotton's entry to the system. The control could be set at any desired temperature. Usually this was something less than two hundred degrees, and to maintain this temperature at the control point, the air at the mixing point would often exceed four hundred degrees on first-stage drying. As long as there was plenty of moisture in the cotton, it withstood this extreme temperature without serious damage. In recent years, we have learned that it is better to locate the control earlier in the system to allow it to react more quickly to changes in moisture conditions.

As mentioned in the discussion of the early USDA-type tower dryer in Chapter 9, a low conveying velocity was used—sometimes as low as nine hundred feet per minute. The shelf spacing was usually seventeen inches, requiring about 5000 cfm. Most of the plants in those days had a capacity of six or seven bales per hour, which would result in about two pounds of air per pound of cotton. This has proven to be a pretty good ratio, but the BTU content from the steam-radiator coils was not enough to bring the temperature of the air up to an efficient drying level.

When the gin manufacturers started making tower dryers, for reasons unknown they chose a much narrower shelf spacing, generally as low as nine inches; they also gradually increased the number of shelves to twenty-three or twenty-four shelves. These arrangements presented a number of problems, including high power consumption and a lot of trouble and expensive maintenance on the rotary seals (vacuum feeders). Fortunately, they have recently significantly improved performance by increasing the shelf spacing and cutting down on the number of shelves—ideas I put into effect more than thirty years ago.

Continental Gin Company made a dryer that consisted of the use of screw conveyor sections mounted side by side. These sections could be any length, but they were usually about sixteen feet long, with a sixteen-inch screw conveyor mounted in an enclosed conveyor box. Heated air, introduced at the inlet end of the conveyor box, followed the flow of cotton as it was conveyed and tumbled along the conveyor. At the end of the conveyor, the cotton was transferred to another conveyor, parallel to the first, and conveyed in the opposite direction, with the heated air flowing over and around the cotton. This was commonly referred to as a trough dryer.

Some of these dryers were two-pass systems and some were four-pass (that was the highest number of passes I saw, although there may have been more). These dryers enjoyed fairly good sales for a number of years, but they were never efficient. The fiber-to-fiber exposure to heated air was not as good as that in the tower dryers. It seems that none of the drying efforts that tumbled the cotton in bulk were efficient. In some cases, where two stages of drying were used, both a tower dryer and a trough dryer would be used, a different one for each stage.

Continental also introduced a counterflow dryer (figure 116), a unit consisting of a vertical box with spiked cylinders mounted inside in a vertical row along the centerline of the box, or chamber. Adjacent to the cylinders on each side were long metal strips mounted on the wall of the box, spaced so that air could flow between them. The cotton entered the top of the box, by gravity, onto the first cylinder, which knocked it onto the metal strips. These metal strips were sloped downward so the cotton could slide down them to the next cylinder. This process was repeated from one cylinder to the next. I believe there were four of these

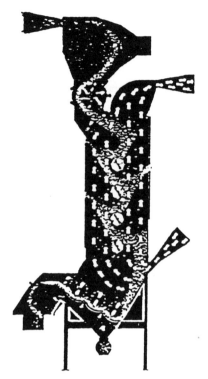

Figure 116. Continental Gin Company counterflow dryer

cylinders in the stack. Heated air entered the bottom of the box and traveled upward against the flow of cotton, thus the name counterflow.

The box containing the spiked cylinders and metal strips was mounted on top of a three-cylinder inclined cleaner of conventional design. There is no doubt about the merits of the counterflow principle for drying, but this unit was too small to be effective and the cost of installing it was excessive. These dryers, which sold through the 1950s, were generally made only in six-foot widths. Plants sold after that time generally had a capacity higher than this narrow width would handle. When I went to the Boswell company in 1964, they had several plants equipped with these counterflow dryers.

The plants at Boswell were 5-90 saw Continental plants, operated at about ten to twelve bales per hour. At this rate, these dryers operated reasonably well. As I increased the capacity of these plants, it became necessary to split the flow and in doing this I added tower dryers, placing the counterflow dryers in series with, and following, the towers. This was done primarily to make use of the three-cylinder cleaner under the counterflow dryers. The cotton and heated air from the tower entered a centrifugal air separator at the top of the counterflow chamber. At this point, the cotton centrifugally separated into the drying chamber; the air bypassed the unit and was piped around to the discharge of the dryer. There, the cotton reentered the air and was conveyed to the hot-air cleaner, where the cotton and air were separated. We used these dryers until all the 5-90 saw plants were replaced by higher-capacity plants.

In the late 1930s, Murray started manufacturing an entirely different type of dryer, originally called the Rylander. The name reportedly came from the man who sold manufacturing rights to the unit to the Murray company. The early literature refers to the dryer as a No. 18 Reel-Type Dryer, 18 apparently referring to the length of the unit. This dryer consisted of a large tube, five or six feet in diameter, with a spiral conveyor inside it. The spiral, or reel, was covered with a screen, except at the inlet end where the cotton entered. The cotton was fed in at the top by gravity and tumbled inside the screen drum by the spiral conveyor. As the cotton tumbled, trash sifted through into a trash conveyor in the bottom. Heated air, introduced through a long slot in the side of the tube, penetrated the tumbling cotton. In earlier units, a stack is shown at the discharge end for the hot air to escape to the atmosphere; in the later units, the hot air discharged at the end, along with the cotton, and served as the conveying air to the cylinder cleaner (acting as the air separator). As first introduced, this dryer had rather limited capacity, but as the capacity of gin plants increased Murray made a larger unit, the eighty-four-inch—the measurement referring to the size of the reel. In this unit, the screen was replaced by a rod-grid screening surface. This method of drying was never highly successful, primarily because the cotton traveled in large masses; the necessary fiber-to-fiber contact with the heated air was not possible (figure 117).

Early in the development of drying in the ginning process, the Murray company made a tower dryer, offered when a customer preferred that type of system. They did not make a serious effort to sell it because the reel dryer was more profitable.

In the 1940s, Murray made another effort to capture a larger part of the market with the introduction of a variation of the stub tower dryer over a cleaner. It consisted of a tower-type chamber with shelves, with a cleaner cylinder at each end of each shelf. The cotton was conveyed into the top of the chamber by heated air, then across the shelf to the first cleaner cylinder. The cylinders had screening surfaces behind them, and the cotton was carried over these surfaces by the

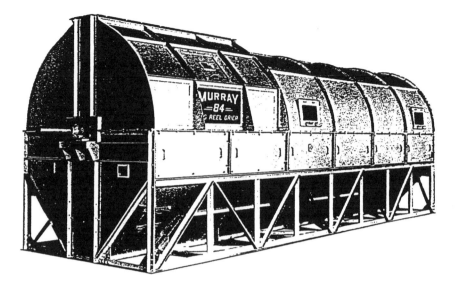

Figure 117. Reel dryer manufactured by the Murray company

cylinders. When the cotton reached the bottom shelf, it and the heated air were discharged into the cylinder cleaner under the unit.

This dryer, called a Multi-Unit, sold quite well; however, as the capacity of the gin plants increased, it did not have the drying capabilities to compete with tower dryers. The cleaning by this unit, with the cotton going around the cylinders at each end of the shelf, was disappointing. The heated air passed through the screening surface, which, it might be thought, would be effective in removing trash; however, the air, having passed through into the trash chamber, had to return through the same screening surface, and it brought back with it a significant amount of trash.

Another early effort to dry cotton was the Lummus Thermo cleaner (figure 118). This unit was unusual. It consisted of a chamber about twelve feet long and four feet wide. It was located in the cotton line between the wagon and the unloading separator (at the time this unit was introduced, cotton was brought to the gin in wagons). The cotton and conveying air were fed into the chamber at the bottom of one end, onto two cylinders that had blades mounted on a shaft at an angle so that, as they rotated, they conveyed the cotton. Above the cylinders was a series of vertical steam coils, spaced across the chamber. As the blades rotated, the cotton was pitched upward between the coils, where it became heated. By the time it reached the end of the chamber, a considerable amount of heat had

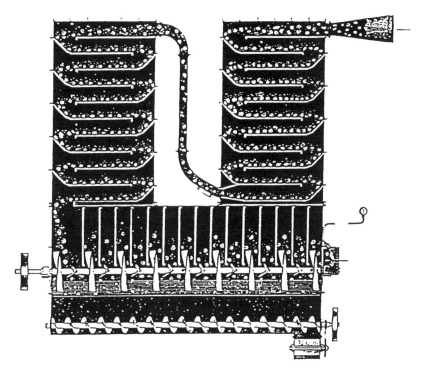

Figure 118. Thermo cleaner

been added from the coils to the air and the cotton. Although this did not remove much moisture, as used with the carefully harvested cotton of the 1930s, this dryer served a useful purpose.

After I arrived on the scene at Lummus, in 1947, more drying was needed and the steam coils were replaced by an eleven-shelf tower mounted on top of the unit. The cotton was conveyed into the tower by heated air and thence discharged into the Thermo cleaner chamber, onto the cylinders with blades, and conveyed to the discharge end of the unit. The heated air then conveyed the cotton to a cleaner, where they were separated. Often, two of these eleven-shelf towers were used in series on top of the unit.

Figure 118 shows the screening surface on the conveying blades. This surface made for an effective cleaner. The agitation of the cotton in hot air is effective both in removing moisture and trash and is particularly effective in opening bolls in stripper-harvested cotton. It is however, limited in capacity, which has almost eliminated its use in modern gins.

Figure 119 shows drawings of early dryers. These drawings present the basic principles clearly. Much of the early drying equipment was limited by the heat units available. Drying temperatures with the low-pressure steam boilers were low. These were soon replaced by direct-fired heaters, but these early units would only produce about one million BTUs. Even if the heat units had been available, there was resistance to drying from the classers and the mill buyers, who claimed that drying the cotton shortened the staple length. However, with the advent of machine-picked cotton, with its high moisture and high content of foreign matter, drying (and a lot of it) became an absolute necessity.

The USDA ginning laboratories had been advocates of low-temperature drying. When machine-picked cotton arrived, they did not adjust their recommendations. Low drying temperatures no doubt produced a stronger and longer fiber, but did not allow the cleaners to perform well enough to remove fine trash. The result was a lower grade, which was costly to the farmer. The manufacturers and the ginners had to demand larger heaters and use of higher temperatures to avoid the heavy discounts on lower grades, due to lack of sufficient drying.

The development of methods of cleaning the lint via lint cleaners relieved a lot of the pressure on both seed-cotton cleaning and drying. Whether this produced a better spinning quality at the mill is still an open question, but once the classers got a look at this combed cotton, lint cleaners became indispensable to cotton ginners.

Conditioners

In my first ten years at Lummus, we introduced a complete new line of successful gin machinery that included significant innovations. However, I was not satisfied with one aspect of ginning at this time: seed-cotton conditioning. I was fascinated and challenged by this problem. I wanted to find a way not only to dry the cotton (we were having some success at this with the tower dryers) but to be able to condition the cotton to the proper moisture level for cleaning and ginning, regardless of whether it came to the gin at 4 percent or 20 percent moisture. I also believed (as I still do today) that the power and fuel requirements, just to evaporate a few pounds of moisture from the cotton, were excessive.

I believed that the conditioning could be done in one unit—for both removal or addition of moisture—and went to work to design such a unit. My plans included a parallel flow tower, with a two-thousand-feet-per-minute shelf velocity. I chose a six-foot wide tower with a twenty-four-inch shelf spacing, making it necessary to move twenty-four hundred cubic feet per minute across the shelves. In order to add moisture when needed, I knew that I would have to work with a

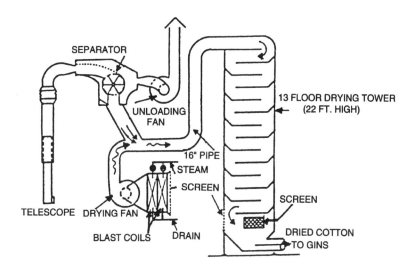

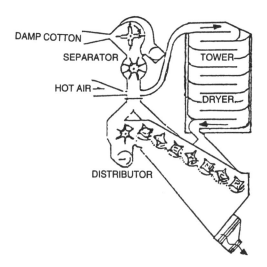

Figure 119. Early dryers (Top) the 1932 Government tower dryer, (Bottom) tower dryer and inclined cleaner, "push-pull" type (from Charles A. Bennett, *Cotton Ginning Systems in the United States and Auxiliary Developments*, Cotton Gin and Oil Mill Press, 1962).

volume of air far less than twenty-four hundred cubic feet per minute. A logical approach would be to use a smaller volume of air to convey the cotton into and out of the unit, and recirculate enough to maintain the desired shelf velocity. I chose to use six thousand cubic feet per minute as the primary air for twelve to sixteen bales per hour, and recirculate an additional eighteen hundred.

During experimental work, one particularly sticky problem was how to separate the cotton from the air to be recirculated. At that time, we had not made a separator to handle such a large volume of air. We had done extensive work with the superjet to separate trash from lint cotton, and had done some work with this idea on seed cotton. In view of this experience, I used the centrifugal method of separating the cotton from the air to be recirculated. The cotton was skimmed off in a thin stream along with the desired amount of air and a thirty-six-inch vane axial fan moved the larger volume of air back to the inlet of the tower. This appeared to be a workable arrangement, but it required field-testing. It was not quite what I had started out to develop, but I believed the unit could be modified for moisture control after it was tested.

Bennett commented in *Cotton Ginning Systems in the United States and Auxillary Developments* (Cotton Gin and Oil Mill Press, 1962) that "In 1958 the Lummus Cotton Gin Company brought to the market a combination dryer, conditioner, and cleaner known to the trade as a Super Volume Cotton Conditioner. This equipment is a good example of American ingenuity and development in promoting flexible apparatus for regions needing a variety of treatments, ranging from drying on the one hand, to cleaning, extracting, and humidifying on the other." The cross section is shown in figure 120.

The first of these units went to the Delta Pine and Land Company at Scott, Mississippi, in a 5-90 saw Murray plant that had a capacity of about ten bales per hour. The conditioner was successful at this capacity and created a lot of interest in the trade. Several units were sold for the following season and prospects for its future looked good. However, a problem developed with the air-flow, resulting in a lowered shelf velocity. I had been aware from the beginning that the vane axial fan handling the recirculated air had to operate against the static pressure drop across the tower (calculated to be about 4.5 to 5 inches WC, which was about the range of the fan). However, in operation, lint built up on the vanes behind the propeller blades, reducing the efficiency of the fan. In addition, the friction of the propeller blades against the lint sometimes resulted in a fire. To avoid the fires, we cut the vanes back, which further reduced the efficiency of the fan, and the shelf velocity dropped below a safe conveying velocity. A number of modifications could have been made to increase the shelf velocity. The most

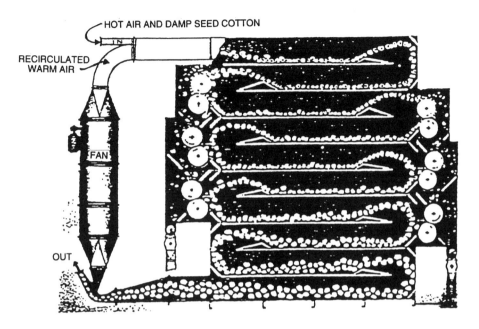

IMPROVED METHOD OF RECIRCULATING DRYING AIR IN LARGE
AIR VOLUME DRYER, SUCH AS THE LUMMUS SUPER VOLUME
CONDITIONER USING 24,000 CFM.

Figure 120. The Super Volume Conditioner

obvious was to use a centrifugal fan that would operate against the higher pressure drop. Before I was able to make them I left Lummus to join Continental. (I applied for and obtained a patent on this unit, but it was issued after I left Lummus.) Lummus sold this unit as a second-stage dryer because there was not enough shelf velocity to convey the heavier cotton through it at first stage.

Some of the outstanding features of this system I subsequently successfully incorporated into other drying systems: I have never resorted to the conventional tower dryer in the intervening years. The volume of air used for this system was unheard of for drying at this time. The shelves were sixteen feet long, but only nine shelves were used. At the end of each shelf was what I called a *bump up*—a device that played a important part in the efficiency of the dryer. As the cotton passed over this bump up, it was dispersed like a flushed covey of quails, allowing the individual fibers to be exposed to the drying air. I theorized that once the cotton was dispersed over the bump up, and had reached the proper stage of moisture removal, it would stay in its state of fluffiness and be conveyed on through the dryer in suspension, thus offering some measure of moisture control. If the proper moisture level had not been reached, the mass would reform into a batt-like layer and move along the surface of the shelf in bulk, until it reached the next bump up, where the process would be repeated. The cotton that had reached a moisture-removal level that permitted it to become fluffy and stay in suspension gave up its trash readily—which, of course, is one of the purposes of the drying process.

The large volume of air is helpful in getting a good fiber-to-fiber exposure to the heated air, but a much lower volume will absorb sufficient moisture if the temperature is kept at a good level for moisture transfer. At the time of the introduction of this unit, standard tower dryers were using about six thousand feet of air per minute for ten bales per hour, maximum, and the heaters and fans in existing plants were set up for this volume. I therefore chose this volume for the primary air. The primary air at this low static pressure had a low power requirement and the recirculated air also required low power. With the potential this dryer had for moisture removal, this could have been a cost-effective unit. The placement of a centrifugal fan (see figure 121) would have permitted recirculation of the necessary volume of air, and this would have eliminated the problem of low velocity in the tower. This arrangement was for gins of thirty-five years ago.

A further detail to mention is that a three-saw stick machine was attached to each end of the unit. The bump ups tossed the cotton on to the first extractor cylinder of the stick machine and the retained portion was doffed back into the flow going into the next shelf. The reclaimed cotton from the next two cylinders was doffed back onto the lower shelves. The problem with the arrangement was the low shelf velocity, which tossed the cotton onto the extractor cylinders in wads, making extraction not as efficient as it might have been.

During my stay at Continental, I had little time to devote to drying equipment, although we did devote considerable effort to temperature controls, which were sensitive to the moisture content of the cotton. We found (and this is still generally true more than twenty-five years later) that it took too long to bring the mass of metal—to which the drying air was exposed—to a desired tempera-ture; similarly, the time it took for this mass to lose its residual heat was also too long for controls to be effective.

Little work of any significance was done by any other manufacturers on improving methods of drying. The conventional tower dryer, with the limitations I have pointed out, was accepted as the standard. I believe that it was during this period that the Murray company enlarged their big reel dryer to an eighty-four-inch-diameter reel. This was an improvement (from a capacity standpoint) over the smaller unit, but it was never generally accepted. Some are still in operation

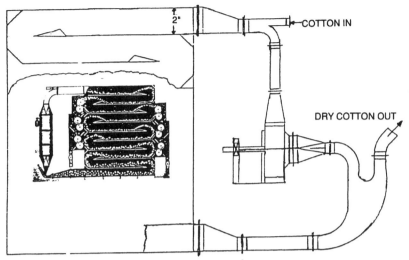

VOLUME OF AIR TO BE RECIRCULATED SHOULD VARY WITH
VOLUME OF COTTON.

FOR UP TO 20 BALES/HOUR, RECIRCULATE 15,000 CFM WITH 3
MILLION BTU HEATER. ABOVE 20 BALES/HOUR, RECIRCULATE
12,000 CFM WITH 4 MILLION BTU HEATER.

Figure 121. A method of recirculating air through a centrifugal fan

(mostly overseas), but even the larger unit is too limited in both cotton-flow capacity and moisture removal to meet the needs of modern cotton gins.

My next opportunity to work on conditioning came after I joined the Boswell company. In 1966, after improving the drying in the old 5-90 plants and prompted by increased capacities of our plants, I made my first move away from Boswell's conventional drying. I installed a six-foot-wide by twelve-foot-long tower with nine shelves on twenty-four-inch spacings. This arrangement operated at a shelf velocity of two thousand feet per minute, requiring twenty-four hundred cubic feet per minute—the same as the supervolume cotton conditioner. As figure 122 shows, bump ups were used at the ends of the shelves. This was one of the most efficient moisture removal units in operation at this time.

In 1967, we ran tests to determine moisture-reduction in the tower (Table 3). At comparatively low temperatures, this arrangement would reduce the moisture content from the 17-18 percent range to around 6 percent, although at only about 18-20 bph. The bump ups disperse the cotton at the end of the shelves, creating slippage. The only additional drying needed was enough hot-air exposure in the cleaners to keep the cotton in good condition for cleaning. The power required

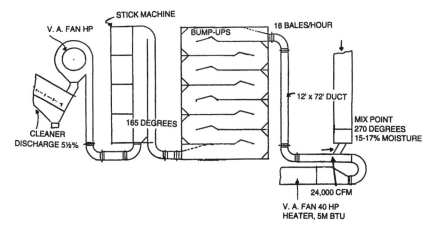

Figure 122. Six-foot by twelve-foot tower with twenty-four-inch shelf spacings used at Boswell

for each of these push-pull fans was only 40 hp. This arrangement operated for many years with tremendous results and today—thirty years later— manufacturers have come around to using higher volumes of air.

The temperature numbers from Table 3 indicate a temperature drop of about 100 degrees across the tower. This drop is not all due to radiation losses. There is also a drop of 10 percentage points in moisture, demonstrating that there is moisture transfer in the tower.

One negative factor with this arrangement is the BTUs required to heat this volume of air. However, because neither a split system nor multiple stages are required, it is economical when compared with conventional systems. There is only a forty-two-inch vane axial fan with a 40-hp motor pushing and pulling on the separator. The separator has a plain screen drum with a scroll arranged so the velocity of the air around the screen drum does not allow any cotton to adhere to

Table 3. 1967 Test results from tower in figure 122

LOAD	TEMP. AT 1	TEMP. AT 2	MOISTURE AT M.P.	MOISTURE AT 2
1	270°	165°	15-17%	6½%
2	270°	165°	15-17%	6½%
3	270°	165°	13-15%	6%
4	270°	165°	13-15%	6½%
5	270°	165°	17-18%	6½%
6	270°	165°	12%	5½%

the screen. The cotton discharges into a cleaner, in this case a ninety-six-inch-wide device, with a vacuum feeder at the discharge. The separator is desirable because of the larger volume of air. This separator and cleaner have been used since 1967, in spite of the fact that the plant capacity was increased from 18 bph to about 32 bph. This was accomplished primarily by the conversion of the existing 119 saw stands to 141s and the addition of a fourth stand.

For the 1967 season, I designed another combination cleaning-and-drying system in an effort to meet the needs of the 40-bph superplant we planned to build. We placed this system in our Melga gin to evaluate its potential. It consisted of "in line" ten-foot-wide cleaners, with a drying system using a high volume of air. The cotton left the tower dryer through a rectangular duct, ten feet wide. The duct delivered the cotton to a centrifugal separating unit; thence the cotton was delivered to a single-saw extractor unit. The air turned down through a duct adjacent to the one that delivered it to the extractor cylinder. The cotton delivered to the extractor cylinder was carried past the grid bars. About one-third of the cotton was slung off through the grids, along with a large percentage of the trash. This sling-off material entered a ten-foot-wide, horizontal six-cylinder cleaner. This cleaner discharged into a second cleaner of the same design, which brought the cotton back and discharged it into the same hot-air duct from which it had been separated initially. This was a efficient system. However, the testing of its ability to handle even higher capacities had to wait until the superplant was built.

When the supercapacity plant went into the final planning stages, we again had to look at a drying system to handle forty bales per hour (none had ever been designed). We felt we had a good start on this system from the results we achieved at Melga during the 1967 season. For this new plant, James Boswell made it clear that he wanted a system that would handle any moisture content in the cotton that could be harvested under reasonable conditions. Prior to this time, harvesting was delayed when moisture content was high. Boswell wanted to avoid this delay and to meet his requirement, we expanded the Melga arrangement to handle 50,000 cfm of air. To heat this volume of air, we needed larger heaters than those offered in the industry. Our normal supplier, Continental, got their heaters from McConnell Engineering in Birmingham, Alabama, with whom I had had previous dealings. I got a discouraging reply: they would be glad to sell me heaters off the shelf but they were not interested in designing a special heater. I looked for other sources of heaters. In 1966, Samuel Jackson had supplied me with a heater producing 4.5 million BTUs by combining three of his humid-air units. A simple heater, it had worked well, although it was not large enough for the present projects larger volume of air. I went to Jackson for help and he indicated interest; but he was not in the position financially to do the engineering work necessary, so we agreed to help with this problem.

We needed a total of eighteen million BTUs to heat the 50,000 cfm of primary air. The system was designed to separate out 25,000 cfm of the primary air after the tower dryers, discharging 25,000 cfm to the atmosphere through a cylinder cleaner. A separate set of fans and heaters was used to add back the 25,000 cfm of fresh air to the system, so the drying would continue through the system with a total of 50,000 cfm. We were heating a total of 75,000 cfm at the end of the system; 25,000 cfm of this air went to two incline cleaners over the distributor. The remainder was separated through another large-volume separator through two forty-two-inch vane axle fans in series, which discharged to the atmosphere (as at Melga).

The heaters were designed, delivered, and installed; however, we encountered serious problems with fires, caused by sparks, due to too much fuel being burned without proper air mixture. These heaters would have been successful for lower volumes of air, but we had a tremendous problem with fire throughout that first season. I decided to skim the sparks off centrifugally through an elbow in the line of primary air. We were using two vane axial fans in two lines (a total of four) with a six million-BTU heater following each pair of these forty-two-inch fans. Following the tower dryers, a separator dumped a part of the air to the atmosphere. Another set of vane axial fans and a six million-BTU heater added fresh hot air to the system. The primary air made a 180-degree turn and picked up the cotton under an outfit feed bin. In the end of this turn, I pushed the joint apart and placed a spacer in it, with a piece of metal to act as a skimmer—an arrangement that skimmed the sparks rather successfully. We were able to complete the season, but it was well into the next season before we got this worked out satisfactorily.

The next season, Jackson designed another set of heaters, using an entirely different principle for burning the fuel. Highly successful in producing a good clean flame with plenty of BTUs, the heaters featured a long, narrow slot, with the edges machined and accurately spaced to allow adjustment. These heaters had one weakness, and it caused them to fail. Impurities in the propane fuel would stop up the narrow orifice, reducing the BTUs produced. Somehow we got through the second season. For the third season Jackson again redesigned the heaters—an enlarged version of the heaters he tried first—and this time we had a much more satisfactory arrangement.

The plant had four stacks of machines: two of stick machines and two of two six-cylinder cleaners, making a total of two stick machines and twenty-four cylinders of cleaning. For trash removal and fiber quality, this arrangement was outstanding. Not more than one-third of the cotton was ever subjected to all of the cleaning. The arrangement proved to be efficient and the fibers retained good quality.

At the end of the line of cleaners and extractors was the large rotating screen separator described earlier; then the cotton split into two streams, each stream going to a seven-cylinder, ninety-six-inch cleaner feeding the distributor from each end with an overflow hopper in the center of the six gin stands (see figure 13, Chapter 5). This drying system had one negative factor: the high volume of air used caused a loss of BTUs into the air.

I designed a system for use at Boswell in 1975 in which only the air needed to do the drying was used. This was the beginning of the hot-shelf drying system (see later in this chapter). A large volume of primary air was used in the tower, but a high percentage was recirculated through the system (figure 123). A pull fan followed the separator and following the fan a two-way valve allowed used air to escape and fresh air to enter. This valve was controlled by a *dew cell* that received a pilot stream of used air from the return line (figure 124). The dew cell actuated a pneumatic cylinder attached to valves that allowed fresh air in and used air out. To pass the used air back through the heater, it is necessary to use some type of filter, or screen, to prevent lint tags from going through the heaters. A high percentage of air can be recirculated, but the amount will vary with seed-cotton moisture. Moisture content under 12 percent did not require any fresh air; consequently, the valves did not open. Although we did not have any high-moisture cotton that season, it appeared that 2000-3000 cfm would carry away sufficient moisture under most normal conditions: this was a hot-shelf dryer and the recirculated drying air temperature could be kept at good drying temperature.

One of the most important aspects of this system is the low volume of air being discharged to the atmosphere, reducing the cost of emission control significantly. If it is ever determined that the emission from the heaters is a significant hazard, the recirculation of this polluted air may prove to be even more significant.

After this 1975 testing, I retired from Boswell. The next season Boswell abandoned the recirculation concept and began experimenting with incinerating the gin trash, using the heat for drying. They chose this plant for the experiment and because the cost of heat would no longer be a factor, the hot-shelf tower arrangement was used as a conventional tower.

After leaving Boswell, I concluded that the hot-shelf dryer could be simplified by narrowing the shelves to twelve inches and using 12,000 cfm instead of the 24,000 cfm in the original unit. I turned to my friends at Elbow Gin in Visalia and from this work the present version of this very popular drying system evolved. One basic change coming out of this work was the abandoning of the parallel flow

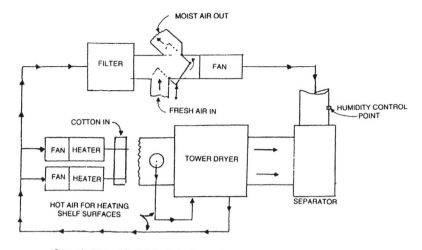

MOIST AIR OUT

FILTER

FAN

FRESH AIR IN

HUMIDITY CONTROL
POINT

COTTON IN

FAN | HEATER

FAN | HEATER

TOWER DRYER

SEPARATOR

HOT AIR FOR HEATING
SHELF SURFACES

Schematic diagram of Seed-Cotton Drying System with humidity
detection to control the amount of air recirculated. This system also utilized
drying air heated by conduction from heated shelf surfaces to maintain good
drying temperature throughout the system.

Figure 123. Boswell tower using recirculated air

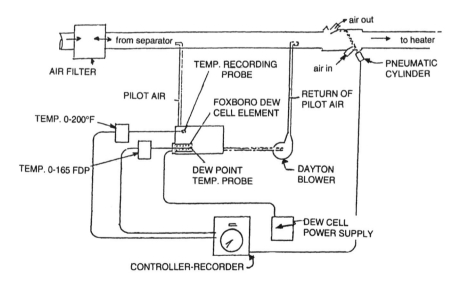

air out

from separator

to heater

AIR FILTER

TEMP. RECORDING
PROBE

air in

PNEUMATIC
CYLINDER

PILOT AIR

FOXBORO DEW
CELL ELEMENT

RETURN OF
PILOT AIR

TEMP. 0-200°F

TEMP. 0-165 FDP

DEW POINT
TEMP. PROBE

DAYTON
BLOWER

DEW CELL
POWER SUPPLY

CONTROLLER-RECORDER

Figure 124. Control system for air recirculation using a dew cell

of the heat-chamber air and the use of turbulent-flow air. This resulted in a much more efficient heat transfer from the heat chambers to the cotton shelves.

In the meantime, two other California plants had installed the hot-shelf dryer with the parallel-flow heat chambers, four units in each plant. One of the arrangements went into the Sayler Gin in Corcoran. This was the world's first 60-bph plant. The original version at Boswell was patented (#4,031,593). The later, and current, version with the turbulent-flow heat chambers was also patented (#5,233,764).

The basic premise of the hot-shelf system is to use lower volumes of air, reducing power costs significantly. The temperature drop toward the end of the drying process is avoided by adding BTUs to the drying air as it passes through the system. This is accomplished through an arrangement of heat chambers between the shelves; the heat is transferred to the drying air. The heat chamber air may be recirculated back to the mixing point, where it becomes a part of the primary drying air.

The present system consists of a six-foot by twelve-foot by sixteen-foot tower with nine shelves, seven of which are heated from seven heat chambers between them. The shelves are twelve inches deep; the heat chambers are also twelve inches. It is desirable to maintain at least a two-thousand-foot-per-minute shelf velocity. For the seventy-two-inch-wide by twelve-inch-deep shelf spacing, a minimum of 12,000 cfm of primary air is required.

The preferred arrangement is shown in figures 125 and 126. A high-efficiency air-foil blower with a 40-hp motor and a six million-BTU heater is recommended to supply the primary air. About 8000 cfm of this air first passes through the heat chambers and then returns to the mixing point. On its way to this point, it is joined by the other approximately 4000 cfm of the primary air to convey the cotton through the drying system. With the heat-chamber air at about three hundred degrees Fahrenheit, there is excellent moisture removal with a low mixing-point temperature. With the control point near the top of the tower, the heat units available can easily provide a two-hundred-degree control-point temperature and a two-hundred-degree temperature entering the cleaner, when needed for high-moisture cotton.

Figures 127 and 128 show the piggyback cleaner arrangements. The arrangement allows the air, which exits the tower at two hundred degrees, to enter the cleaners hotter than do other dryers, enhancing the efficiency of trash removal and fully completing the drying process. There is sufficient heat in the drying air to provide efficient drying and cleaning through at least three cleaners in series.

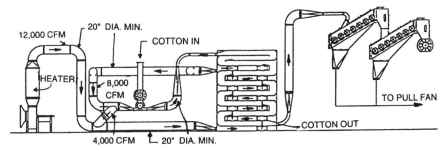

Figure 125. Hot-shelf dryer with turbulent-flow heat chambers

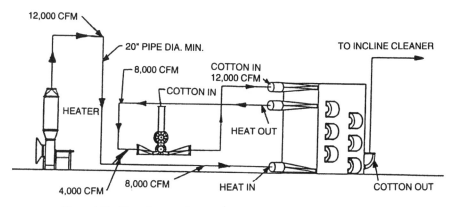

Figure 126. Flow diagram showing elbows on outside of tower for figure 125

The seal should be in the last cleaner, some of the air being removed through each cleaner by a pull fan.

Figure 126—a flow diagram of the above arrangement—shows the elbows on the outside of the tower, carrying the hot air from one heat chamber to the next. These are on both sides of the tower, with half of the air flowing through each set of elbows.

Figure 129 shows another (the original) arrangement, with the shelf heat entering parallel to the cotton flow. The shelf heat is supplied by a separate fan and heater, is recirculated, and is separate from the primary air. This arrangement can also be used with the current turbulent-flow model.

In these early units, we had difficulty sealing the heat chambers to prevent entry of cotton and trash. A cylindrical screen was placed ahead of the fan providing the air for the heat chambers; this screened out foreign matter that might

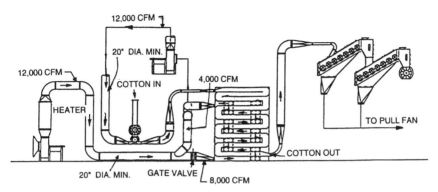

Figure 127. Piggyback cleaner arrangement

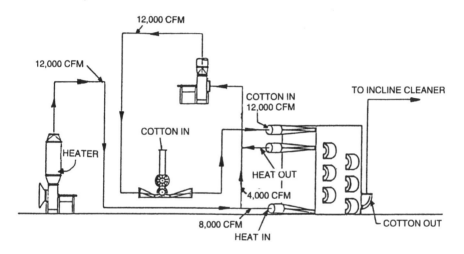

Figure 128. Flow diagram for figure 127

have caught fire when going through the heater (figure 129). This screen also lets in fresh air for combustion. This leakage is not a problem with the current turbulent-flow model.

As shown in figures 130 and 131, the hot air enters the heat chambers from elbows on each side of the tower and collides in the center. This collision of air is the origin of the term *turbulent flow*. Compared with a laminar (normal) flow of air, the turbulence creates a near-ideal environment in the heat chamber for heat transfer to the cotton shelves.

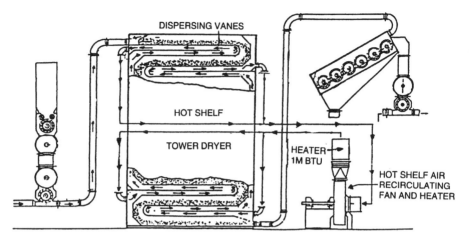

Figure 129. Arrangement showing heat shelf entering parallel to the cotton flow.

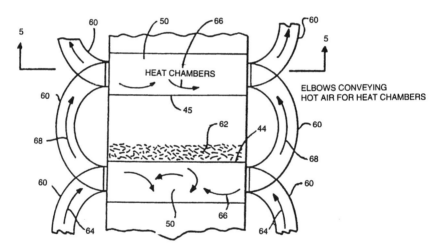

Figure 130. Elbows that convey hot air for turbulent flow

Turbulence can aid in heat transfer. It is in direct proportion to the intensity of the collision and the temperature of the air. With the 8000 cfm recommended for the heat chambers, approximately seven hundred thousand BTUs can be added to the primary air (air conveying the cotton) as this turbulent flow takes place. This can result in exit temperatures about fifty degrees higher than otherwise, raising exit temperatures to around two hundred degrees—where drying efficiency is three

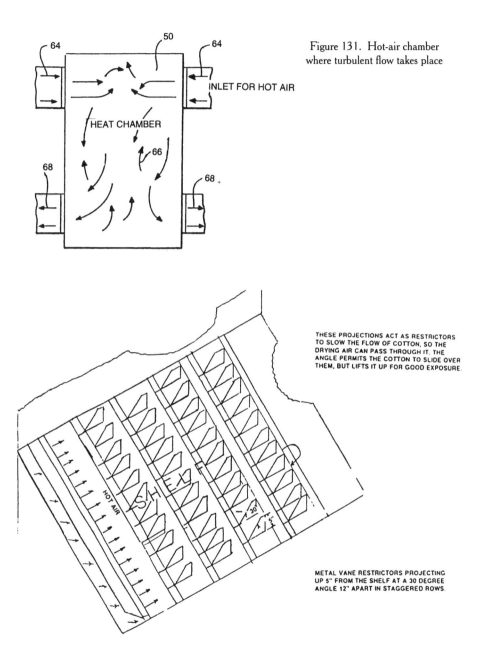

Figure 131. Hot-air chamber where turbulent flow takes place

64   50   64

INLET FOR HOT AIR

HEAT CHAMBER

66

68   68

THESE PROJECTIONS ACT AS RESTRICTORS TO SLOW THE FLOW OF COTTON, SO THE DRYING AIR CAN PASS THROUGH IT. THE ANGLE PERMITS THE COTTON TO SLIDE OVER THEM, BUT LIFTS IT UP FOR GOOD EXPOSURE.

HOT AIR

30°

5"

METAL VANE RESTRICTORS PROJECTING UP 5" FROM THE SHELF AT A 30 DEGREE ANGLE 12" APART IN STAGGERED ROWS.

Figure 132. Cross section of vanes on shelves, further expediting moisture transfer

is three times as great as at 150 degrees (figures 130 and 131). The hot-shelf dryer has been used for some time (patent #4,031,593), but the turbulent-flow feature is relatively new (patent #5,233,764).

Another feature adding significantly to the moisture transfer are the vanes on the surface of the shelves (figure 132). These vanes are fourteen-gauge sheet-metal blades placed upright on the shelves. The cotton rides up a thirty-degree angle over the vanes, which project up five inches from the shelf. The vanes are spaced usually twelve inches apart in staggered rows across the shelf (the pattern of placement is of no great significance). Without significant resistance to air flow, these vanes lift the cotton, allowing the air to pass through the mass and providing excellent fiber-to-fiber exposure. In modern terminology, this provides for *high slippage*. The vanes play an important part in the efficiency of the drying.

It is important to emphasize the dryer mixing-point temperature. Many systems using high temperatures to dry high-moisture cotton do so because of the heat loss as the cotton travels through their systems, although it is a well-accepted theory that high mixing-point temperatures can cause fiber damage. During a test of a hot-shelf arrangement in which only one fan and heater were being used for two hot-shelf tower heat chambers (and only 20 hp, which is not enough to provide the best heat-transfer velocity), we observed the following results: mixing point temperature on no. 1 tower was 260 degrees Fahrenheit; temperature at the control point in the second shelf of the tower was 175 degrees; temperature in the discharge duct from the tower to the cleaner was 175 degrees; the mixing-point temperature for the second tower was 260 degrees and at the control point, 190 degrees; discharge of the tower was 190 degrees. These observations illustrate that enough heat units can be added to get the cotton to the cleaner at the same temperature it enters the tower.

We also turned the shelf heat off to determine what the mixing point temperature would have to be to allow discharge from the tower to be 175 degrees. For the first dryer, the mixing point had to be 475 degrees and for the second-stage dryer 315 degrees to achieve the same 190 degrees with shelf heat on. High volume instrument (HVI) fiber tests were made on these samples and the higher temperatures showed considerable damage, as would be expected. The fiber length was reduced from 1.12 inches to 1.09 inches, and the strength reduced proportionally.

With all drying systems where the highest temperature is applied at the high end of the moisture content (mixing point), the high moisture evaporates quickly and the temperature drops rapidly. That is the easy part, and may be a high percentage of the drying needed. However, with the falling rate of drying, the falling temperature, and the short exposure, the drying stops before it is finished. This drop in temperature must be avoided to complete the drying in this short exposure time. The hot-shelf system avoids the temperature drop and does not quit until the cotton is through the entire system. These features enable a single system to remove up to 10 percentage points of moisture (other systems remove 2 or 3 percent).

In recent years, there has been negative publicity about tower drying systems. In *Design Precepts for Towerless Drying*, Sam Jackson stated: "Several years ago, the J.G. Boswell Company conducted tests which showed that the cotton fiber did not lose any moisture to the air either in the conveying pipes or in the tower dryer" (1987, reprinted by Cotton Gin and Oil Mill Press, 1989). His conclusion is drawn from tests conducted by Robert C. Eckley (consulting engineer, Corcoran, CA) during the 1983 through 1987 seasons at Boswell. The results of these tests were reported in a paper by Eckley entitled: "New Drying Concepts/System" and presented to the Beltwide Conference held in New Orleans in 1988. Eckley referenced the Boswell tests and stated: "I chose to alternate test shelves beginning with the top one. Each shelf's sample was run through a 10 saw test gin with an extractor feeder in order to separate the sample into lint, trash and seed. Each component was then placed in a sample can and sealed, oven dried and tested." He further stated that, much to his surprise, he found no significant difference in the moisture content in any of the three components during the time they were in the tower.

The key point that makes these tests invalid is that cotton fibers cannot be taken from a hot drying chamber, carried by hand to a small ginning unit, run through the feeder and gin, and not approach equilibrium with the ambient air. Essentially, all final samples will have the same moisture content. Researchers continue to repeat this mistake. Lint moisture at the gin stand is compared with that at the lint slide. Once the lint is exposed to the doffing air in the gin stand and lint cleaners and conveyed to the condenser, the lint moisture may be completely different from what it was upon entering the gin stand.

The manufacturers of tower dryers deserve some of the criticism that towers have encountered. As gin plants increased their production rates, in many cases no effort was made to adapt the system to this change. Twenty-three shelf towers with eight-inch to nine-inch shelf spacing are a complete failure at modern-day capacities. The pressure drop is so great that it is not practicable to force enough air through them to dry cotton efficiently. As evaporation occurs, BTUs are used and the temperature drops. This drop in most cases involving high-moisture cotton

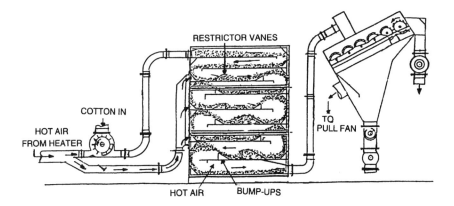

Figure 133. Vandergriff even-heat dryer (patent #4,143,470)

will seriously reduce the rate of drying. In many cases, a high mixing-point temperature will still permit the exit temperature to drop to 150 degrees or less.

The hot-shelf tower drying arrangement is a result of more than thirty years of study and research in seed-cotton conditioning. An attractive option for the ginning industry, it makes sense in terms of cost, drying efficiency, and maintenance of fiber quality. Its principal feature is its ability to add heat downstream to keep the temperature up to a good drying level throughout the entire drying cycle and into the separating cleaner.

The Even-Heat Tower Dryer

Another unit that adds heat downstream is the even-heat dryer (figure 133). The dryer air is split, with a part of it picking up the cotton at the mixing point and the remainder entering a chamber at the end of the tower. From this chamber, the fresh hot air enters the tower through one-inch slots on the bottom of the shelf. This one inch-slot, seventy-two inches long, will deliver 2000 cfm at a four-thousand-foot velocity. It is desirable to increase the shelf spacing for each slot to maintain the two-thousand-foot-per-minute shelf velocity. This 2000 cfm through the one-inch slot would suggest increasing the shelf spacing by two inches. Three slots are shown, which would add 6000 cfm to the primary air. With an initial ten-inch shelf spacing on the first two shelves and 10,000 cfm, the total volume would be 16,000 cfm. This is a larger volume than is desirable for separation through one cleaner. It is suggested that two or three piggyback cleaners be used (figure 127) with the hot-shelf dryer arrangement, or about one-half the air could be recirculated with the supervolume conditioner (figure 120) referred to earlier in this chapter.

An important feature of this unit is the restrictor vanes (figure 133). With nozzles blasting the cotton against the vanes, a high-slippage condition is created for efficient moisture transfer. These vanes are also used on my hot-shelf dryers. In figure 125, what appears to be a vane at the end of each shelf is actually a bump up, as is used in all my tower dryers.

These two tower dryers with heat added downstream are the most efficient dryers available today. The other manufacturers are finally recognizing that keeping the temperature up through the drying cycle is important. In some cases, this is being done by using larger volumes of air to reduce the temperature drop. One manufacturer is doing both, using a larger volume and adding heat downstream.

The Vandergriff Fountain Dryer

I have had extensive experience with fountain dryers. I supplied my friend Sam Jackson with an early design for a fountain dryer (figure 134), which he modified (figure 135) and developed into his own popular fountain dryer. I also designed an efficient fountain dryer of my own (figure 136). The cotton is projected into a tubular chamber and flows upward to the top. The chamber should be at least twelve feet high (fifteen to twenty feet is ideal). The chamber should be tapered slightly so that the top will not be more than seventy-two inches in diameter. This long taper is important in providing maximum slippage between the cotton going up and coming down. A strong turbulence will be created by the friction between the upward and downward flows. This turbulence causes the cotton to spin in and out of the two streams, making for a longer and more thorough exposure.

The dryer shown in figure 136 is a true fountain. The cotton enters the center and is sprayed in a 360-degree circle in its upward and downward travel. This provides for a far greater exposure of the fibers to the air. There is also a more sophisticated version of this arrangement (figure 137) that consists of a tubular exposure chamber, mounted vertically. The cotton to be dried is conveyed vertically at a high velocity to the unit by heated air through an orifice in the bottom center of the tube. An inlet velocity of at least four thousand feet per minute is desirable. The cotton to be dried is in suspension and will generally follow the action of the air.

A short distance into the chamber, the area expands to about three times that of the inlet nozzle. But the initial velocity will slow a little through this section.

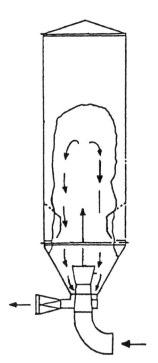

Figure 134. Original design sent to Samuel Jackson.

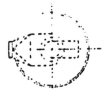

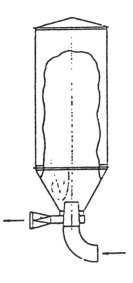

Figure 135. Samuel Jackson's returned sketch dated November 14, 1969 and labeled Vandergriff Conditioning Fountain.

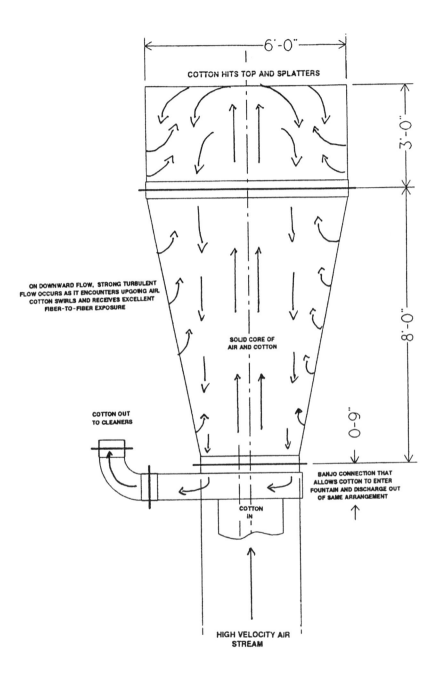

Figure 136. Simple version of Vandergriff fountain dryer (patent # 5,533,276)

Figure 137. More sophisticated version of
Vandergriff fountain dryer

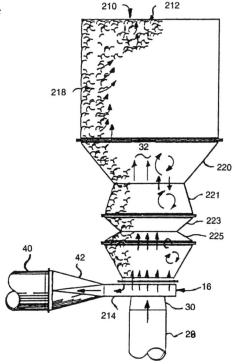

The flow of the air (and cotton) will be referred to as a *column*. This column passes through a slight restriction, creating a turbulence around it that is significant in the downward flow, after the column is broken up by blasting against the top of the chamber. Following this first restriction, the area increases for a short distance, adding to the turbulence (an important factor in exposing the fibers to be dried). The area is again restricted, for the same reason that the first restriction was created—each creates slippage between the air and the materials. The column will slow down as it travels through the upper portion of the tube—the part with the expanded area—but will maintain enough velocity to be blasted against the flat surface of the top of the chamber. It will then splatter to the outer surfaces of the tube wall. The diameter of this section of the tube is not critical, but a larger area will slow the flow rate for an increased exposure time. (The diameters at all sections ideally vary with the volume of material to be dried, which in turn suggests variations in air volume. I prefer an air volume of about one pound of standard air per pound of material. One thousand pounds of material (seed cotton) per minute

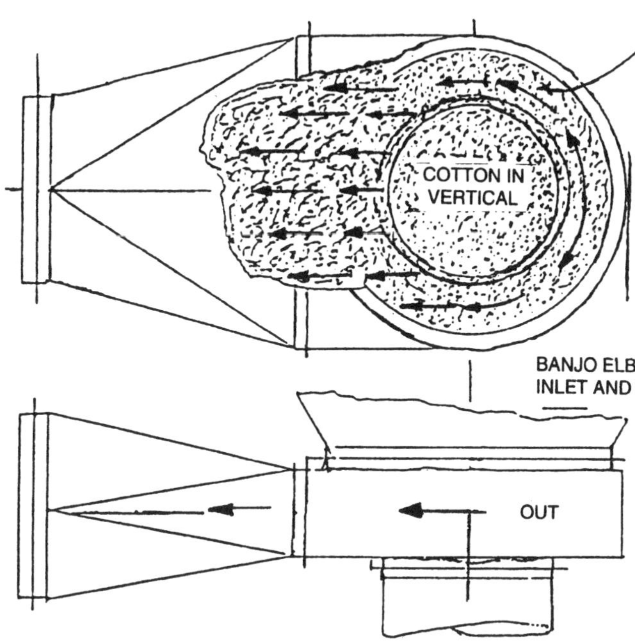

COTTON DISCHARGES AROUND INCOMING FLOW,
SEPARATED FROM IT BY THE DIFFERENCE IN
DIRECTION AND VELOCITY.

Figure 138. Banjo connection on Vandergriff fountain dryer (patent #4,845,860)

would then require about 13,000-14,000 cfm, and the seed-cotton rate would be about 40 bph.)

In the downward passage, the initial velocity of the air and cotton mixture will be greatly reduced by the reversal of its direction in the upper chamber. It will flow down the tapered surfaces leading from the upper chamber and the cotton will receive excellent exposure to the air, as well as being aided by the downward movement of the air. As the mixture of air and cotton enters this first restricted area, it is met by the upward flow of the rising air currents created by the upward-moving column. This will result in turbulence, causing the material to change directions a number of times. The resulting slippage between the air and the cotton results in excellent moisture transfer. The restrictions do not impede the downward flow of cotton because this air is traveling at high velocity, assuring movement through the restriction. The material in the flow is subjected to severe turbulence and direction changes, which provides thorough exposure of the individual fibers to the heated air. This arrangement is the ideal form of slippage between product and air.

Another unique feature of this unit is the manner in which the column of air and fibrous material enter and discharge through the same banjo connection; they are not separated by mechanical means (figure 138). The column of air carrying the fibrous material is rigid enough at the high velocity to permit the outward flow to discharge around the incoming flow, creating more slippage, and to prevent bridging. The slippage in this unit is far greater than that of the Jackson fountain dryer.

Vandergriff High-Slippage Dryer

I also have designed what I call a high-slippage dryer. Although the hot-shelf system is my preferred arrangement, this system is much simpler. To use the process of pulling the seed locks apart while they are in the hot air, which improves drying efficiency, I have devised an arrangement of cylinders with long pins spaced apart to permit free air flow between them. The seed cotton may be conveyed to the unit by the drying air and is directed against the pins of the first cylinder. The pins are rotating in the direction of air and cotton flow, but at a much slower rate of travel. While the cotton flow is restricted by the pins, the high velocity air stretches the seed locks. As the cylinder rotates, the cotton is released. As the cotton leaves the pins, it is directed to a flat metal surface inclined to deflect the mass into the pins of the next cylinder. Again, the cotton is restricted by the slower-moving pins, while the high-velocity air continues its pulling action until it is released to be deflected into the next set of pins (figure 139).

The action is repeated by the multiple arrangement of cylinders and pins. The cylinders are preferably spaced apart sufficiently to permit the cotton to be deflected upward into the down-going side of the cylinders to provide a longer exposure to the air. The preferred spacing is such that the space between them is about one-half the diameter of the cylinder. A cylinder made by welding three-inch pins to each of the four sides of a four-inch square bar is satisfactory.

This high-slippage dryer was a result of the success of the cross blow box shown in figure 140. I have used this method to feed cotton into the dryer air since 1974. This method of feeding the cotton into a high-velocity air flow eliminates problems with the rotary seal (vacuum feeder) at this point. (These vacuum feeders are often a problem where they drop the cotton onto a high-velocity stream of air. The cotton rides the top of the air and builds up until it is picked up by the up-going side of the feeder. This recirculation soon tears the flights off the feeder cylin-

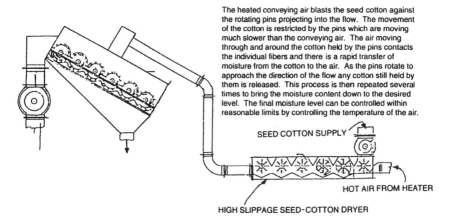

The heated conveying air blasts the seed cotton against the rotating pins projecting into the flow. The movement of the cotton is restricted by the pins which are moving much slower than the conveying air. The air moving through and around the cotton held by the pins contacts the individual fibers and there is a rapid transfer of moisture from the cotton to the air. As the pins rotate to approach the direction of the flow any cotton still held by them is released. This process is then repeated several times to bring the moisture content down to the desired level. The final moisture level can be controlled within reasonable limits by controlling the temperature of the air.

SEED COTTON SUPPLY

HOT AIR FROM HEATER

HIGH SLIPPAGE SEED-COTTON DRYER

Figure 139. A high-slippage dryer arrangement

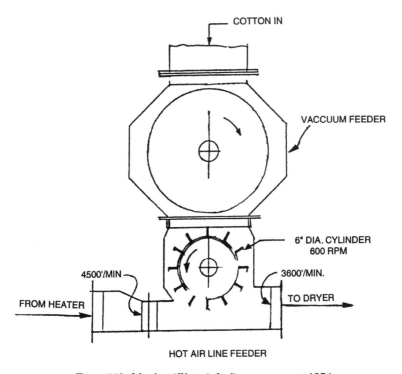

COTTON IN

VACCUUM FEEDER

6" DIA. CYLINDER
600 RPM

4500'/MIN

3600'/MIN.

FROM HEATER

TO DRYER

HOT AIR LINE FEEDER

Figure 140. Vandergriff hot-air feeding arrangement, 1974

der.) The cross blow box with a standard cleaner cylinder pushes the cotton into the air stream and eliminates recirculation. These units have become quite common.

Today, slippage is being exaggerated by some in the industry to the extent of forcing all of the drying air through the cotton held by the pins. This is accomplished by placing a scroll close to the pins and releasing the drying air through a nozzle directed at the pins and around the scroll. This is what is now referred to as a high-slip dryer.

The first cylinder in my high-slippage unit may be under the vacuum feeder and serve the purpose of the original cross blow box used in 1974. This is a low-pressure system compared with the high-pressure nozzle used with the high-slip unit. Of course, the cotton can be introduced into the air ahead of the unit if desired.

Air Conveying

Air handling of material is well documented in various publications. One theory promoted by industry authorities states that the hot air in the drying system has increased conveying capacity over ambient air because of its increased volume.

For many years, I have not considered the increased velocity from hot air as a factor in conveying. I base my theory on information from Buffalo Forge Company's book *Fan Engineering* (sixth edition, Buffalo, New York, 1961). The dynamics and physics of air conveying have not changed over the years and I have used this information for a long time. In the chapter "Exhausting and Conveying," the weight of the air, rather than the volume, is used as a measure of conveying ability. From the formulas used in that chapter, it can be seen that a weight ratio of air to material is used, not a volume ratio. Pressure loss due to air movement, conveying, acceleration, and fan inlets can be determined from these pages. These factors are all based on standard air having a weight of 0.075 pounds per cubic foot. Over the years, my calculations for air conveying have been based on using one pound of air per pound of seed cotton. This would be 13.3 cubic feet of standard air per pound of seed cotton.

A simple example of the use of these formulas (pp. 615-619, formulas 344-345) is to first determine the weight of the material to be conveyed per minute. For 30 bph, or about 800 pounds of seed cotton per minute at a ratio of 1:1,800 pounds of air would be required: 800 × 13.3 is 10,640 cfm. If we choose a conveying velocity of 4000 feet per minute, the pipe would have to have a cross sectional area of 2.564 square feet. A round pipe with this area would need to be twenty-two inches in diameter. The length of pipe required will need to be decided, and from this the pressure loss for air movement in the pipe can be determined. For each fifty diameters of pipe, there will be one velocity head loss, which at four thousand feet per minute is one inch WC. Keep in mind that the loss varies by the square of the velocity. If the velocity is five thousand feet per minute, then the loss for fifty diameters is $(5000/4000)^2$, or 1.56 inches. There are numerous tables and charts for determining the pressure loss for various velocities and pipe sizes.

An important factor to consider in pressure loss in a system is the loss in the elbows. The minimum loss is when the centerline radius is more than twice the diameter of the pipe. This results in about 0.25 velocity head, or 0.25-inch at four thousand feet per minute. Few elbows have a radius this large, but—and I want to emphasize this—the loss goes up rapidly as the radius is shortened. With the loss due to air movement in the piping determined, we can calculate the loss due to conveying the material through the pipes. The formula for this is (Ratio/3.5) + 1 × the air loss. In the example, the ratio is 1. Then we have 1/3.5 + 1 = 1.285 inches air movement loss.

Another pressure loss that can be calculated is that for acceleration. This is the loss resulting from starting the seed cotton to moving at the mixing point and bringing it up to conveying velocity. The formula for this is 2.25 × R × PV (velocity head.) In this example, R is 1 and velocity head is 1 at 4000 feet per minute. The acceleration loss then would be 2.25 × 1 × 1, or 2.25 inches WC.

The fan inlet loss is usually considered to be one velocity head, which in this case is one inch WC. However, many of the fan inlets in cotton gins have much higher losses, such as a short radius elbow on the inlet. Banjo connections also have high losses.

Many aspects of air handling are technical. Numerous publications are available. The one generally used by engineers I know in the industry is the previously mentioned *Fan Engineering*. I also recommend handbooks published by the American Society of Heating and Ventilating.

It would be difficult to handle enough air through the hot-shelf drying system to maintain the 1:1 ratio of material to air weight for capacities above forty bales per hour. For this reason, this system is not recommended for more than this capacity. However, it is being used for capacities of up to 50 bph with an air volume of about 13,500 cfm. These air volumes are much greater than needed for the necessary moisture transfer when the temperature is kept at the recommended level throughout the system. For example, to remove 10 percentage points of moisture from forty bales per hour would require that the air absorb 33.3 pounds per minute. Adding this water to nine hundred pounds of air (33.3/900) results in adding 0.037 pounds of water per pound of dry air. If we add 0.01 pounds of water per pound of air for the moisture in the ambient air, we have a total of 0.047 pounds of water per pound of dry air. From Table 2 in Chapter 9, air has a relative humidity of only 9 percent at two hundred degrees Fahrenheit. Even after absorbing this large amount of water, the air still has good drying capacity.

Keeping the temperature up throughout the drying cycle is important. If the temperature drops to 150 degrees, the relative humidity triples and the drying capacity is only one-third of what it would be at 200 degrees. Only the hot-shelf dryer can accomplish this. Others are using more than twice as much air and are not able to maintain a good drying temperature throughout the system when high moisture is present.

11   Condensers

Condensers were used in gins to separate the conveying air from the ginned lint and form the lint into a batt. They were an early logical development: in the earliest days, the brush doffing system of the gin blew the loose lint into a lint room or into an open space and the lint was difficult to handle in this form; hence, a method was sought to separate the lint from the air and condense it into what became known as a batt. This was accomplished by the placement of a rotating screen drum onto which the lint was deposited. The air escaped through the screen of the drum and out at its ends. This type of condensing reduced the volume of the lint and made it much easier to transfer it to the press, which at that time was outside the building.

When Munger developed system ginning, he made a condenser that received the lint from a battery of two or more gins and delivered the batt of lint to a double box press. This arrangement became known in the trade as a *battery condenser*. The housing of these early condensers was made of wood and to form a seal between the end of the drum and the condenser housing, a rubber strip was nailed to the wall and laid over the end of the screen drum. Condensers were made this way for at least fifty years.

An interesting story related to the development of condensers was told by my friend, the late John A. Streun, chief engineer at Hardwicke Etter. This story must be prefaced, however. The Daniel Pratt Company was established in 1838. About fifty years after the establishment of the company, Munger developed his battery condenser. In 1900, when Continental Gin Company was formed, Pratt became part of Continental, who chose to use 1838 as the beginning date of the merged companies. Thus, Continental Gin also took credit for the development of the battery condenser. This condenser was an "over-shot" unit—and another fifty years later, in 1938, Continental changed the direction of the rotation of the screen drum, making it an "under-shot condenser." Streun's comment at the time was: "It took Continental fifty years to learn that they needed a battery condenser, and another fifty years to find out they were running it backwards." Flash forward another fifty years and Continental has changed back to an over-shot condenser. At this date (1996) I am not sure which way they are running their condenser.

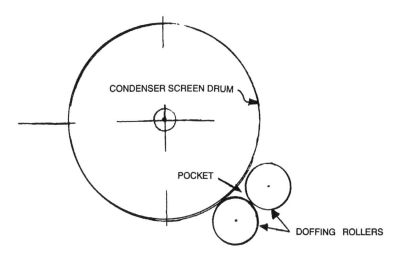

Figure 141. Condensers with two large doffing rollers

As long as the lint was delivered to the battery condenser by the air from the gin stand doffing system under a slight positive pressure, these units were more or less trouble free. The doffing rollers did not have to seal and doffing was improved if the rollers were run with a slight gap between them. This ensured that the batt coming off the condenser drum would thread between the rollers. Some condensers had two large doffing rollers, one of them having rubber flights to wipe the lint from the screen. This arrangement was troublesome because there was no leakage of air to start the batt between the rollers—especially so when starting to gin with only a trickle of lint from the condenser. This lint accumulated in the pocket formed by the two doffing rollers and the curvature of the condenser drum. The accumulation built until it was large enough for the two rollers to pinch it; it then came through as a wad of lint (figure 141).

Wadding due to no air leakage became troublesome when it became necessary to operate condensers with a *negative* pressure to accommodate lint cleaners. Not all companies used the rubber flights on the condenser doffing rollers to seal them. Others used smooth rollers, which worked fine as long as they were run slightly apart and under positive pressure, so the air would aid in starting the batt between them.

At Lummus in the late 1940s when we started working with the superjet cleaner, the battery condenser had to operate with about four-inch negative pressure, which resulted in a serious doffing problem. The condenser problem was not serious in the multi-jet because the gin saw doffing operation used a slight negative pressure in the condenser. The superjet arrangement was the first effort to operate a cotton gin battery condenser under high vacuum. To operate efficiently, the pocket between the three curved surfaces of the rollers and screen drum had to be reduced to a minimum. This was done by using two five-inch-diameter doffing rollers, which initially had a smooth surface. Because the rollers ran tightly together, friction turned the roller next to the screen, referred to as the floating roller, against the screen. The roller had to be mounted so that it could adjust to the thickness of the batt and move up as the batt passed between the rollers. The rollers were spring-loaded to permit movement in both directions under tension. In new condensers, the floating roller is now stationary. The lint batt passes between this stationary roller and the condenser screen, which has to have enough clearance to accommodate the thickness of the batt and avoid damaging the drum.

The condenser operated with two smooth rollers for a couple of seasons, but they were somewhat troublesome. We cut grooves in the stationary roller doffing the screen, which made the doffing action more positive, but it was still not completely trouble free. My staff, in particular Don Van Doorn, spent considerable time experimenting and designing a groove in the doffing roller to ensure that it would doff the screen and positively thread the lint between the rollers. This final groove design is still in use today, over forty years later.

The next step was to put gears on the doffing roller shaft. The gears were cut so that the rollers could spread apart as the batt passed between them. This required a special hob to cut this kind of variable pitch gear. We confirmed the industry adage, "don't run a steel gear with a steel gear," they will not last long. We switched to using one steel and one cast iron gear, which proved a much more satisfactory arrangement. Over a period of twenty-five years we kept experimenting with different materials—even rawhide. Finally, we used roller chain drives for the doffing rollers. When other lint cleaners came into use a few years later and a high negative pressure was needed for their operation as well, the problems with doffing and sealing under vacuum were generally behind us.

The other troublesome spot with condensers was the sealing strips or flashing that sealed between the end of the condenser screen drum and the condenser wall. I discovered that condensers that only discharge air on one end do not need a seal on the end opposite the air discharge. By sealing the end of the drum with a metal cover, the need for flashing replacement for that end is eliminated. Any lint that might collect between the metal cover of the drum and the condenser wall could be eliminated by placing air holes in the head plate, allowing the vacuum inside the housing to pull air through these holes, washing out any accumulation of lint in this space. A reverse air current generated by this vacuum could prevent any lint from escaping between the end of the drum and the wall of the condenser.

With the early wooden frame condensers, a light flashing was nailed to the wall—probably the most successful method of sealing this opening. However, when the wood was replaced with a metal housing, attempts were made to improve the method of sealing. Most engineers believed that a heavier flashing bolted to a metal ring would be ideal and last indefinitely. At Hardwicke Etter in the late 1930s, I learned this was not true. I found that the heavier the flashing and the tighter the seal, the quicker it would tear off. The tight seal pinches the fibers and starts a roll of lint that gets larger as the drum turns. This roll would continue to build until it tore the flashing off, or wedged and locked the rotation of the drum. The factory kept sending me heavier flashing, two ply then three ply. I was practically sleeping and eating in the condenser. I finally put some light flashing on the wall of the condenser, let it lay lightly on the end of the drum, and moved out of the condenser never to use heavy flashing again.

There are several methods of sealing the ends of the condenser drum that would take the flashing out of the flow of lint. One design would eliminate the flashing completely on condensers under vacuum: allow a reverse air flow to prevent the fibers from escaping from the condenser.

As to which way to rotate the drum, over or under, one company uses "under shot" and a doffing roller with flexible flights to wipe the drum. This is generally the simplest and most trouble-free arrangement. To use the same type of doffing roller on an "over shot" condenser is generally troublesome, because the air current created by the roller causes the cotton to follow the doffing roller around and back into the condenser.

There is one other aspect about condensers that has been debated through the years, and that is what size condenser to use, and how much screen area is needed. The area should be sized to handle the air. The volume of cotton is not a significant factor. The drum speed can be controlled to produce the desired batt thickness, regardless of the volume of cotton or diameter of the drum, but if the pressure drop is too great with the proper batt thickness, then a larger screen area is needed. Many battery condensers are larger than necessary.

Humidifying the Lint at the Battery Condenser

During the development of the first high capacity gin plants, one of the major drawbacks was the dry cotton coming out of the battery condenser into the press.

This low density cotton would not allow the press feeding mechanism to handle forty and later up to sixty bales per hour capacities. At the J. G. Boswell Company in 1968, we added a belt feed to the standard Continental pusher to improve the performance. However, we found that the low density of a big charge of lint would not permit the pusher that fed the press charging hopper to go all the way in. A layer of lint was left on top of the pusher and when the tramper foot passed the face of the pusher, this lint batt would be pulled between the face of the pusher and the press box. This would prevent the dogs from dropping back into position to hold the charge down. When the press cycled and the boxes rotated, this batt of cotton would occasionally lay over the top of the box and wedge against the floor. Its removal would cause considerable delay in the press completing its cycle.

It was not readily apparent as to what allowed this batt to lay over the top of the box. After much analysis, I concluded that we had to add moisture to the dry cotton to increase its density. Sprayed water had been used for a number of years to add weight to the lint, but this was only surface moisture and did not sufficiently increase the density. Also, water caused problems by wetting the metal surfaces. I was using Sam Jackson's humid air units to humidify cotton at the feeder hopper, and Jackson suggested that this humid air might be used to humidify the lint batt. I found that by blowing my breath on a dry sample, the moisture level could be raised from 4.5-5 percent to 7-8 percent almost instantaneously.

In 1972, I decided to try introducing air from the humid air unit through the batt just above the doffing rollers. Increasing the moisture content almost completely solved our press feeding problem. Most of our cotton was reaching the condenser at 4.5-5 percent moisture, primarily due to the low ambient humidity of the area. With this new arrangement, we could easily raise the moisture of the lint to 7-8 percent, and seal it in the polyethylene package. Boswell equipped their plant with this arrangement (figure 142) and over a period of intervening years, we sold millions of dollars worth of water. The addition of moisture also reduced the load on the hydraulic system and press structure. An added bonus was the mill customer liked the humidified lint in our clean package.

The use of this lint humidifying arrangement never spread in any significant numbers beyond California until higher capacity gins were built in other areas. Maintaining an even feed was not such a critical problem in areas where normal humidity ranged 50 percent or higher. Lint will gain or lose moisture from its initial moisture in relation to the relative humidity of the air to which it is exposed. The lint does not enter the gin stand at a given moisture content and come out at the press at the same moisture. The moisture content between these two points can vary widely depending on the humidity and temperature of the conveying air

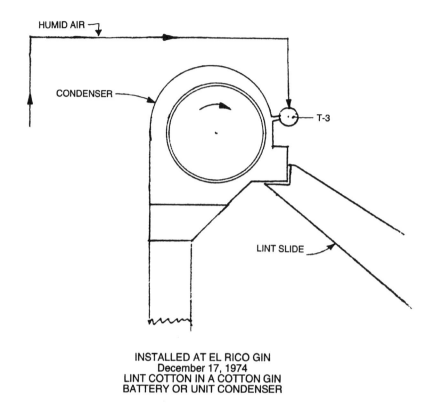

INSTALLED AT EL RICO GIN
December 17, 1974
LINT COTTON IN A COTTON GIN
BATTERY OR UNIT CONDENSER

Figure 142. Arrangement for introducing humid air above the doffing rollers

between the gin stands and the press. If the humidity of the conveying air is 50 percent and the temperature is eighty degrees, the cotton will reach the press at 6.5 percent moisture, even though it may enter the gin stand at 5 percent (Table 2).

It took some time before other high-capacity plants made use of this moisture restoration. One of the first systems to do so was Farmers Co-op Gin, managed by Carlton Hooper. He was a former employee of mine at J. G. Boswell and was well informed on what we were doing. The sketch in figure 143, is a crude arrangement that operated for over twenty years at one of his plants.

Farmers Co-op Gin established a condenser screen cleaning procedure whereby once a day, the back door on the condenser was opened and the screen cleaned with a steel wire brush to remove any wet fibers sticking to the screen. This procedure took less than ten minutes. The negative aspect of this method of adding moisture to the lint batt on the condenser screen was occasional conden-

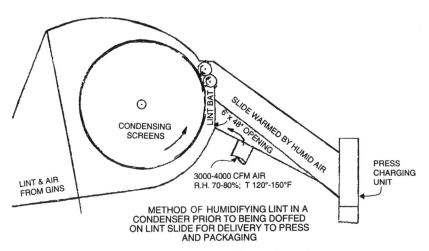

Figure 143. Arrangement at Farmers Co-op Gin

sation on the screen and sometimes the doffing rollers. Ambient conditions vary considerably from daytime to nighttime, and the air can become too humid when the temperature is low, such as at night or early morning.

It is difficult to control the humidity of the air. The wet-bulb temperature can be reasonably controlled by the humid air unit burner. This burner heats the water spray through which the air passes, and this spray is recirculated from a tank. The temperature of this water is essentially the wet-bulb temperature of the air. The closer the dry-bulb temperature is to the wet-bulb temperature, the higher the humidity. If these two temperatures are the same, the saturation point is reached and condensation results. Sometimes this saturation may occur where the humid air contacts metal surfaces colder than the air. Condensation from saturation usually occurs at night or early morning, when the dry-bulb temperature is lowest and reaches that of the wet-bulb temperature.

The opposite of this condition occurs when the ambient temperature increases during the day. The original humid air units would provide a wet-bulb temperature of about 135 degrees Fahrenheit. If the dry-bulb temperature does not exceed this, the humid air will give up sufficient moisture to the cotton. Sometimes the lint cotton itself will become so warm it will lower the humidity of the air as the air penetrates it. To improve this, it sometimes helps to add a fine water spray to the lint before it reaches the condenser to drop its temperature a few degrees. This of course is equivalent to lowering the dry-bulb temperature and raising the humidity (see figure 144).

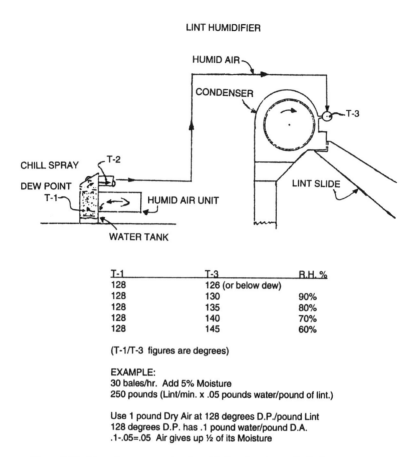

LINT HUMIDIFIER

T-1	T-3	R.H. %
128	126 (or below dew)	
128	130	90%
128	135	80%
128	140	70%
128	145	60%

(T-1/T-3 figures are degrees)

EXAMPLE:
30 bales/hr. Add 5% Moisture
250 pounds (Lint/min. x .05 pounds water/pound of lint.)

Use 1 pound Dry Air at 128 degrees D.P./pound Lint
128 degrees D.P. has .1 pound water/pound D.A.
.1-.05=.05 Air gives up ½ of its Moisture

Figure 144. Use of water spray in a humid air unit to lower dry-bulb temperature.

To compensate for the increase in the dry-bulb temperature as the afternoon temperature increases, a thermocouple was placed on the metal of the condenser near the air inlet. The spray nozzles were arranged into three banks, with a solenoid valve on each bank. At night and in the morning, only one bank would be actuated. As the ambient dry-bulb temperature increased, a second bank would kick in and a higher temperature would kick in the third bank. A fine spray nozzle was placed in the top of the humid air unit to cool the humid air if the dry-bulb temperature continued to rise after all the spray nozzles were activated. Without this system, sufficient moisture could not be added during the high-temperature, low-humidity afternoons. Jackson since has added features that automatically compensate for these changing conditions.

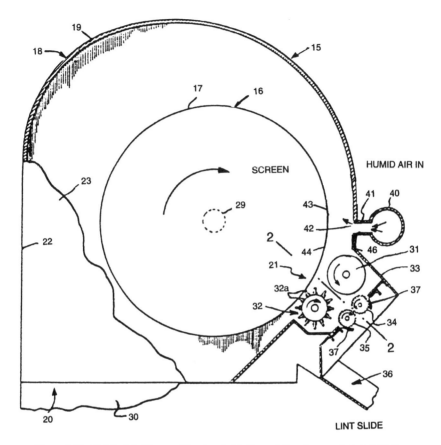

Figure 145. Original doffing modification, J. G. Boswell Co. (patent # 4,140,503)

To improve the problem of condensation on the condenser screen that would sometimes partially blind the screen, I designed a new combination of doffing rollers. A large diameter roller with stiff rubber flights was placed next to the screen (figure 145). The purpose of this arrangement was to doff the lint from the screen and wipe the wet fibers from the screen at the same time. A second large-diameter steel smooth roller was placed well away from the screen and the doffing roller to guide the batt into the sealing rollers. The original five-inch steel sealing rollers were placed in front of the large roller to receive the batt, wipe the doffing roller, and seal the doffing chamber against the vacuum in the condenser. They also compressed the humidified batt. This modification was done around 1973 and quickly became standard in all Boswell condensers, which were all of the overshot variety.

When Lummus Cotton Gin Company developed a press that would operate at high capacity, they encountered the press feeding problem on the dry, low-density cotton. During this time, I was acting as a consultant for Sayler-American in Corcoran, California, who had built a high-capacity Lummus plant in 1982. To improve the press feeding rate, I had them install the arrangement that was in use at Boswell (figure 145). Karl Smith Inc. of Corcoran, California manufactured this arrangement for them. This plant, with 5-158 saw gins, was capable of ginning at a higher rate than other plants on which this device had been used, so it needed some modification to meet their needs.

One of the most serious problems was the speed at which the small five-inch doffing rollers had to run for this capacity. At this speed, the rollers generated an air current that followed the surface of the roller and tended to carry the lint batt with it and feed it back into the condenser. To remedy this, Karl Smith designed an air chamber adjacent to the doffing rollers with a air nozzle that would blow the lint away from the rollers. The air supply was heated, which kept the doffing rollers dry as well. This proved to be successful, and Karl and I secured a joint patent on the arrangement to be used with my original device. This enabled the press feeder to handle a large volume of cotton. The press cycle time was improved to the point that the plant would operate at sixty bales per hour. I believe this was the first gin plant to operate consistently at this capacity. Lummus was so excited that they insisted on securing the manufacturing rights to the patent from us. There are only a few plants capable of such capacities and those that do use this arrangement, known in the trade as the "Hot Lips" (figure 146).

In my later work with Consolidated Cotton Gin Company, I had to provide a condenser arrangement that would humidify the lint to expedite press operation in some of the high-capacity plants they had been building. They used an undershot condenser, which uses a different doffing roller arrangement. I designed an arrangement similar to that described earlier at Farmers Co-op Gin, where the humid air enters under the doffing rollers. In this arrangement, large compression rollers were added following the standard doffing rollers; a modification that has proven to be successful (figure 147).

This is a much simpler arrangement than that sold to Lummus, because with the large compression rollers, the air chamber and air nozzle to help doff them are not needed. At the present time these two Vandergriff patented systems are dominating the field. In either arrangement, the bottom of the lint slide is heated by applying hot, humid air on its way to the condenser through a passage under the slide. The passage is formed by placing a false bottom in the slide forming a five-inch to six-inch duct through which the air passes. In some cases, a separate

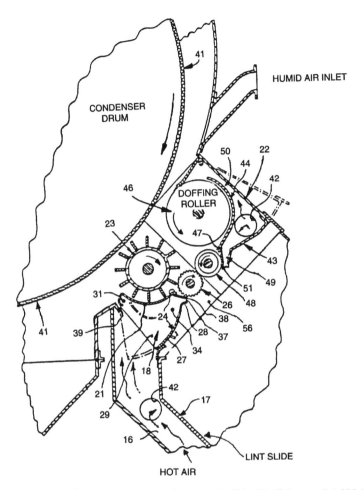

Figure 146. Sayler-American arrangement known as the "Hot Lips" (patent # 4,999,881)

source of heat is used to heat the slide. Heating the slide is necessary to prevent condensation due to the humidified cotton cooling and giving up its moisture.

The desirability of adding moisture to the lint batt on a condenser screen is well established. As we move into the mid-1990s and more super capacity plants are built, we constantly encounter new problems. A case in point is the thickness of the batt on the screen drum of the condenser. The thickness is determined by the speed of the drum and the ginning rate. At sixty bales per hour, what is the desirable batt thickness? Is there enough screen area available to permit this high

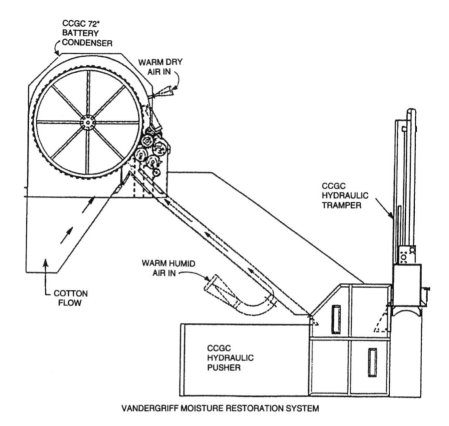

Figure 147. Consolidated arrangement (patent # 5,381,587)

capacity with its large volume of air, without excessive pressure loss across the screen? It has been common practice to create a vacuum of about five-inch WC from a vane axial fan in the discharge of the condenser to move the cotton from the lint cleaners and gin stands. Such vacuum is about the limit of vane axial fans. Today, centrifugal high-efficiency fans are being used to handle the larger volume of air from the large units.

These new conditions offer some interesting possible solutions. This discussion is about battery condensers, not unit condensers. I have found that approximately 0.20 to 0.30 pounds of lint per square foot of batt from a battery condenser is a reasonable thickness that will let air flow through with an acceptable resistance. A seventy-two-inch condenser with the drum running at 20 rpm, receiving lint at the rate of forty bales per hour would have a batt thickness of about 0.20 pounds per square foot. This is a reasonable batt thickness, although it would vary due to operator preference. To maintain a 0.20 batt thickness at sixty bales per hour, it would be necessary to have a seventy-two-inch condenser drum run at 30 rpm, instead of 20 rpm, or about five hundred feet per minute batt speed. If the drum speed is maintained at 20 rpm, the batt would weigh 0.30 pounds per square foot. This thicker batt offers significantly more resistance to air flow, creating a problem. This resistance also varies with the screen area exposed and condenser design. Some condensers of the undershot type have a large part of the screen blocked off to control the batt uniformity. Some condenser designs block off too much of the screen area to handle the air, lint volume, or both, causing excessive resistance to the air flow. This pressure loss across the screen drum maybe several inches WC resulting in excessive power requirements and more problems with the doffing.

One factor in the pressure loss in some of the undershot condensers is the way the air and lint are applied. Figure 148 is a commonly used undershot condenser. Note that the air and lint are directed at the screen furthermost from the doffing rollers. As the screen drum rotates, clean screen is exposed. But the lint immediately blocks this clean screen, forcing the air to pass through the batt on the screen drum. Figure 149 shows the same condenser with the inlet transition reversed, so that the air and lint are directed at the area toward the doffing rollers. The lint will essentially continue its initial direction, while most of the air can discharge through the clean screen with low resistance. This can make a significant difference in the pressure loss across the condenser screen, saving power and permitting the doffing arrangement to operate more trouble free.

Another significant factor affecting condensers in high capacity plants, is the large volume of air. This volume may be in the range of 50,000-60,000 cfm, and may be even higher when the cotton from each gin stand is split into two lint cleaners. This makes it necessary for the condenser to handle the air from eight or ten lint cleaners. With four or five stand plants, a simple solution to this problem would be to skim off the desired amount of the air ahead of the condenser and let this air go directly to the condenser fan, or another fan. A method of accomplishing this is shown in figure 150. This skimmer can be placed in any convenient place, but most likely under, or near the condenser would be preferable. A variation of this would be to return the air to the top of the condenser (see figure 151).

When humidifying lint in this undershot condenser, warm air is usually pushed in the top of the condenser to pass it through the screen and remove any free moisture that has condensed from the humid air. Putting this large volume of air through the screen eliminates the problem with raw moisture on the screen. And, if for no other reason, it would be practical to skim off some of the air into the top of the condenser for this purpose.

A condensing and air separating unit, operating under vacuum, having a rotating screen drum with doffing rollers which doff the bat of fibers into the atmosphere of the condensing chamber, permitting the screen doffing rollers to perform the doffing action without having to perform the troublesome function of sealing against the pressure difference inside and outside the condensing chamber. Humid air is forced through the bat ahead of the doffing rollers to raise the moisture content to about 8%. The bat passes from the doffing rollers to a pair of sealing and compression rollers where it is compressed to reduce its density to aid pressing and packaging.

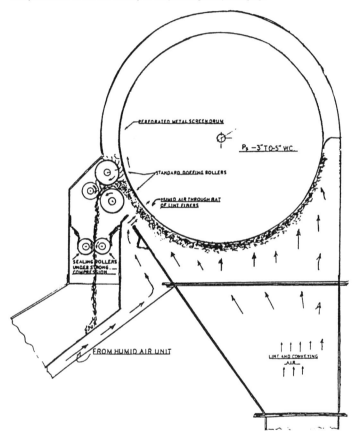

Figure 148. Consolidated Cotton Gin Co. Condenser

Some manufacturers have built and are building battery condensers with screens as large as ninety inches (or larger) in diameter to handle up to 80,000 cfm. Screen drums of eighty inches in diameter are now common. These large diameter units make it difficult to maintain accuracy and are expensive to build. When subjected to six-inch to ten-inch vacuum, the walls of the unit have to be

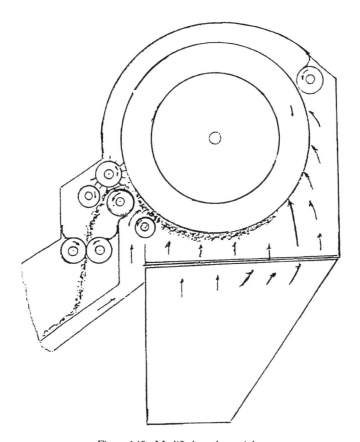

Figure 149. Modified condenser inlet

extremely rigid to avoid collapse. With the use of this skimmer arrangement, the
need for these super large condensers is eliminated. In the future, I am sure we
will see this arrangement used extensively with fifty-inch and sixty-inch condensers
replacing the super size.

The concept of adding moisture to the cotton via the condenser has been of
great benefit to the industry. It removed one of the great bottlenecks to high capacity
by allowing the press to handle higher volumes of cotton, increasing the capacity
of the plant tremendously. Starting with the first forty-bale-per-hour plant at
Boswell in the late 60s, to plants operating at sixty bales per hour today. Who can
fathom what is next. One thing is for sure, it would be difficult if not impossible
to obtain high capacities without applying humid air at the condenser prior to batt

TO CONDENSER

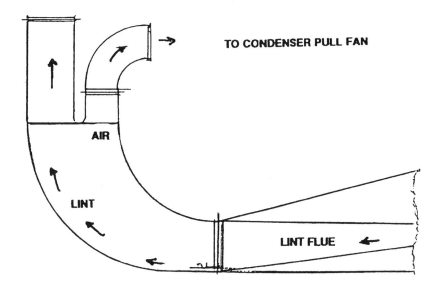

Figure 150. Means to reduce the air volume going to a battery condenser

compression. The added moisture is also welcomed by the textile mills, who prefer cotton packaged at levels of around 8 percent moisture. The final benefit and one of equal importance is the benefit of adding weight to the lint cotton in the form of moisture, which allows the grower to sell this, adding to profits substantially.

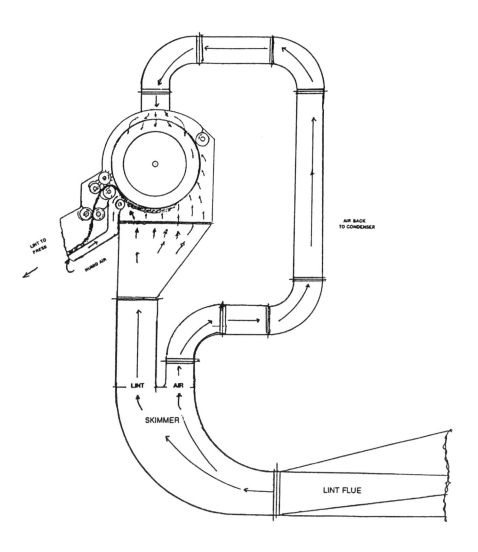

Figure 151. Variation that passes air to the top of the condenser

12 Roller Ginning

Early History

The growth and use of cotton dates back to at least the fourth century BC. Before the process became mechanized, cotton fibers were separated from the seeds by hand. Hand pulling the lint from the seed was a very slow process. The earliest means of mechanically removing the lint from the seed was that of pinching the lint between two rotating small-diameter sticks. The sticks were about three-quarters of an inch in diameter, small enough to reject the seed and pull the lint off the seed. The sticks were powered by hand in various ways, and rolling the lint between two sticks is no doubt the origin of the term *roller ginning*.

The first cotton produced in the United States was of the sea-island variety. Sea-island cotton is an extra-long staple cotton with what is known as black seed. The cotton fibers are only attached to one end of the seed and are easy to remove. On plantations in the United States slaves were used to hand-pull long-staple cotton from the seed but they could only supply a very small amount of lint for the market. This variety of cotton is almost always roller ginned. When this long-staple black seed cotton is saw ginned, it has a distinctly different appearance from the roller-ginned cotton because the fibers are not firmly attached to the seed. Textile mills have no standards by which to judge this different appearance and thus, it is deemed not suitable for saw ginning. In comparison, the seeds of upland varieties of cotton have fibers attached all over—usually referred to as fuzzy seed. The users of upland cotton ginned on a roller gin have had the same problem with a lack of standards for classing the cotton. Over the long history of roller ginning, thousands of variations of methods of mechanically rolling the lint off the seed have been used.

In 1840, the McCarthy Roller Gin was patented and became the dominant roller gin for many years to come. The patented method positioned a stationary knife tightly against a ginning roller and a reciprocating knife blade was used to dislodge the seed from the pinch point (see figure 152). This same principle is used in modern-day roller ginning.

The stationary knife on the McCarthy unit was mounted vertically with the ginning edge pointing down. The moving blade was mounted in guides on each end of the frame. It was moved up and down by means of an eccentric arrangement

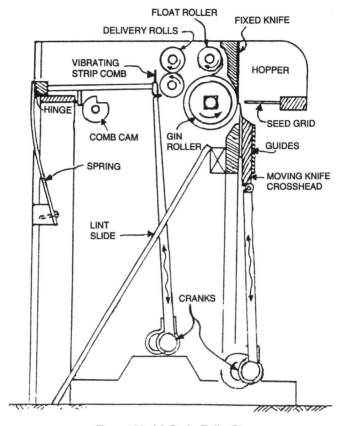

Figure 152. McCarthy Roller Gin

on a rotating shaft near the bottom of the frame. The moving knife traveled over the stationary knife pushing the seed a distance of about one half the staple length of the cotton (this distance is known as "overlap") and then returned to a position below the edge of the stationary knife. The overlap had to be adjustable to accommodate cotton of significantly different staple lengths.

The reason for releasing the seed at a position of about one half the length of the staple is to permit the seed to return to the stationary knife edge. At this stage, the seed still has fibers attached at the point of release. These fibers are pinched between the stationary knife and the ginning rollers, which pulls the seed back to the knife. The remaining fibers are then removed. If the overlap is too great, the seed may be pushed off with the fibers still attached and the seed would not be fully ginned. The speed of reciprocation of the moving knife on the early gins was probably in the range of four hundred oscillations per minute.

The ginning roller was composed of coarse leather, grooved to permit motes and other foreign objects to pass under the knife. The first gins had rollers with a diameter of about four inches. However, they were soon increased to about seven inches in diameter. Cotton was fed to the ginning roller from a rack mounted in the frame opposite the moving and stationary knives. A mechanically operated pusher pushed the cotton against the ginning roll between the strokes of the moving knife. This rack also had grids that allowed the seed to fall through (figure 153). Although the feed through this opening was intermittent, a continuous batt could still be deposited on the ginning roller.

For a period of well over one hundred years, this type of roller gin with the reciprocating knife was the predominant form used and its use spread throughout the world. It is still used today in many areas outside the United States. In the United States, improvements such as methods of feeding, larger ginning rollers that can run at higher speeds, better mechanical parts to permit higher speeds of the reciprocating knife, and preparation of cotton by pre-cleaning and drying have all contributed to its increased efficiency. Other countries throughout the Middle East, Egypt, and Sudan, for example, still produce gins using the reciprocating principle in various forms. Because the capacity of this type of gin is low per unit, many units are needed to make up a plant. It is not uncommon to find them used in batteries of one hundred or more units.

Since their invention, mechanics, engineers, ginners, and others were constantly striving to improve the capacity of these low-production roller gins. There were many efforts to replace the reciprocating knife with a rotary knife. Many of these efforts are covered by patents but none reached commercial success.

A promising effort to replace the reciprocating knife in the McCarthy gin was made in the late 1950s by the personnel at the USDA ginning laboratory in Messilla Park, New Mexico. They developed and made a pilot model of a roller gin called a Flight Bar Gin (see figure 154). It had a series of bars mounted on a pair of chains, the bars running parallel to the stationary knife. The bars were spaced apart so that as they moved over the knife, they would push the seed off the knife. The chain continued around a sprocket located so that the bar would pull away from the knife to release the seed at the proper overlap. The cotton was fed to the ginning roller between the bars.

This design had one serious mechanical fault that was not evident in the pilot model. After only a short period of operation, the wear on the chain and the sprockets was enough to let the bars rotate and slide over the seed on the knife

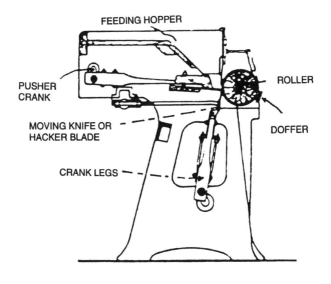

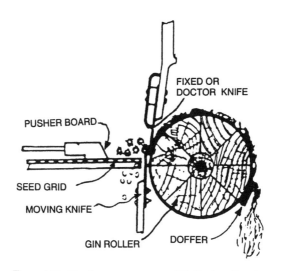

Figure 153. Feeding arrangement on McCarthy roller gin

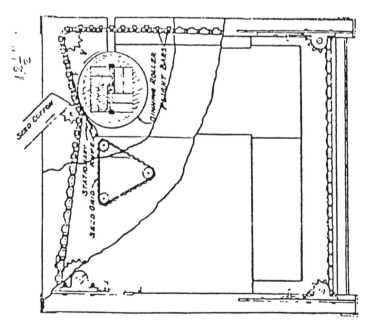

Figure 154. USDA Flight Bar Gin

surface. At this point it became necessary to tighten the chain, but this occurred too often to make the operation practical under actual field conditions.

I was president of Continental Gin Company at this time and we believed in the merits of this USDA prototype unit. Accordingly, several full-sized units were built and incorporated in two gin plants. The plants were built in 1962 and when operated under normal conditions, these units did not function efficiently. Unless we could come up with some successful modifications, the company would have suffered a substantial loss.

I had some knowledge of the old reciprocating knife roller gins and I was aware of the overlap principle. I thought about exploring the possibility of using a rotating member to replace the moving knife that removed the seed from the ginning point. I knew that as far back as 1872, rotating knives of various types had been tried without much success, but none of them had taken into consideration the critical overlap feature. I experimented first with long-staple cotton with a critical overlap of three-quarters of an inch; that is the seed should be released after it traveled about three-quarters of an inch over the surface of the knife. I found that using one-half-inch blades on a $1^{15}/16$-inch diameter shaft or a $2^{15}/16$-inch OD cylinder, would move the seed three-quarters·of an inch from the ginning edge of the knife leaving it slightly less than one-quarter inch away from the surface of the knife. The release point would vary with the taper on the top surface of the knife. I had a six-blade rotary knife made up—the number an arbitrary figure chosen as a manufacturing convenience.

At this time, we had a Flight Bar Gin in our experimental plant. The chains and sprockets were removed and this six-blade rotabar was mounted in the ginning position. I have vivid recollections of this because it was installed and tested on Thanksgiving Day in 1962. The ginning roller and stationary knife arrangement was not changed and remains today about the same as it was in the Flight Bar Gin. Despite the simplicity of the arrangement—no chains, no reciprocating knifes—the results incorporating the rotabar feature were outstanding.

The chief engineer of Hardwicke Etter watched the installation of this first unit carefully and, after seeing our results, converted their gins almost as fast as ours. Hardwicke Etter applied for a patent for this modified gin before I did and, although they did not try to patent the rotabar, their application did cover some other features of the gin. In my application, the patent examiner disallowed the use of the overlap principle in conjunction with the rotabar. A valid patent was eventually issued in my name and assigned to Continental Gin Company after I left for Boswell. The patent was somewhat limited, although the use of an air cylinder to move the ginning roller up and down was thoroughly covered. Also, the rotating blade was protected by Claim One in my patent, as long as the ginning roller rim speed was greater than the rotating knife rim speed. (Several years later I continued to discover that the two surfaces speeds should be about the same.) Hardwicke Etter's model continued to use my rotabar arrangement and speed ratio between the ginning roller and rotating knife. Why Continental did not challenge this potential infringement of Claim One of my patent is a mystery.

For Continental Gin Company, converting the two existing plants using the Flight Bar Gin to the Rotabar Gin was able to fend off a financial loss. It also provided a commercial potential that resulted in sales of a few of these gins in the long-staple area. The demand was limited, however, and Continental chose not to pursue it aggressively.

After 1962 many gins using the reciprocating knife principle began to be replaced with the rotabar. Some areas such as Egypt, with its fine quality fiber, are slow to change from ginning with the reciprocal blade because after it is ginned the cotton appears different from that produced by other forms of ginning. The reciprocating knife creates a continuous batt, whereas the rotabar delivers the cotton in lumps. This results in a different appearance in the sample and bale. There may not be any difference in the actual spinning quality but the appearance makes it unacceptable to many buyers.

My next opportunity to work with a roller gin came when I was with the J. G. Boswell Company. In 1973, we became interested in exploring the economics of using roller ginning on our Acala cotton grown on our own ranches. The possibility of roller ginning this cotton had been discussed for quite some time, but no one had tested its potential. We were encouraged by some of the Japanese textile mills that there may be a limited demand for a better quality of fiber, which we believed could be achieved by roller ginning. Some growers became interested enough to haul some cotton to a roller gin in Arizona for testing, a distance of about four hundred miles.

In November 1973, we purchased from Hardwicke Etter Company one forty-inch Hi-Cap Roller Gin equipped with a forty-inch extractor feeder. The rotating blade arrangement was the one I designed at Continental in 1962. Arrangements were made with our ranch division to save about 150 bales of field-stored cotton for test purposes after the 1973 season. We installed this roller gin in place of one of our 90 saw gins in our No. 3 plant in Corcoran, California, and began testing in January 1974. This installation gave me a chance to continue the investigation of the optimum speed, diameter, and configuration of the rotating blade. Nothing had been done in this direction since my work at Continental Gin Company in 1962.

Acala cotton is a long-staple upland cotton that has a shorter staple length when compared with the long-staple Pima cotton on which the development had first been used. The first modification involved shortening the overlap for this shorter staple cotton. The logical approach would be to reduce the diameter of the rotating blade assembly. To do this and maintain the needed rigidity was a challenge. Analysis indicated that the rotating blade should be about two inches in diameter to release the seed after about $1/2$ to $5/8$ of an inch of movement, the exact amount depending on the size of the seed.

To arrive at a suitable configuration for a rotating blade of two-inch O.D., both the number of revolutions per minute and the optimum number of blades are key factors. A study of the relationship of the surface speed of the rotating blade to that of the ginning roller indicated that the ratio should approach 1:1. During the development stage at Continental, there was no testing done to determine the best configuration and speed ratios to be used. If the ginning roller approaches the ginning point fully covered with cotton and the surface speed of the rotating blade is slightly less than that of the ginning roller, there is intermittent build-up of cotton ahead of the rotating blade as each blade comes into ginning position. These build-ups overload the ginning capacity of the ginning roller and knife, resulting in the necessity to cut back the feed. The build-ups can be eliminated by setting the surface speeds of the two rollers, the rotabar and the ginning roller, close to the same, i.e., 1:1. This required the two-inch rotabar to run above 700 rpm, which is approximately the same tip speed as the ginning roller. At this speed and at high capacity, little unginned cotton was carried over the stationary knife (figures 155 and 156).

With the revolutions per minute established, the question of the optimum number blades on the rotabar can be determined. After the seed is pushed away from the ginning roller to the release position, it must have time to return to the ginning point before the next blade moves to the ginning point. The travel of the ginning roller surface must be enough to pull the seed back to the knife before the next blade reaches the knife edge. We decided to try a four-point blade assembly made from a 1.5-inch square bar with diagonal dimension of 2.12 inches. This is reasonably close to the calculated two-inch diameter (see figure 157).

As testing progressed, we found that a roller ahead of the rotating blade assembly was helpful in getting a heavy feed of cotton to flow smoothly under the rotabar (figure 158). The feeder was modified to enable it to maintain an even feed and to separate the cotton into single seed locks. This was accomplished by speeding up the extractor cylinder, placing some brushes against it to pull the

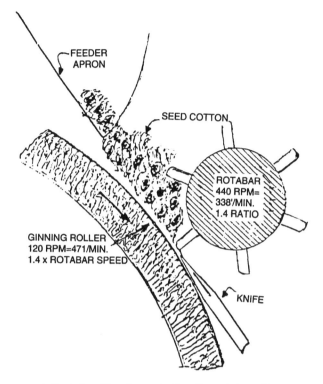

An illustration of how the seed cotton piles up between the rotabar blades when the surface speed of the ginning roller is faster than the surface speed of the rotabar. This is the normal way all roller gins are set up to operate, but it results in unginned cotton being pushed over the knife with the seed. The seed cotton is not flowing smoothly to the ginning point.

Figure 155. Illustration of what happens when surface speed of the ginning roller is faster than surface speed of rotabar.

cotton apart, and changing the doffing arrangement so it would doff directly onto the rotabar.

With these modifications, we were able to gin at a rate of about two bales per hour on the upland cotton—a capacity unheard of. One bale per hour had been tops on this variety of cotton and usually much less. Another interesting aspect of rotabar roller ginning on the upland cotton was that the amount of residual lint left on the seed was reduced to as low as 6.6 percent, which translates into approximately fifty more pounds of lint per bale. Saw-ginned upland cotton

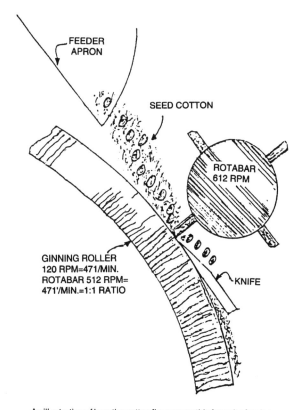

An illustration of how the cotton flows smoothly from the feeder
apron to the rotabar when the surface speed of the rotabar
and the ginning roller are approximately the same. The cotton
does not wad up in front of the rotabar blade, and all of the
seeds are ginned as they pass over the knife edge. The
capacity is greatly increased with practically no carry over.

Figure 156. Illustration of what happens when surface speed of rotabar and the ginning roller
are approximately the same.

leaves an average of about 12 percent residual lint. The next step would be to get
the spinning quality to improve.

We continued experimentation for mill testing. We were not able to find a
significant difference in spinning quality from any standpoint, either from the
full-scale testing at the mill or from small-scale spinning tests performed at the
Textile Research Center, Texas Tech University. We also had this cotton tested
at U.S. Testing Co. Inc. in Memphis. The results showed there was a significant

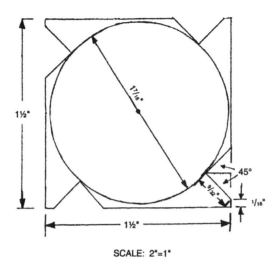

SCALE: 2"=1"

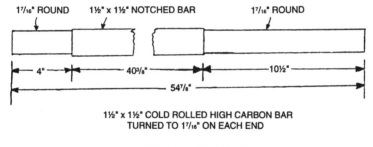

1½" x 1½" COLD ROLLED HIGH CARBON BAR
TURNED TO 1⁷/₁₆" ON EACH END

ROTABAR MODIFICATION
FOR ROLLER GIN

Figure 157. Rotabar modification for roller gin, J. G. Boswell Co., 1973.

difference in short fiber content and fiber strength of the cotton that had been roller ginned, but this did not translate into improved quality of the yarn. The results for roller ginning were: P.S.1 of 93,000; span length, 1.15 inches; uniformity ratio, 4.7; fibers shorter than ½ inches, array method, 8.9 percent. Saw ginning results on the same cotton were: P.S.1 of 90,000; span length, 1.11 inches; uniformity ratio, 4.4; and short fibers, 15.5 percent.

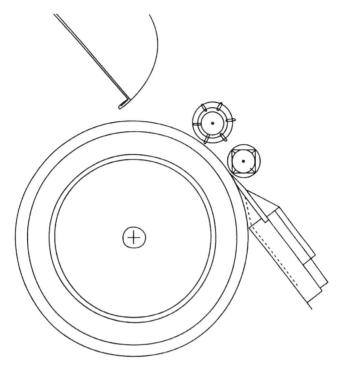

ROTOR BAR ROLLER GIN MODIFICATION, SMALLER ROTABAR
FOR SHORTER STAPLE COTTON (1" TO 1¼")

Figure 158. Modified arrangement with auxiliary roller prior to rotabar.

We repeated the testing the next year and again the results were disappointing, so we gave up the idea of roller ginning upland cotton. However, the
modifications made to the rotabar were significant improvements, and I incorporated them into other systems. In the intervening years since the issuance of my
patent in the early 1960s, there was little market for roller gins in the United States
and my patent has expired.

In 1976 in Egypt, there was interest to test the rotabar principle on Egyptian
extra-long staple cotton. I was asked by Continental to adapt the modifications
tested at Boswell to the situation in Egypt. I included the four-blade rotabar that
had been a successful development, although I used a larger diameter rotabar for
the longer staple cotton.

I began with a two-inch, square rotabar with the corners milled to what we
had done with the 1.5-inch, square bar at Boswell. Because the flat surface of the

bar was far enough away from the ginning roller, unginned cotton was allowed to pass under the rotabar as it passed over the knife. In an effort to correct this problem, I bonded flexible material to the square bar to hold the cotton to the ginning roller. This was successful as far as principle was concerned, but it was difficult to find a material that could be permanently bonded to the metal and stand the wear and tear over time.

During the 1976 testing I determined that if the blades of the rotabar could be spiraled, this would accomplish what we were trying to do with the flexible material bonded to the square rotabar. The engineering department at Continental made a drawing of the four-blade spiral rotabar (figure 159). One of these rotabars was made-up and tested promptly. The results were better than we expected. The ginning was more complete primarily because the side motion imparted to the seed locks better exposed the fibers to the pinch point. Once a few fibers were caught by the pinch point, the fibers adjacent to those caught were pulled into the pinch point as well. Because the action of delivering the lint to the pinch point is continuous, the rotation of the rotabar is smooth. Contrast this action to the straight-blade rotabar that intermittently removes the seed from the pinch point where they have accumulated between blade passings. They all will be removed in one motion, which sometimes causes the rotabar to vibrate or chatter. The spiral rotabar eliminated this problem.

The development of the spiral rotabar made so much sense and was so successful, I thought it would be easy to obtain a patent. Unfortunately, the examiner cited many ineffective spiral cylinders used for many purposes, although none covered my use. The patent that was granted was limited to a specific number of turns of the blades, which was equivalent to no patent at all, because even one tenth of a turn more or less than that specified would not infringe on the patent (figure 160).

Although we were still not happy with our feeder, we believed our roller gin arrangement would perform reasonably well and shipped a unit to Egypt for testing late in 1976. Joe Fermon, the agent for Continental Gin Company in Africa, made the arrangements for the testing. (Fermon is now the sole owner of Continental Eagle Corporation, the successor to Continental Gin Company.) The tests were done in a roller gin location outside of Alexandria. It was soon obvious that our results would be poor from the standpoint of capacity. It was raining. The cotton was damp from the high humidity and no seed cotton drying was available in any of the plants. There was no pre-cleaning available to open the cotton and prepare it for roller ginning. Given these conditions, the capacity was low, less than one bale per hour. This was still an improvement over the McCarthy type of

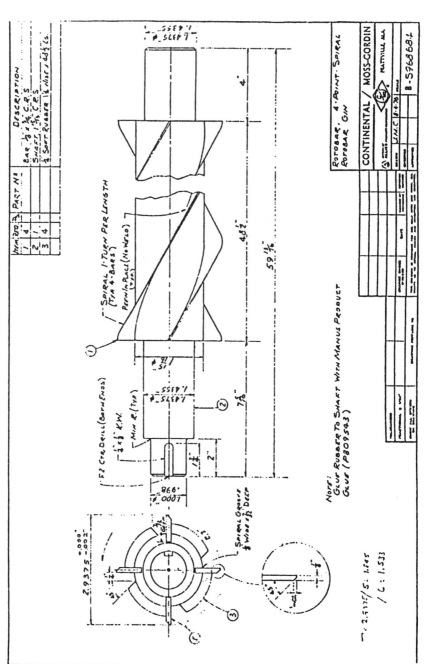

Figure 159. Four-blade spiral rotabar designed by Vandergriff, 8/4/76.

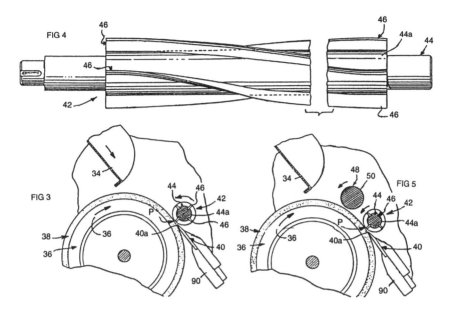

Figure 160. Spiral rotabar (patent #4,153,976)

gin using the reciprocating principle, but the appearance of the cotton from the rotabar was also not acceptable to the Egyptian market. Although not a successful endeavor, we did learn that for a rotabar gin to perform successfully, it is necessary for the cotton to be dry, single-locked, and fluffed by the use of pre-cleaning and a feeder.

In the 1970s, long-staple cotton made a come back. Our modifications had shown that the capacity of the rotabar roller gin could be doubled by using a spiraled rotabar and running it at the proper speed, as well as properly preparing the cotton for ginning. Because of the limited nature of my patent, roller gin manufacturers could make minor modifications and use this arrangement immediately. During this time, the Hardwicke Etter Company, which had dominated the market in this area, was bought out by Lummus Cotton Gin Company. Lummus then applied the spiral rotabar arrangement to their roller gins as well.

There is some misconception in the industry that the spiral rotabar was developed at the USDA ginning laboratory at Mesilla Park, New Mexico. The USDA ginning lab reported on test results on the spiral rotabar. The report stated that in September 1978, a spiral rotary knife was taken to Santo Tomas Co-op Gin for testing in one of their stands: "The spiral knife worked well. The ginner thought the knife would gin faster, perhaps because there was less vibration with the knife at a given feed rate. Increased feed rates, if the edge of the stationary knife stays clear, results in increased ginning rates, therefore lower roller surface temperatures improved roller material wear life. Improved ginning rate and improved roller life have been the comments heard about the spiral knives installed (by gin managers) in two of this valley's gins."(M. N. Gillum, C. G. Leonard, T. E. Wright, and E. A. Le Blanc, "Increasing ginning rate on the rotary knife roller gin stand," Annual Report—Mesilla Park, April 1977-January 1979, pp. 220-38). These tests were performed after my testing at Continental Gin Company and in Egypt. Although the USDA laboratory report makes no claim or comment as to the development of the spiral knife, the industry generally gives them credit for the development.

There is much misinformation in the industry concerning the history of the modern roller gin, for example, M. N. Gillum stated: "The Rotary Knife Roller Gin evolved between 1955 and 1963 through the efforts of the Southwestern Cotton Ginning Research Laboratory, the gin equipment manufacturers, and private ginneries." ("High speed roller ginning" *Transactions of the ASAE*, Volume 28(3), pp. 959-68, 1985). If the personnel of the Southwest Ginning Laboratory had developed a successful rotating knife to replace the reciprocating knife of a roller gin during the period between 1955 and 1963, the public would surely have known about it. This lab had no knowledge or input in the design of the rotating knife I made in November of 1962.

In studying the performance of the rotabar gin, I developed a theory that if a single seed lock could be deposited on each square inch of the ginning roller with the proper rotabar configuration and stationary knife setting, a forty-inch gin would have the potential to gin four bales per hour with practically no "carry over" over the stationary knife. Figure 161 illustrates one variation of the ideas tried at this gin. The following description is from my research notes.

> This rotary knife gin, commonly referred to as the rotabar gin, has not realized its full potential because no successful means of feeding a uniform single layer of seed cotton to the pinch point has been developed. The commonly used feeders present a patchwork of clumps of multi-layered seed locks, which utilize a small percentage of the rotary knife length at any given instant, while over-feeding short sections of the ginning area. A more recent analysis of this problem has led me to the discovery that in making use of the rotary knife, the principle of feeding a batt of seed cotton from a reserve, to the ginning area, such as was done with the old reciprocating knife gin, has been overlooked.
>
> I have determined that there are about 2000 seed locks [seeds with their attached fibers] per pound of seed cotton. This figure will vary widely, but it will serve

for purposes of illustration. Also, about 1500 pounds of seed cotton is required to produce a 500 pound bale of lint. There are then, about 3,000,000 seed locks required to produce a standard bale of lint. A rotary knife having six blades and operating at 400 rpm would have 2400 blades per minute passing the ginning point. Because nominal capacity of the present Rotabar gins do not exceed about one bale per hour, or 3,000,000 seed locks per hour, (which is 50,000 per minute) each blade passing would handle an average of only 20.8 seed locks. The standard 40-inch length unit should easily handle three to four times this number of seed locks per blade passing if *presented in a uniform, single layer*. I have devised a novel means for accomplishing this. It consists of a feed roller and feed plate with sufficient storage ahead of the feed roller to permit a batt of seed cotton to be formed between the feed roller and feed plate. The feed roller has a compressible surface, and is spaced from the feed plate to compress the batt into a single layer of seed locks. This arrangement receives the seed cotton from the standard feeder at a controlled rate, and this rate is correlated with the speed of the feed roller to form a batt with the desired number of seed locks per inch of travel. The pinch point of the feed plate is located so that the blades of the rotary knife draw the batt of seed locks as they are released from the pinch point. The compressible surface of the feed roller prevents the batt from being drawn from the bite before being released, which would upset the controlled rated of flow to the rotary blades.

A practical arrangement for feeding 100,000 seed locks per minute, (enough to produce 1000 pounds of lint per hour) would be a 6-inch diameter feed roller 40 inches long at 40 rpm and having a reserve storage sufficient to form a batt containing 3.3 seed locks per square inch. The feed roller-feed plate relationship is such that the batt is compressed to single layer thickness at the release point. The feed roller feeds the batt over the edge of the feed plate directly to the blades of the rotary knife. The compression holds the batt so that the blade removes it in single seed locks and draws the fibers at a 5:1 ratio from the bite. The 5:1 ratio is obtained by operating the 3-inch diameter rotary knife at 400 rpm versus the 6-inch feed roller at 40 rpm. With the 3-inch diameter rotary knife having six blades, there is approximately 1.5 inches between blades, and while a blade travels this distance, the batt moves one-fifth this distance, or .3 inches. This .3-inch of batt forty inches long theoretically contains .3 x 40 x 3.3 seed locks per square inch, or 39.6 seed locks per blade passing. This is about one seed lock per inch of length of the ginning roller per blade passing, which is considerably less than the maximum that can be handled with a good single layer distribution, yet about double the ginning rate without this feed mechanism.

In 1982, I had an opportunity to test this theory at Valley Industries Roller Gin at Wenden, Arizona at the invitation of the manager, Jim Downing. The arrangement shown in figure 161 would have been successful if the scroll under the feed roller had been more rigid. The spring tension necessary to hold the batt caused the scroll that was acting as a feed plate to bow in the center and release the cotton in wads. I had a heavier feed plate made with stronger spring tension.

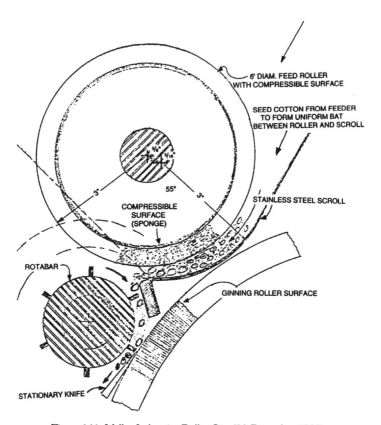

6' DIAM. FEED ROLLER
WITH COMPRESSIBLE SURFACE

SEED COTTON FROM FEEDER
TO FORM UNIFORM BAT
BETWEEN ROLLER AND SCROLL

55°

COMPRESSIBLE
SURFACE
(SPONGE)

STAINLESS STEEL SCROLL

ROTABAR

GINNING ROLLER SURFACE

STATIONARY KNIFE

Figure 161. Valley Industries Roller Gin (30 December 1980)

I could not test this modification until the next season. Unfortunately, the plant was sold and the new ownership canceled my research and development privileges.

My next opportunity to pursue any roller gin work would be with Consolidated HGM Corporation in 1988. I had been hired by them in 1986 to design a new gin stand, which ultimately became the Consolidated 164 Saw Gin. When they asked me in 1988 to design a roller gin and feeder for them, I was excited and anxious to apply and further refine my theories to a totally new unit. I worked with a local engineering firm in Visalia, California to make the initial detailed drawings. In this new unit, we used the device previously described at Valley Industries, with a heavy feed plate and strong spring tension. Instead of allowing the rotabar to take the cotton from the feed plate, we used a separate doffer that directed the cotton to the rotabar. This showed considerable promise, but the arrangement for driving the feed roller had a variable speed motor. Even at maximum speed, we could not run the feed roller fast enough to obtain a thin enough batt. Before we could get our changes made, the cooperating gin completed the season. This delayed any further work until the next season.

A unique feature of this feeding arrangement was that the roller was covered with a knobby tread surface (figure 162). The configuration of this surface was such that a single seed lock would fit into the pocket between the knobs. By compressing a batt of seed cotton against this surface with a feed plate, the seed locks are pushed into the pockets. This also helped to maintain an even feed of single seed locks to the ginning roller. I was not satisfied with the wobble-disc doffer. It is not possible to locate it so that the rotabar would doff directly into the knife because of the small diameter of the rotabar. An auxiliary rotabar could have been located so that it would doff the knobby tread cylinder into the rotabar, or rotating blade.

The preparation of the cotton by the feeder is extremely important to the success of the roller gin. One of the problems in preparing the cotton properly for roller ginning is the loss of seed through cleaning and extracting, because the lint on the black seed is loosely attached. To avoid seed loss and to separate the cotton effectively into single seed locks, I designed a special feeder. Its purpose was to pre-gin the cotton as much as possible without damaging the fiber and avoiding seed loss. The machine consisted of two stacked four-cylinder sections (figure 163). The cylinders are eight inches in diameter, which obtains the maximum centrifugal action. The metal screening surfaces under the top cylinders have holes small enough to avoid seed loss. The feeder also has deflectors over the back cylinders to start the seed lock separation process. As the cotton passes under the cylinders, it is subjected to more separation and fluffing. The screening surfaces are wrapped fifteen degrees further around the cylinders than the standard. This is the same contour used on the feeder I designed at Lummus in 1949 and is still present on the Lummus 700 feeder. The screen projecting higher between the cylinders results in a more drastic action on the cotton to pull seed locks apart as it is transferred from one cylinder to the next.

The last of this group of four cylinders discharges on top of the next group of cylinders, and the cotton is again subjected to separation action as it passes over the top of them (see figure 163). Between each pair of cylinders is a sharp blade projecting to an adjustable height. As the cotton is transferred between the cylinders, it is drawn over these blades and the seed is stripped from the fibers. This pre-ginning results in a beautiful smooth flow of fluffy cotton to the ginning knife.

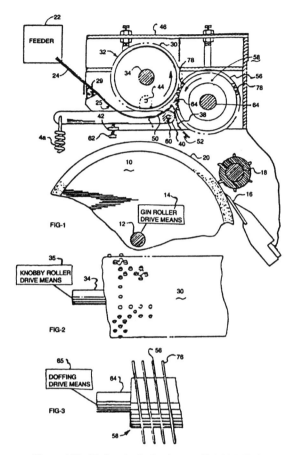

Figure 162. Roller gin feeder (patent # 4,914,786)

The small diameter cylinders are run at high speed, in the range of 1000 rpm, which adds to the pre-ginning action. There are no screens under the bottom cylinders, only metal scrolls, so there is no loss of ginned seed. This arrangement does not have the benefit of trash removal because seed loss would be too great and the cleaning provided by the high-speed rotabar more than offsets the loss of cleaning from these cylinders.

The cross section shown in figure 163 shows provisions for heat in the feeder, it is equipped for adding a small amount of hot air, and this is recommended for a more efficient operation. There is an outlet duct at the back of the lower group of cylinders to remove the hot air. Even if heat is not used, it is still desirable to

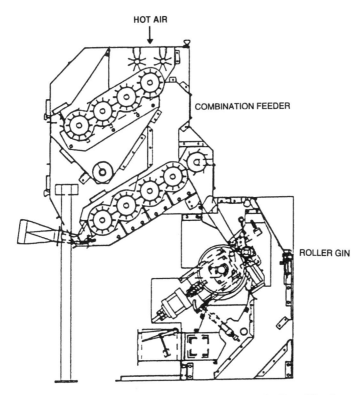

Figure 163. Cross sectional drawing of arrangement for Consolidated.

remove a small amount of air here to eliminate the dust and lint fly at the discharge of the feeder.

The roller gin itself is a basic rotabar roller with a fifteen-inch diameter ginning roller—the same configuration that I have worked with since 1962. The four-blade spiral rotabar was also a key part of the unit. The rim speed of the rotabar should run at least as fast as that of the ginning roller. With a fifteen-inch diameter ginning roller at 120 rpm, the three-inch (approximate) rotabar would have to run at 600 rpm.

The setting of the stationary knife to the ginning roller had become well established over the years. A typical knife is a flat bar of AISI 01 oil-hardened tool steel hardened to 53-54 Rockwell C and is 3¾ inches wide and one-quarter inch thick. The length varies with the make of gin. At the end there is a one-inch section that tapers to 1/32 inch. The square edges at the thin end should be beveled slightly with sandpaper or a file so it will not cut the ginning roller and will allow the release of the fiber more readily. The knife is located approximately tangentially to the ginning roller. It is mounted so that it can be tilted and adjusted slightly up and down. The final adjustment should be so that a thin gauge (0.005 to 0.010 inches) can be started between the upper edge of the knife and the ginning roller with air pressure holding the ginning roller in ginning position.

The ginning roller pressure against the knife on a forty-inch roller is about 2800 psi. Because the knife has a thin cross section, this pressure makes it necessary to use strong supports for the knife. The knife support is attached at each end of the frame by gussets welded to the head plates of the gin. This one-inch plate is backed up by a heavy support bar to maintain rigidity of the knife support. A second one-inch plate is bolted to the top of the first one-inch plate. The second plate is bolted across the bottom edge and there are adjusting set screws across the top of the plate. The knife blade is clamped between these two heavy plates. The top set screws can be adjusted to spring or bow the heavy plate, allowing the knife pressure to be evenly distributed across the ginning roller.

To adjust the knife pressure, it is common practice to operate the ginning roller with some pressure on the knife, feeling the ginning roller by hand to find the hot strips. The set screws are then adjusted to eliminate the hot spots. Each manufacturer uses a slightly different support bar arrangement, but the results are generally the same. (A variation I have tested uses a 1¼-inch top plate instead of one-inch and does not use adjusting screws. Although this arrangement operated well, it was never adopted.)

The rotabar is held in position by arms attached to the rotabar bearing at each end and an air cylinder at each end. The air cylinders lift the rotabar away from the knife slightly when no cotton is being fed to the ginning roller. The ginning roller cylinder is held in position against the knife by an air cylinder at each end of the cylinder. The cylinder backs away from the knife when there is no cotton flow. If it remained in ginning position under pressure against the knife, it would overheat. When there is cotton flowing, the roller is insulated by the cotton thus preventing overheating. The ginning roller is also connected to another set of air cylinders through linkage and will back away from the ginning knife when the feed is cut off to prevent over-heating the roller. The air cylinder included was a part of my original 1962 unit (note its position in figure 163).

Three model gins were produced and tested in Lubbock, Texas in September 1989. They were then shipped to a plant in El Frida, Arizona in November 1989. This plant was an operating saw gin. We were able to use the existing seed-cotton cleaning, distributor, press, and other common equipment, but had to install the roller gin and feeders, lint cleaning, and seed-handling equipment. The installation was made in record time and we started operation on 11 November 1989.

One problem we encountered was the hopper over the gins. The gins were located so that the hopper from the distributor over the feeder was on a rather flat angle—the hopper in the distributor did not line up with the feeder hopper. This resulted in the cotton feeding into the feeder intermittently. Nonetheless, the units performed at two bales per hour per gin. The four-blade rotabars at ginning roller surface speed proved to be everything I had expected. Unfortunately, the season ended before we could enjoy fully the fruits of our labor.

Our next experience with this arrangement was to use it in one stand added to the eight-stand Lummus roller gin at Buttonwillow Ginning (Houchin) at Buttonwillow, California. This unit was installed at the end of 1989 season and operated briefly in January 1990. The personnel there did not follow our key recommendations. One critical error was slowing down the speed of the rotabar. The next season began in October 1990. During the hiatus there was a change in gin personnel. Tracy Birklebak was brought in as the new Superintendent. He had a lot of experience with the Lummus roller gin and was open-minded to what I was attempting to do. He cooperated fully and contributed much to the project. The gin was readjusted, tuned up, and the rotabar setting corrected. This was by far the smoothest roller gin operation we had ever seen. Birklebak was so enthused with the four-blade spiral rotabar, he immediately ordered them for all eight of the Lummus gins, which were operating with six-blade rotabars.

The plant could not operate at full capacity because of bottlenecks in other parts of the process. To find out the peak capacity of the test gin we cut back on the others. Without any special adjustments, pressures, or speeds, the gin operated at 2.7 bales per hour. We were pleased to discover that only a few seed locks were passing over the ginning knife because the batt of cotton coming down the feeder apron was so fluffy. Occasionally, a few locks would hit the rotabar too high to go directly under it and they would be knocked back and then go under it. This doubled the layer and the knife would not take all of the locks. This problem occurred in the tests on upland cotton at Boswell in 1974. The solution I devised for them (placing a standard six-blade rotabar ahead of the smaller one to prevent the flow from hitting too high on the rotabar) could not be used here because the addition of a second cylinder ahead of the rotabar was not feasible in this model.

Although I have placed considerable emphasis on the "overlap theory" in my discussion of roller gins, I have some reason to doubt its importance with my present gin. In working with Tracy Birklebak on rotabar speed variations, we increased the speed to as high as 800 rpm. The results did not differ from those obtained at 600-700 rpm. At the higher speed however, it is not necessary for the seed to be released at any specific position because they will be stripped free of the lint that is pinched between the knife and ginning roller. This is more likely to be true of pima cotton, whereas the upland variety, with its firmer fiber attachment, it might not be true.

The ginning roller does not over-heat with higher pressure or higher speed, so both can be increased permitting even higher flow rates. A plant in Australia with our equipment is taking advantage of this factor, allowing them to operate at an average of 2.5 bales per hour over an entire season.

Pima cotton and a variety of long-staple upland cotton is being grown increasingly in California. With the considerable interest created by the performance of this arrangement at Buttonwillow, I was encouraged that there was a developing market for roller gins in California. Unfortunately, at this writing, that has not been the case for Consolidated Cotton Gin Co. On the brighter side, four units that were shipped to Australia as a part of a combination gin have had fabulous results, averaging ten bales per hour on season runs. For the 1996 season, eight units were sold in Australia, an indication that there is hope for the future of our roller gins.

Appendix: Patents

A total of 28 patents have been issued to A. L. Vandergriff.

Holder	Description	Filed	Number	Issued
A. L. Vandergriff	Belt tightener	—	2,513,436	07-04-50
A. L. Vandergriff	Multi-jet air doffer #1	—	2,588,593	03-11-52
A. L. Vandergriff	Thermex feeder	—	2,668,989	02-16-54
A. L. Vandergriff	Feed control	—	2,696,025	12-07-54
A. L. Vandergriff	Multi-jet air doffer #2	—	2,733,401	02-07-56
A. L. Vandergriff	Green-boll trap	—	2,760,235	08-28-56
A. L. Vandergriff & W. C. Pease III	Seed cotton cleaner	05-13-55	2,862,247	12-07-58
A. L. Vandergriff	Sling-off extractor	09-10-53	2,848,635	08-11-59
A. L. Vandergriff	Cotton harvester cleaner	01-19-55	2,745,011	06-11-59
A. L. Vandergriff & W. C. Pease III	88 saw gin	02-24-59	3,091,001	05-28-63
A. L. Vandergriff D. W. Van Doorn	Lint comber	05-13-57	2,912,720	11-17-59
A. L. Vandergriff	Apparatus to remove foreign matter (Stick Machine)	11-24-58	3,046,611	07-31-62
A. L. Vandergriff	Process and apparatus: cleaning/ conditioning seed cotton	09-08-59	3,069,730	12-25-62
A. L. Vandergriff	Process and apparatus: removing lint from condenser	11-21-58	3,029,478	04-17-62
A. L. Vandergriff	Roller cotton gin	07-31-63	3,251,094	05-17-66
A. L. Vandergriff	Hot-shelf seed-cotton dryer: Apparatus and method	10-07-75	4,031,593	06-28-77

Holder	Description	Filed	Number	Issued
A. L. Vandergriff	Roller gin with grooved square rotabar	05-09-77	4,094,043	06-13-78
A. L. Vandergriff	Vapor condenser and lint humidifying system	01-19-78	4,140,503	02-20-79
A. L. Vandergriff	Even-heat parallel-flow tower dryer	08-16-77	4,143,470	03-18-79
A. L. Vandergriff	Roller gin with spiral-blade rotabar	05-09 77	4,153,976	05-15-79
A. L. Vandergriff	Gin rib and seed tube	07-05 79	4,310,949	01-19-82
A. L. Vandergriff	Feeder for cotton gin roller gin	05-08-89	4,914,786	04-10-90
A. L. Vandergriff	Cotton gin seed vanes and seed roll box. Consolidated 164 Gin Stand	—	4,974,294	12-04-90
A. L. Vandergriff	Condensate control apparatus for cotton gin condenser	11-28-89	4,999,881	03-19-91
A. L. Vandergriff	Cotton gin feeder and pre-ginner	03-05-90	5,016,326	05-21-91
A. L. Vandergriff	Turbulent airflow hot-shelf tower dryer	02-07-92	5,233,764	08-11-93
A. L. Vandergriff	Cotton gin condenser with humidification and batt compression	11-15-93	5,381,587	01-17-95
A. L. Vandergriff	Fountain Dryer	07-18-96	5,533,276	07-09-96

Index

W

ROWAN UNIVERSITY
LIBRARY
201 MULLICA HILL RD.
GLASSBORO, NJ 08028-1701

ROWAN COLLEGE OF NEW JERSEY

3 3001 00811 1931

TS 1585 .V36 1997
Vandergriff, A. L. 1910-
Ginning cotton

DATE DUE

~~MAR 1 8 1998~~		
07-26-99		

GAYLORD No. 2333   PRINTED IN U.S.A.